NARRATIVE DISCOURSE

GÉRARD GENETTE

Narrative Discourse

AN ESSAY IN METHOD

Translated by Jane E. Lewin
Foreword by Jonathan Culler

CORNELL UNIVERSITY PRESS

ITHACA, NEW YORK

"Discours du récit," a portion of *Figures III* by Gérard Genette, was published in French, © Editions due Seuil, 1972.

The publisher gratefully acknowledges the financial assistance of the French Ministry of Culture in defraying part of the cost of translation.

First published 1980 by Cornell University Press.
First printing, Cornell Paperbacks, 1983.

Quotations from *Remembrance of Things Past*, by Marcel Proust, translated by C. K. Scott Moncrieff, copyright 1924, 1925, 1927, 1929, 1930, 1932 and renewed 1952, 1953, 1955, 1957, 1958, 1960 by Random House, Inc., are reprinted by permission of Random House, Inc., and Chatto and Windus, Ltd.

Cornell University Press strives to utilize environmentally responsible suppliers and materials to the fullest extent possible in the publishing of its books. Such materials include vegetable-based, low-VOC inks and acid-free papers that are also either recycled, totally chlorine-free, or partly composed of nonwood fibers.

Library of Congress Cataloging in Publication Data

Genette, Gérard, 1930–
   Narrative Discourse.

   Translation of Discours du récit, a portion of the 3d vol. of the author's Figures, essais.
   Bibliography: p.
   Includes index.
   1. Proust, Marcel, 1871–1922. A la recherche du temps perdu.
2. Narration (Rhetoric) I. Title.
PQ2631.R63A791713   808.3'3   79-13499
ISBN 0-8014-1099-1 (cloth)
ISBN 0-8014-9259-9 (pbk.)

Paperback printing   10   9   8   7

Contents

Foreword

Anyone who has begun the study of fiction has encountered terms like *point of view, flashback, omniscient narrator, third-person narrative*. One can't describe the techniques of a novel without such terms, any more than one can describe the workings of a car without the appropriate technical vocabulary. But while someone who wanted to learn about cars would have no trouble finding a manual, there is no comparable work for the student of literature. These basic concepts have been developed in an ad hoc, piecemeal fashion and, paradoxically, though they are supposed to identify all the various elements and possible techniques of the novel, they have not been put together in a systematic way. Even Wayne Booth's *The Rhetoric of Fiction*, from which students of the novel have learned a great deal, is primarily limited to problems of narrative perspective and point of view. There has been no comprehensive survey.

Gérard Genette's *Narrative Discourse* is invaluable because it fills this need for a systematic theory of narrative. As the most thorough attempt we have to identify, name, and illustrate the basic constituents and techniques of narrative, it will prove indispensable to students of fiction, who not only will find in it terms to describe what they have perceived in novels but will also be alerted to the existence of fictional devices which they had previously failed to notice and whose implications they had never been able to consider. Every reader of Genette will find that he becomes a more acute and perceptive analyst of fiction than before.

This is also a major work, however, for those who are interested in narrative theory itself, for it is one of the central achievements of what was called "structuralism." The structuralist study of literature, associated with the names of Roland Barthes, Tzvetan Todorov, Genette, and others, sought not to interpret literature but to investigate its structures and devices. The project, as defined in Barthes's *Critique et vérité* and Todorov's "Poétique" (in *Qu'est-ce que le structuralisme?*), was to develop a poetics which would stand to literature as linguistics stands to language and which therefore would not seek to explain what individual works mean but would attempt to make explicit the system of figures and conventions that enable works to have the forms and meanings they do.[1] Structuralists devoted considerable attention to plot structure, or the "grammar" of plot, as Todorov called it in his *Grammaire du Décaméron*, and to the ways in which details of various kinds in a novel are organized to produce effects of suspense, characters, plot sequences, and thematic and symbolic patterns.[2] Though *Narrative Discourse* does not directly assimilate either of these investigations, it is the centerpiece of the study of narrative, for in attempting to define the forms and figures of narrative discourse Genette must deal with all the complex relations between the narrative and the story it tells. The structures and codes which Barthes and Todorov studied must be taken up and organized by a narrative; this activity is Genette's subject.

But if *Narrative Discourse* is the culmination of structuralist work on narrative and shows, in its terminological exuberance, a Gallic delight in the adventures of thought, it is also wholly conversant with Anglo-American discussions of narrative, which it cites, uses, and occasionally refutes. This is no provincial exercise but a broadly based theoretical study.

It is also, however—and this is doubtless more surprising—a

[1] For discussion and bibliography see Jonathan Culler, *Structuralist Poetics: Structuralism, Linguistics, and the Study of Literature* (Ithaca, N.Y.: Cornell University Press, 1975).

[2] See Roland Barthes, *S/Z* (New York: Hill and Wang, 1974), and Tzvetan Todorov, *The Poetics of Prose* (Ithaca, N.Y.: Cornell University Press; London: Blackwell, 1977).

remarkable study of Proust's *A la recherche du temps perdu*. It is as though Genette had determined to give the lie to the skeptics who maintained that the structural analysis of narrative was suited only to the simplest narratives, like folk tales, and, in an act of bravado, had chosen as his object one of the most complex, subtle, and involuted of narratives. But in fact, this is not an act of bravura. Genette has long been concerned with Proust, and the three volumes of his *Figures*,[3] from which *Narrative Discourse* is taken, contain three other essays on Proust's work.

Given the focus on Proust, our ordinary notions of criticism ask us to choose between two ways of viewing Genette's project: either his real goal is the development of a theory of narrative and Proust's great novel is simply being used as a source of illustrations, or else the theoretical matter is simply a methodological discussion which is justified insofar as it leads to a better understanding of *A la recherche du temps perdu*. In his preface Genette quite rightly refuses to choose between these alternatives, but this does not mean that his work should be viewed as something of a compromise, neither one nor the other. On the contrary, it is an extreme and unusual example of each genre. On the one hand, the fact that it uses Proust so voraciously gives it great theoretical power, for it is forced to take account of all the complexities of Proustian narrative. Not only is this a severe test of categories, which doubtless leads to the discovery of new distinctions, but the theory is constantly confronted with anomalies and must show how they are anomalous. On the other hand, the fact that Genette is trying to elaborate a theory of narrative while studying Proust gives him a signal advantage over other interpreters of the *Recherche*. He need not hasten to offer a thematic interpretation of every incident, decide what is Proust's vision of life, his conception of art. He can dwell on the strangeness of Proustian discourse, constantly pointing out how

---

[3] *Figures* (Paris: Seuil, 1966), *Figures II* (1969), *Figures III* (1972). In addition to the three other discussions of Proust (one in each volume) these collections contain essays dealing with Stendhal, Flaubert, Robbe-Grillet, Barthes, baroque poets, and various issues in literary and rhetorical theory. More recently, Genette has published his immense *Mimologiques* (Seuil, 1976), a study of writings through the ages that have denied the arbitrary nature of the linguistic sign.

bizarre a construction this novel is. Compelled by his special perspective to ask questions about what is usually taken for granted, he continually tells us things we did not know about the book and achieves something that most interpreters do not: he leads us to experience the strangeness of the text.

Since Genette's presentation and Jane Lewin's translation are admirably clear, there is no need to outline the book's argument, and one can introduce it simply by indicating several major areas of interest.

Point of View. One important and original proposal bears on the traditional notion of point of view. Most theorists, Genette argues, have failed to distinguish properly between "*mood* and *voice,* that is to say, between the question *who is the character whose point of view orients the narrative perspective?* and the very different question *who is the narrator?*" Thus, if a story is told from the point of view of a particular character (or, in Genette's terms, *focalized* through that character), the question whether this character is also the narrator, speaking in the first person, or whether the narrator is someone else who speaks of him in the third person, is not a question of the point of view, which is the same in both cases, but a question of voice. And conversely, in what is traditionally called a first-person narrative the point of view can vary, depending on whether events are focalized through the consciousness of the narrator at the moment of narration or through his consciousness at a time in the past when the events took place. Insistence on the difference between narration and focalization is a major revision of the theory of point of view.

Focalization. The notion of focalization leads to some interesting problems in its own right. One commentator, Mieke Bal, has argued persuasively that Genette uses *focalization* to cover two cases which are so different that to treat them as variants of the same phenomenon is to weaken his important new concept.[4] In what Genette calls *internal focalization* the narrative is focused *through* the consciousness of a character, whereas *external focali-*

4 Mieke Bal, "Narration et focalisation," *Poétique,* 29 (February 1977), 107–127.

zation is something altogether different: the narrative is focused *on* a character, not through him. For example, in Hemingway's "The Killers" or in the novels of Dashiell Hammett we are told what the characters do but not what they think or see. To treat this absence of focalization as another sort of focalization reduces the precision of the concept. Bal has proposed emendations to solve the problems which Genette's theory brings to light, and Genette seems quite happy to accept modifications. As he says in his Afterword, the very nature of poetics as a progressive, cumulative enterprise ensures that his formulations will one day be relegated to the rubbish heap. If this happens, it will doubtless be because they have inspired improvements.

The Iterative. Genette's attempt to be comprehensive where ◁— others have proceeded in more piecemeal fashion occasionally leads to the discovery of topics which have not been much discussed but which prove, on investigation, to be extremely important. Studying the possible relationships between the time of story or plot and the time of the narrative, he determines that they may be classified in terms of *order* (events occur in one order but are narrated in another), pace or *duration* (the narrative devotes considerable space to a momentary experience and then leaps over or swiftly summarizes a number of years), and *frequency* (the narrative may repeatedly recount an event that happened only once or may recount once what happened frequently). Now order and pace are well known to students of narrative: the former involves notions like *flashback, foreshadowing,* and beginning *in medias res,* and the latter notions like *scene* and *summary.* But frequency, as it happens, has seldom been discussed, though it turns out to be a major topic. Repetition, a common form of frequency, has emerged as the central technique in certain avant-garde novels, and what Genette calls the *iterative,* in which the narrative tells once that something happened frequently, turns out to have a variety of important functions. Proust, of course, is much given to the iterative mode, but he also employs a fascinating figure which Genette calls the *pseudo-iterative:* when the story narrates as something that happened repeatedly an event whose very particularity makes it seem undeniably singular. Thus, in the long account of what happened every Sunday at Combray are inserted extended conversations, unlikely to have been repeated every week. This mode produces strange narrative effects which have not been discussed; we owe our growing understanding of them to Genette's pioneering investigation of the iterative.

—➤   *Norm and Anomaly.* Genette's definition of the figures of frequency has the result of making anomalous (hence the label "*pseudo*-iterative") a distinctively Proustian mode. Now one might expect an account of narrative based on Proustian examples to work just the other way, making Proust's bizarre techniques the norm; but under each of the major categories—tense, voice, and mood—something typically Proustian is rendered anomalous by the system of distinctions. Discussing voice, Genette concludes that the movement from one level of narrative to another in Proust is often confused and is ruled by transgressions. In the case of mood, not only does Proust prove "inassimilable" to the basic distinction between *mimesis* and *diegesis*, but his "polymodality" is "a scandal" for the system of point of view. At moments when we are looking with Marcel through a window or keyhole and seeing only those actions he can see, we will be told the thoughts of the characters we are supposedly observing. In various ways, as Genette says, "Proust upsets the whole logic of narrative representation."

This may seem an odd conclusion to reach, since in comparison with more recent novelists Proust seems so massively committed to representing a world and a character's experience of it. Doubtless, if Proust can always be caught in flagrant violation of the system, this is because the categories for the description of narrative discourse are in fact based on what we may for convenience call a model of the real world. According to this model, events necessarily take place both in a particular order and a definable number of times. A speaker has certain kinds of information about events and lacks other kinds. He either experienced them or he did not, and generally he stands in a definable relationship to the events he recounts. However true this model may be, there is nothing to prevent narratives from violating it and producing texts which involve impossible combinations. A sentence such as "I watched George reach into his briefcase for something while he thought about whether he might have lamb for dinner that evening" asserts a combination of knowledge and ignorance that in the world would be most unlikely, but novels frequently produce such combinations, though seldom within the space of a single sentence. It may well be that narratives will usually prove anomalous because our models of narrative procedures are always based on models of reality.

But it might also be the case that Genette's work is testimony to the power of the marginal, the supplementary, the exception. It is as though his categories were specifically designed to identify as anomalous the most salient of Proust's techniques, so that in a sense these marginal phenomena, these exceptions, in fact determine the norms; these cases which the system seems to set aside are in fact crucial to it. In its exemplification of this paradoxical logic, Genette's work communicates with the most interesting speculative strain of what is now called "post-structuralism": Jacques Derrida's investigation of the logic of marginality or supplementarity that is always at work in our interpretive schemes.[5] Whether or not one actively pursues these questions, Genette's *Narrative Discourse* is a provocative work, as well as an indispensable tool for students of narrative.

JONATHAN CULLER

Ithaca, New York

[5] See Derrida's *Of Grammatology* (Baltimore: Johns Hopkins University Press, 1977).

Translator's Preface

Marcel Proust's *A la recherche du temps perdu*, whose narrative is "the specific subject of this book," has been translated into English as *Remembrance of Things Past* (by C. K. Scott Moncrieff [vols. 1–6] and Frederick A. Blossom [whose translation of volume 7 was replaced in 1970 by Andreas Mayor's]; 2 vols., New York: Random House, 1934; also published in seven separate volumes by Random House). In this book the French title (which means literally "in search of time lost") is retained, as are the French titles of the seven volumes forming the *Recherche*, listed here with their standard English translations:

Du côté de chez Swann (Swann's Way)
  Part I: *Combray (Overture; Combray)*
  Part II: *Un amour de Swann (Swann in Love)*
  Part III: *Noms de pays: le nom (Place-Names: The Name)*
A l'ombre des jeunes filles en fleurs (Within a Budding Grove)
  Part I: *Autour de Mme. Swann (Madame Swann at Home)*
  Part II: *Noms de pays: le pays (Place-Names: The Place; Seascape, with Frieze of Girls)*
Le Côté de Guermantes (The Guermantes Way)
Sodome et Gomorrhe (Cities of the Plain)
La Prisonnière (The Captive)
Albertine disparue, later changed to *La Fugitive (The Sweet Cheat Gone)*
Le Temps retrouvé (The Past Recaptured)

All quotations from the *Recherche* are from the Scott Moncrieff and Mayor translation, except for a very few (indicated in the notes) which are my translation, at those places where Genette's exposition required a strictly literal rendering. In the notes, page references to the *Recherche* are to both the two-volume Random House translation (1934/1970) and the later three-volume Clarac-Ferré edition (Pléiade, 1954) that is cited by Genette, but in the body of the text, page numbers—or the number of pages in a given section—refer only to the Random House edition.

For quotations from French works other than the *Recherche*, all translations are mine unless the notes indicate otherwise. (Existing translations of other works by Proust and of French critical studies, listed in the Bibliography, have always been used, and in such cases the notes usually cite only the English edition.) For quotations from works originally written in English, the original has been quoted and cited, although Genette sometimes used French translations, as listed in the Bibliography. And for quotations from works originally written in a language other than French or English, I have used and cited published English translations.

I have silently modified the French edition of this book by correcting obvious errors, occasionally supplementing the documentation, and giving both French and English versions of quotations from Proust when the French version seemed essential (mainly in Chapter 3).

The publication history of Proust's novel enters into Genette's discussion (and explains, as well, the occasional discrepancies between English and French versions of the *Recherche*). By 1912, Proust had written a 1300-page novel in three sections: *Du côté de chez Swann, Le Côté de Guermantes,* and *Le Temps retrouvé.* Proust's original first part would have run about 800 pages in print, but the publisher, Grasset, refused to produce a volume of that size; his refusal forced Proust to play around with his material, shifting it to meet the 500-page limit that Grasset imposed for publication in 1913. Then came the war, delaying publication of the remaining two sections—and giving Proust time to alter and expand his manuscripts, which he did assiduously. As a result, when publication was resumed five years later, by Gallimard, it was with a volume entitled *A l'ombre des jeunes filles en fleurs,* formerly planned as the opening chapter of the third volume; and *Sodome et Gomorrhe* was announced. *Le Côté de*

Guermantes I was published in 1920, with *Guermantes II* and *Sodome et Gomorrhe I* following in 1921; *Sodome II* appeared in May 1922. In November 1922 Proust died. *La Prisonnière* came out in 1923, *Albertine disparue* (changed in 1954 to Proust's original title, *La Fugitive*) in 1925, *Le Temps retrouvé* in 1927. Scott Moncrieff and Blossom's translation is based on these volumes.

Proust's method of working was such that the published editions of his novel were rather unreliable—in some cases thoroughly so, as was learned when his manuscripts became available in the 1950's. He revised and expanded incessantly, adding to typescripts and page proofs without mercy. After 1918, in poor health and driving hard to finish his work before death should come, he put his energies into creation rather than supervision, with the result that the volumes published in his lifetime were seen through the press by others, who had a great deal of difficulty coping with the never-ending flow of revisions. The volumes published after his death were based either on manuscripts he had only partially revised or simply on rough drafts, but considerably rearranged and touched up by the original editors, whose first care was to put the drafts in readable and orderly shape. In 1954, however, Pierre Clarac and André Ferré, having had access to the newly available manuscripts, published what is now the standard edition of the novel. They restored the text of the later volumes to the state it had been in when Proust died. For the earlier volumes, to establish their text they struggled with Proust's habit of revising and adding, continually creating his novel, and letting other people—who may have misunderstood his intentions or his handwriting—see the work into print.

Because the French text on which the English translation of *Le Temps retrouvé* was based was the one most changed by the Clarac-Ferré edition of 1954, in 1970 Andreas Mayor published a new English translation based on the Clarac-Ferré text. Mayor's avowed intention, however, was chiefly to please an audience interested in reading a good narrative; therefore he took the same kind of liberty with the restored text that the original French editors had taken with Proust's manuscripts.

JANE E. LEWIN

Bethesda, Maryland

NARRATIVE DISCOURSE

Preface

The specific subject of this book is the narrative in *A la recherche du temps perdu*. This statement immediately calls for two comments, of differing importance. The first bears on the nature of the Proustian corpus. Everyone today knows that the work whose canonic text was established in 1954 by the Clarac-Ferré edition is but the latest form of a work Proust labored at during his whole life, as it were, a work whose earlier versions are, for the most part, scattered among *Les Plaisirs et les jours* (1896), *Pastiches et mélanges* (1919), the various posthumous collections or previously unpublished works entitled *Chroniques* (1927), *Jean Santeuil* (1952), and *Contre Sainte-Beuve* (1954),[1] and the eighty-odd notebooks deposited in the manuscript room of the Bibliothèque Nationale beginning in 1962. For this reason, plus the forced interruption of November 18, 1922, the *Recherche*, more than all other works, must not be considered *closed*; and therefore it is always legitimate and sometimes necessary to appeal to one or another of its variants for comparison with the "definitive" text. The same is true with respect to the handling of the narrative. We cannot fail to appreciate, for example, how much

[1] The dates given here are those of the first publication, but my references are naturally to the Clarac-Sandre edition in two volumes—*Jean Santeuil* preceded by *Les Plaisirs et les jours*; *Contre Sainte-Beuve* preceded by *Pastiches et mélanges* and followed by *Essais et articles* (Pléiade, 1971)—which contain numerous previously unpublished writings. Even so, while waiting for the critical edition of the *Recherche* we must sometimes continue to turn to the Fallois edition of the *Contre Sainte-Beuve* for certain pages taken from the *Cahiers*.

perspective and significance the discovery of the *Santeuil* text in the "third person" brings to the narrative system adopted in the *Recherche*. Therefore while my study will bear mainly on the final work, I will occasionally take into account its antecedents, considering them not for their own sake, which would make little sense, but for the light they can add.

The second comment concerns the method, or rather the approach, adopted here. Readers may already have observed that neither the title nor the subtitle of this book mentions what I have just designated as its specific subject. The reason is neither coyness nor deliberate inflation of the subject. The fact is that quite often, and in a way that may exasperate some readers, Proustian narrative will seem neglected in favor of more general considerations; or, as they say nowadays, criticism will seem pushed aside by "literary theory," and more precisely by the theory of narrative or *narratology*. I could justify and clarify this ambiguous situation in two very different ways. I could either—as others have done elsewhere—frankly put the specific subject at the service of the general aim, and critical analysis at the service of theory: in that case the *Recherche* would be only a pretext, a reservoir of examples, and a flow of illustration for a narrative poetics in which the specific features of the *Recherche* would vanish into the transcendence of "laws of the genre." Or, on the other hand, I could subordinate poetics to criticism and turn the concepts, classifications, and procedures proposed here into so many ad hoc instruments exclusively intended to allow a more precise description of Proustian narrative in its particularity, the "theoretical" detour being imposed each time by the requirements of methodological clarification.

I confess my reluctance—or my inability—to choose between these two apparently incompatible systems of defense. It seems to me impossible to treat the *Recherche du temps perdu* as a mere example of what is supposedly narrative in general, or novelistic narrative, or narrative in autobiographical form, or narrative of God knows what other class, species, or variety. The specificity of Proustian narrative taken as a whole is *irreducible*, and any extrapolation would be a mistake in method; the *Recherche* illustrates only itself. But, on the other hand, that specificity is not

undecomposable, and each of its analyzable features lends itself to
some connection, comparison, or putting into perspective. Like
every work, like every organism, the *Recherche* is made up of
elements that are universal, or at least transindividual, which it
assembles into a specific synthesis, into a particular totality. To
analyze it is to go not from the general to the particular, but
indeed from the particular to the general: from that incompa-
rable being that is the *Recherche* to those extremely ordinary elements, figures, and techniques of general use and common cur-
rency that I call anachronies, the iterative, focalizations,
paralipses, and so on. What I propose here is essentially a
method of analysis; I must therefore recognize that by seeking
the specific I find the universal, and that by wishing to put
theory at the service of criticism I put criticism, against my will,
at the service of theory. This is the paradox of every poetics, and
doubtless of every other activity of knowledge as well: always
torn between those two unavoidable commonplaces—that there
are no objects except particular ones and no science except of the
general—but always finding comfort and something like attrac-
tion in this other, slightly less widespread truth, that the general
is at the heart of the particular, and therefore (contrary to the
common preconception) the knowable is at the heart of the
mysterious.

But to answer for methodological giddiness, even strabismus,
by invoking science perhaps involves some fraud. I will therefore plead the same case differently: perhaps the real relationship between "theoretical" dryness and critical meticulousness
is one of refreshing rotation and mutual entertainment. May the
reader also find in that relationship a sort of periodic diversion,
like the insomniac turning over and over in search of a better
position: *amant alterna Camenae.* [2]

[2] [Translator's note.] "Alternate strains are to the Muses dear." Virgil, *Ec-
logues,* III.59, trans. James Rhoades, *The Poems of Virgil* (Chicago: Encyclopaedia
Britannica, 1952).

Introduction

RÉCIT

We currently use the word *narrative*[1] without paying attention to, even at times without noticing, its ambiguity, and some of the difficulties of narratology are perhaps due to this confusion. It seems to me that if we want to begin to see clearly in this area, we must plainly distinguish under this term three distinct notions.

A first meaning—the one nowadays most evident and most central in common usage—has *narrative* refer to the narrative statement, the oral or written discourse that undertakes to tell of an event or a series of events: thus we would term *narrative of Ulysses* the speech given by the hero to the Phaeacians in Books IX-XII of the *Odyssey*, and also these four books themselves, that is, the section of Homeric text that purports to be the faithful transcription of that speech.

A second meaning, less widespread but current today among analysts and theoreticians of narrative content, has *narrative* refer to the succession of events, real or fictitious, that are the subjects of this discourse, and to their several relations of linking, opposition, repetition, etc. "Analysis of narrative" in this sense means the study of a totality of actions and situations taken in themselves, without regard to the medium, linguistic or other, through which knowledge of that totality comes to us: an

---

[1] [Translator's note.] The French word is *récit;* in Genette's text it functions as "narrative" does in English, and it has been so translated throughout.

example would be the adventures experienced by Ulysses from
the fall of Troy to his arrival on Calypso's island.

A third meaning, apparently the oldest, has *narrative* refer
once more to an event: not, however, the event that is recounted, but the event that consists of someone recounting
something: the act of narrating taken in itself. We thus say that
Books IX-XII of the *Odyssey* are devoted to the narrative of Ulysses in the same way that we say Book XXII is devoted to the
slaughter of the suitors: recounting his adventures is just as
much an action as slaughtering his wife's suitors is, and if it goes
without saying that the existence of those adventures in no way
depends on the action of telling (supposing that, like Ulysses,
we look on them as real), it is just as evident that the narrative
discourse ("narrative of Ulysses" in the first meaning of the
term) depends absolutely on that action of telling, since the
narrative discourse is *produced* by the action of telling in the
same way that any statement is the product of an act of enunciating. If, on the other hand, we take Ulysses to be a liar and the
adventures he recounts to be fictitious, then the importance of
the act of narrating expands, for on it depend not only the existence of the discourse but also the fiction of the existence of the
actions that it "relates." The same thing can obviously be said of
the narrating act of Homer himself wherever he undertakes to
tell directly the account of the adventures of Ulysses. Without a
narrating act, therefore, there is no statement, and sometimes
even no narrative content. So it is surprising that until now the
theory of narrative has been so little concerned with the problems of narrative enunciating, concentrating almost all its attention on the statement and its contents, as though it were completely secondary, for example, that the adventures of Ulysses
should be recounted sometimes by Homer and sometimes by
Ulysses himself. Yet we know (and I will return to this later) that
Plato long ago found this subject worth his attention.

As its title indicates, or almost indicates, my study basically
has to do with the most widespread meaning of the term narrative, that is, with narrative discourse, which in literature, and
particularly in the case that interests me, happens to be a narrative *text*. But, as we will see, analysis of narrative discourse as I

understand it constantly implies a study of relationships: on the one hand the relationship between a discourse and the events that it recounts (narrative in its second meaning), on the other hand the relationship between the same discourse and the act that produces it, actually (Homer) or fictively (Ulysses) (narrative in its third meaning). Starting now, therefore, in order to avoid confusion and semantic difficulties, we must designate each of these three aspects of narrative reality by univocal terms. I propose, without insisting on the obvious reasons for my choice of terms, to use the word *story* for the signified or narrative content (even if this content turns out, in a given case, to be low in dramatic intensity or fullness of incident), to use the word *narrative* for the signifier, statement, discourse or narrative text itself, and to use the word *narrating* for the producing narrative action and, by extension, the whole of the real or fictional situation in which that action takes place.[2]

My subject here is therefore *narrative*, in the limited sense that I will henceforth assign to that term. It is fairly evident, I think, that of the three levels we have just sorted out, the level of narrative discourse is the only one directly available to textual analysis, which is itself the only instrument of examination at our disposal in the field of literary narrative, and particularly fictional narrative. If we wanted to study on their own account, let us say, the events recounted by Michelet in his *Histoire de France*, we could have recourse to all sorts of documents external to that work and concerned with the history of France; or, if we wanted to study on its own account the writing of that work, we could use other documents, just as external to Michelet's text, concerned with his life and his work during the years that he

---

[2] [Translator's note.] "Story" is the French *histoire* (tell a story—*raconter une histoire*); the gerund "narrating" is an English rendering of the French noun *narration*, and it is the rendering that will be adhered to throughout. In a note at this point Genette speaks of the acceptability of his terms with respect to current French usage, and apropos of *histoire* ("story"), he refers to Tzvetan Todorov's by now "fairly well accepted . . . proposal to differentiate 'narrative as discourse' (first meaning) and 'narrative as story' (second meaning)." He also explains his use of a term generally unfamiliar in America but used frequently in this book: "With the same meaning ["story"], I will also use the term *diegesis*, which comes to us from the theoreticians of cinematographic narrative."

devoted to that text. Such a resource is not available to someone interested in either the events recounted by the narrative that the *Recherche du temps perdu* constitutes or the narrating act from which it arises: no document external to the *Recherche*, and particularly not a good biography of Marcel Proust, if one existed,[3] could teach us about either those events or that act, since both of these are fictional and both set on stage, not Marcel Proust, but the hero and supposed narrator of his novel. I do not mean to suggest that the narrative content of the *Recherche* has no connection with the life of its author, but simply that this connection is not such that the latter can be used for a rigorous analysis of the former (any more than the reverse). As to the narrating that produced the narrative, the act of Marcel[4] recounting his past life, we will be careful from this point on not to confuse it with the act of Proust writing the *Recherche du temps perdu*. I will come back to this subject later; it is enough for the time being to remember that the 521 pages of *Du côté de chez Swann* (Grasset edition) published in November 1913 and written by Proust some years before that date are supposed (in the present state of the fiction) to have been written by the narrator well after the war. It is thus the narrative, and that alone, that informs us here both of the events that it recounts and of the activity that supposedly gave birth to it. In other words, our knowledge of the two (the events and the action of writing) must be indirect, unavoidably mediated by the narrative discourse, inasmuch as the events are the very subject of that discourse and the activity of writing leaves in it traces, signs or indices that we can pick up and interpret—traces such as the presence of a first-person pronoun to mark the oneness of character and narrator, or a verb in the past tense to indicate that a recounted action occurred prior to the narrating action, not to mention more direct and more

---

[3] The bad ones present no inconvenience here, since their main defect consists of coolly attributing to Proust what Proust says of Marcel, to Illiers what he says of Combray, to Cabourg what he says of Balbec, and so on—a technique debatable in itself, but not dangerous for us: except for the names, such books never step outside the *Recherche*.

[4] Here, to refer to both the hero and the narrator of the *Recherche*, we are keeping this controversial Christian name. I will explain this in the last chapter.

explicit indications. Story and narrating thus exist for me only by means of the intermediary of the narrative. But reciprocally the narrative (the narrated discourse) can only be such to the extent that it tells a story, without which it would not be narrative (like, let us say, Spinoza's *Ethics*), and to the extent that it is uttered by someone, without which (like, for example, a collection of archeological documents) it would not in itself be a discourse. As narrative, it lives by its relationship to the story that it recounts; as discourse, it lives by its relationship to the narrating that utters it.

Analysis of narrative discourse will thus be for me, essentially, a study of the relationships between narrative and story, between narrative and narrating, and (to the extent that they are inscribed in the narrative discourse) between story and narrating. This position leads me to propose a new demarcation of the field of study. My starting point will be the division put forth in 1966 by Tzvetan Todorov.[5] This division classed the problems of narrative in three categories: that of *tense*, "in which the relationship between the time of the story and the time of the discourse is expressed"; that of *aspect*, "or the way in which the story is perceived by the narrator"; that of *mood*, in other words, "the type of discourse used by the narrator." I adopt, without any amendment, the first category with the definition that I have just cited, illustrated by Todorov with remarks on "temporal distortions" (that is, infidelities to the chronological order of events) and on relationships of linking, alternation, or embedding among the different lines of action that make up the story, but he added considerations about the "time of [narrative] enunciating" and the time of narrative "perception" (which he assimilated to the time of the *writing* and the *reading*) that seem to me to exceed the limits of his own definition. I for my part will hold those considerations in reserve for another order of problems, obviously connected to the relationships between narrative and narrating. The category of aspect[6] basically covered *vision*

[5] Tzvetan Todorov, "Les Catégories du récit littéraire," *Communications*, 8 (1966).

[6] Rechristened "vision" in *Littérature et signification* (1967) and in *Qu'est-ce que le structuralisme?* (1968).

REGISTER

questions of narrative "point of view"; and that of mood[7]
gathered together the problems of "distance" that American critics in the Jamesian tradition generally treat in terms of opposition between *showing* ("representation" in Todorov's vocabulary) and *telling* ("narration"), a resurgence of the Platonic
categories of *mimesis* (perfect imitation) and *diegesis* (pure narrative), the various ways of representing the speech of characters,
and the modes of explicit or implicit presence in the narrative of
narrator and reader. Just as with the "time of enunciating," here
too I think it is necessary to cut off the last series of problems, in
that it focuses on the act of narrating and its protagonists; on the
other hand, we must gather into a single large category—let us
provisionally call it that of the modalities of representation or the
degrees of mimesis—all the rest of what Todorov split between
aspect and mood. This redistribution thus ends us up with a
division substantially different from the one that inspired it, a
division that I will now formulate on its own account, having
recourse for my terms to a kind of linguistic metaphor that
should certainly not be taken too literally.

Since any narrative, even one as extensive and complex as the
Recherche du temps perdu,[8] is a linguistic production undertaking
to tell of one or several events, it is perhaps legitimate to treat it
as the development—monstrous, if you will—given to a *verbal*
form, in the grammatical sense of the term: the expansion of a
verb. *I walk, Pierre has come* are for me minimal forms of narrative, and inversely the *Odyssey* or the *Recherche* is only, in a
certain way, an amplification (in the rhetorical sense) of statements such as *Ulysses comes home to Ithaca* or *Marcel becomes a
writer.* This perhaps authorizes us to organize, or at any rate to
formulate, the problems of analyzing narrative discourse according to categories borrowed from the grammar of verbs,

---

[7] Rechristened "register" in 1967 and 1968.

[8] Is it necessary to specify that by treating this work as a narrative here we do
not by any means intend to limit it to that aspect? An aspect too often neglected
by critics, but one Proust himself never lost sight of. Thus he speaks of "that
invisible vocation of which these volumes are the *history*" (RH I, 1002/P II, 397; my
emphasis).

categories that I will reduce here to three basic classes of determinations: those dealing with temporal relations between narrative and story, which I will arrange under the heading of *tense;* those dealing with modalities (forms and degrees) of narrative "representation," and thus with the *mood* of the narrative; and finally, those dealing with the way in which the narrating itself is implicated in the narrative, narrating in the sense in which I have defined it, that is, the narrative situation or its instance,[10] and along with that its two protagonists: the narrator and his audience, real or implied. We might be tempted to set this third determination under the heading of "person," but, for reasons that will be clear below, I prefer to adopt a term whose psychological connotations are a little less pronounced (very little less, alas), a term to which I will give a conceptual extension noticeably larger than "person"—an extension in which the "person" (referring to the traditional opposition between "first-person" and "third-person" narratives) will be merely one facet among others: this term is *voice,* whose grammatical meaning Vendryès, for example, defined thus: "Mode of action of the verb in its relations with the subject."[11] Of course, what he is referring to is the subject of the statement, whereas for us *voice,* since it deals with the narrating, will refer to a relation with the subject (and more generally with the instance) of the enunciat-

[9] The term is used here with a sense very close to its linguistic meaning, if we refer, for example, to this definition in the *Littré* dictionary: "Name given to the different forms of the verb that are used to affirm more or less the thing in question, and to express . . . the different points of view from which the life or the action is looked at."

[10] In the sense in which Benveniste speaks of "instance of discourse" (*Problems in General Linguistics*, trans. M. E. Meek [Coral Gables, Fla., 1971], pp. 217-222). [Translator's note: "instance" with this very particular sense appears throughout Genette's text. In Benveniste's essay ("The Nature of Pronouns"), the "instances of discourse" are defined as "the discrete and always unique acts by which the language is actualized in speech by a speaker" (p. 217); "[each] instance is unique by definition" (p. 218). The narrating instance, then, refers to something like the narrating situation, the narrative matrix—the entire set of conditions (human, temporal, spatial) out of which a narrative statement is produced.]

[11] Quoted in the *Petit Robert* dictionary, under *Voix.*

ing: once more, these terms are merely borrowed, and I make no pretense of basing them on rigorous homologies.[12]

As we have seen, the three classes proposed here, which designate fields of study and determine the arrangement of the chapters that follow,[13] do not overlap with but sort out in a more complex way the three categories defined earlier designating the levels of definition of narrative: *tense* and *mood* both operate at the level of connections between *story* and *narrative*, while *voice* designates the connections between both *narrating* and *narrative* and *narrating* and *story*. We will be careful, however, not to hypostatize these terms, not to convert into substance what is each time merely a matter of relationships.

[12] Another—purely Proustological—justification for the use of this term: the existence of Marcel Muller's valuable book entitled *Les Voix narratives dans "A la recherche du temps perdu"* (Geneva, 1965).

[13] The first three (Order, Duration, Frequency) deal with time; the fourth, with mood; the fifth and last, with voice.

1 Order

Narrative Time?

Narrative is a . . . doubly temporal sequence . . . : There is the time of the thing told and the time of the narrative (the time of the signified and the time of the signifier). This duality not only renders possible all the temporal distortions that are commonplace in narratives (three years of the hero's life summed up in two sentences of a novel or in a few shots of a "frequentative" montage in film, etc.). More basically, it invites us to consider that one of the functions of narrative is to invent one time scheme in terms of another time scheme.[1]

The temporal duality so sharply emphasized here, and referred to by German theoreticians as the opposition between *erzählte Zeit* (story time) and *Erzählzeit* (narrative time),[2] is a typical characteristic not only of cinematic narrative but also of oral narrative, at all its levels of aesthetic elaboration, including the fully "literary" level of epic recitation or dramatic narration (the narrative of Théramène,[3] for example). It is less relevant

[1] Christian Metz, *Film Language: A Semiotics of the Cinema*, trans. Michael Taylor (New York, 1974), p. 18. [Translator's note: I have altered this translation slightly so as to align its terms with the terms used throughout this book.]
[2] See Gunther Müller, "Erzählzeit und erzählte Zeit," *Festschrift für P. Kluckhohn und Hermann Schneider*, 1948; rpt. in *Morphologische Poetik* (Tübingen, 1968).
[3] [Translator's note.] A character in Racine's *Phèdre*, proverbial for his narration of Hippolytus' death.

perhaps in other forms of narrative expression, such as the
roman-photo[4] or the comic strip (or a pictorial strip, like the pre-
della of Urbino, or an embroidered strip, like the "tapestry" of
Queen Matilda), which, while making up sequences of images
and thus requiring a successive or diachronic reading, also lend
themselves to, and even invite, a kind of global and synchronic
look—or at least a look whose direction is no longer determined
by the sequence of images. The status of written literary narrative in this respect is even more difficult to establish. Like the
oral or cinematic narrative, it can only be "consumed," and
therefore actualized, in a *time* that is obviously reading time,
and even if the sequentiality of its components can be under-
mined by a capricious, repetitive, or selective reading, that un-
dermining nonetheless stops short of perfect analexia: one can
run a film backwards, image by image, but one cannot read a
text backwards, letter by letter, or even word by word, or even
sentence by sentence, without its ceasing to be a text. Books are
a little more constrained than people sometimes say they are by
the celebrated *linearity* of the linguistic signifier, which is easier
to deny in theory than eliminate in fact. However, there is no
question here of identifying the status of written narrative (literary or not) with that of oral narrative. The temporality of written
narrative is to some extent conditional or instrumental; produced
in time, like everything else, written narrative exists in space and
as space, and the time needed for "consuming" it is the time
needed for *crossing* or *traversing* it, like a road or a field. The
narrative text, like every other text, has no other temporality than
what it borrows, metonymically, from its own reading.

   This state of affairs, we will see below, has certain consequences for our discussion, and at times we will have to correct,
or try to correct, the effects of metonymic displacement; but we
must first take that displacement for granted, since it forms part
of the narrative game, and therefore accept literally the quasi-
fiction of *Erzählzeit*, this false time standing in for a true time
and to be treated—with the combination of reservation and ac-
quiescence that this involves—as a *pseudo-time*.

---

[4] [Translator's note.] Magazine with love stories told in photographs.

Having taken these precautions, we will study relations between the time of the story and the (pseudo-) time of the narrative according to what seem to me to be three essential determinations: connections between the temporal *order* of succession of the events in the story and the pseudo-temporal order of their arrangement in the narrative, which will be the subject of the first chapter; connections between the variable *duration* of these events or story sections and the pseudo-duration (in fact, length of text) of their telling in the narrative—connections, thus, of *speed*—which will be the subject of the second chapter; finally, connections of *frequency,* that is (to limit myself to an approximate formulation), relations between the repetitive capacities of the story and those of the narrative, relations to which the third chapter will be devoted.

Anachronies

To study the temporal order of a narrative is to compare the order in which events or temporal sections are arranged in the narrative discourse with the order of succession these same events or temporal segments have in the story, to the extent that story order is explicitly indicated by the narrative itself or inferable from one or another indirect clue. Obviously this reconstitution is not always possible, and it becomes useless for certain extreme cases like the novels of Robbe-Grillet, where temporal reference is deliberately sabotaged. It is just as obvious that in the classical narrative, on the other hand, reconstitution is most often not only possible, because in those texts narrative discourse never inverts the order of events without saying so, but also necessary, and precisely for the same reason: when a narrative segment begins with an indication like "Three months earlier, ... " we must take into account both that this scene comes *after* in the narrative, and that it is supposed to have come *before* in the story: each of these, or rather the relationship between them (of contrast or of dissonance), is basic to the narrative text, and suppressing this relationship by eliminating one of its members is not only not sticking to the text, but is quite simply killing it.

Pinpointing and measuring these narrative *anachronies* (as I

will call the various types of discordance between the two order-
ings of story and narrative) implicitly assume the existence of a
kind of zero degree that would be a condition of perfect temporal correspondence between narrative and story. This point of
reference is more hypothetical than real. Folklore narrative
habitually conforms, at least in its major articulations, to
chronological order, but our (Western) literary tradition, in contrast, was inaugurated by a characteristic effect of anachrony. In
the eighth line of the *Iliad*, the narrator, having evoked the
quarrel between Achilles and Agamemnon that he proclaims as
the starting point of his narrative (*ex hou de ta prôta*), goes back
about ten days to reveal the cause of the quarrel in some 140
retrospective lines (affront to Chryses—Apollo's anger—
plague). We know that this beginning *in medias res,* followed by
an expository return to an earlier period of time, will become
one of the formal topoi of epic, and we also know how faithfully
the style of novelistic narration follows in this respect the style of
its remote ancestor,[5] even in the heart of the "realistic"
nineteenth century. To be convinced of this one need only think
of certain of Balzac's openings, such as those in *César Birotteau* or
La Duchesse de Langeais. D'Arthez directs Lucien de Rubempré to
follow this principle,[6] and Balzac himself chides Stendhal for not
having begun the *Chartreuse* with the Waterloo episode, reducing "everything that precedes it to some narrative by or about
Fabrice while he lies wounded in the Flemish village."[7] We will
thus not be so foolish as to claim that anachrony is either a rarity
or a modern invention. On the contrary, it is one of the traditional resources of literary narration.

Furthermore, if we look a little more closely at the opening
lines of the *Iliad* just referred to, we see that their temporal

[5] A testimony *a contrario* is this appraisal Huet gives of Jamblique's *Babyloniques:*
"The arrangement of his design lacks art. He has roughly followed temporal
order, and did not toss the reader immediately into the middle of the subject as
Homer did" (*Traité de l'origine des romans,* 1670, p. 157).

[6] "Step into the action first. Grab your subject sometimes sideways, sometimes from the rear; finally, vary your plans, so as never to be the same" (Balzac,
Illusions perdues, Garnier ed., p. 230).

[7] Balzac, *Etudes sur M. Beyle* (Geneva, 1943), p. 69.

movement is still more complex. Here they are in the translation of Andrew Lang, Walter Leaf, and Ernest Myers:

> Sing, goddess, the wrath of Achilles Peleus' son, the ruinous wrath that brought on the Achaians woes innumerable, and hurled down into Hades many strong souls of heroes, and gave their bodies to be a prey to dogs and all winged fowls; and so the counsel of Zeus wrought out its accomplishment from the day when first strife parted Atreides king of men and noble Achilles.
> Who then among the gods set the twain at strife and variance? Even the son of Leto and of Zeus; for he in anger at the king sent a sore plague upon the host, that the folk began to perish, because Atreides had done dishonour to Chryses the priest.[8]

Thus, the first narrative subject Homer refers to is the *wrath of Achilles*; the second is the *miseries of the Greeks*, which are in fact its consequence; but the third is the *quarrel between Achilles and Agamemnon*, which is its immediate cause and thus precedes it; then, continuing to go back explicitly from cause to cause: the *plague*, cause of the quarrel, and finally the *affront to Chryses*, cause of the plague. The five constituent elements of this opening, which I will name A, B, C, D, and E according to the order of their appearance in the narrative, occupy in the story, respectively, the chronological positions 4, 5, 3, 2, and 1: hence this formula that will synthesize the sequential relationships more or less well: A4–B5–C3–D2–E1. We are fairly close to an evenly retrograde movement.[9]

We must now go into greater detail in our analysis of anachronies. I take a fairly typical example from *Jean Santeuil*. The situation is one that will appear in various forms in the *Recherche*: the future has become present but does not resemble the idea of it that one had in the past. Jean, after several years, again

---

[8] Homer, *The Iliad*, trans. Andrew Lang, Walter Leaf, and Ernest Myers (New York: Modern Library, n.d.), Book I, ll.1-11. [Translator's note: Genette's reference in the text is to the French translation by Paul Mazon (Paris, 1962).]

[9] And even more so if we take into account the first—nonnarrative—section, in the present tense of the narrating instance (in Benveniste's sense), which thus comes at the last possible moment: "Sing, goddess."

finds the hotel where Marie Kossichef, whom he once loved, lives, and compares the impressions he has today with those that he once thought he would be experiencing today:

> Sometimes passing in front of the hotel he remembered the rainy days when he used to bring his nursemaid that far, on a pilgrimage. But he remembered them without the melancholy that he then thought he would surely some day savor on feeling that he no longer loved her. For this melancholy, projected in anticipation prior to the indifference that lay ahead, came from his love. And this love existed no more.[10]

The temporal analysis of such a text consists first of numbering the sections according to their change of position in story time. We discover here, in brief, nine sections divided between two temporal positions that we will designate 2 (*now*) and 1 (*once*), setting aside their iterative nature ("sometimes"). Section A goes in position 2 ("Sometimes passing in front of the hotel he remembered"), B in position 1 ("the rainy days when he used to bring his nursemaid that far, on a pilgrimage"), C in 2 ("But he remembered them without"), D in 1 ("the melancholy that he then thought"), E in 2 ("he would surely some day savor on feeling that he no longer loved her"), F in 1 ("For this melancholy, projected in anticipation"), G in 2 ("prior to the indifference that lay ahead"), H in 1 ("came from his love"), I in 2 ("And this love existed no more"). The formula of temporal positions, then, is as follows:

$$A2-B1-C2-D1-E2-F1-G2-H1-I2,$$

thus, a perfect zigzag. We will observe in passing that on a first reading the difficulty of this text comes from the apparently systematic way in which Proust eliminates the most elementary temporal indicators (once, now), so that the reader must supply

---

[10] *Jean Santeuil*, Pléiade ed., p. 674. [Translator's note: the rendering given in the English edition—trans. Gerard Hopkins (New York, 1956), p. 496—is very free; for purposes of Genette's analysis, I have used a literal translation of my own.]

them himself in order to know where he is. But simply picking out the positions does not exhaust temporal analysis, even temporal analysis restricted to questions of sequence, and does not allow us to determine the status of the anachronies: we have yet to define the relationships connecting sections to each other.

If we take section *A* as the narrative starting point, and therefore as being in an autonomous position, we can obviously define section *B* as *retrospective*, and this retrospection we may call subjective in the sense that it is adopted by the character himself, with the narrative doing no more than reporting his present thoughts ("he remembered . . . "); *B* is thus temporally subordinate to *A*: it is defined as retrospective *in relation* to *A*. *C* continues with a simple return to the initial position, without subordination. *D* is again retrospective, but this time the retrospection is adopted directly by the text: apparently it is the narrator who mentions the absence of melancholy, even if this absence is noticed by the hero. *E* brings us back to the present, but in a totally different way from *C*, for this time the present is envisaged as emerging from the past and "from the point of view" of that past: it is not a simple return to the present but an *anticipation* (subjective, obviously) of the present from within the past; *E* is thus subordinated to *D* as *D* is to *C*, whereas *C*, like *A*, was autonomous. *F* brings us again to position 1 (the past), on a higher level than anticipation *E*: simple return again, but return to 1, that is, to a subordinate position. *G* is again an anticipation, but this time an objective one, for the Jean of the earlier time foresaw the end that was to come to his love precisely as, not indifference, but melancholy at loss of love. *H*, like *F*, is a simple return to 1. *I*, finally, is (like *C*) a simple return to 2, that is, to the starting point.

This brief fragment thus offers us in miniature a quite variegated sample of the several possible temporal relationships: subjective and objective retrospections, subjective and objective anticipations, and simple returns to each of these two positions. As the distinction between subjective and objective anachronies is not a matter of temporality but arises from other categories that we will come to in the chapter on mood, we will neutralize it for the moment. Moreover, to avoid the psychological connotations of such terms as "anticipation" or "retrospection," which automatically evoke subjective phenomena, we will eliminate these terms most of the time in favor of two others that are more neutral, designating as *prolepsis* any narrative maneuver that consists of narrating or evoking in advance an event that will take place later, designating as *analepsis* any evocation after the fact of an event that took place earlier than the point in the story where we are at any given moment, and reserving the general term *anachrony* to designate all forms of discordance between the two temporal orders of story and narrative (we will see later that these discordances are not entirely limited to analepsis and prolepsis).[11]

This analysis of syntactic relationships (subordination and coordination) between sections now allows us to replace our first formula, which admitted only positions, with a second, which recognizes connections and interlockings:

$$A2[B1]C2[D1(E2)F1(G2)H1]I2$$

Here we clearly see the difference in status between sections *A*, *C*, and *I* on the one hand, and *E* and *G* on the other, all of which occupy the same temporal position but not at the same hierarchical level. We also see that the dynamic relationships (analepses and prolepses) come at the openings of brackets or parentheses, with the closings corresponding to simple returns. Finally, we observe that this fragment is perfectly self-contained, with the starting positions at each level scrupulously reinstated: we will see that this is not always the case. Of course, numerical relationships allow us to recognize analepses and pro-

---

[11] Here begin the problems (and disgraces) of terminology. *Prolepsis* and *analepsis* offer the advantage of being—through their roots—part of a grammatical-rhetorical family some of whose other members will serve us later; on the other hand, we will have to play on the opposition between the root *-lepse*—which in Greek refers to the fact of taking, whence, in narrative, assuming responsibility for and taking on (prolepsis: to take on something in advance; analepsis: to take on something after the event)—and the root *-lipse* (as in *ellipsis* or *paralipsis*) which refers, on the contrary, to the fact of leaving out, passing by without any mention. But no prefix taken from Greek allows us to subsume the antithesis *pro/ana*. Whence our recourse to *anachrony*, which is perfectly clear but lies outside the system, and whose prefix interferes regrettably with *analepsis*. Regrettably, but significantly.

lepses, but we can clarify the formula even further, like this, for example:

$$A2[B1]C2[\overbrace{D1(E2)F1(G2)}^{A \quad A}H1]I2$$
$$\underset{P \quad P}{}$$

This fragment presented the obvious advantage (didactically) of a temporal structure limited to two positions. That situation is fairly rare, however, and before leaving the micronarrative level behind, we will take from *Sodome et Gomorrhe* a text that is much more complex (even if we reduce it, as we shall, to its basic temporal positions, ignoring a few nuances), and that illustrates well the temporal omnipresence characteristic of Proustian narrative. We are at the soirée given by the Prince de Guermantes, and Swann has just told Marcel of the Prince's conversion to Dreyfusism which, with a naive partiality, he sees as proof of intelligence. This is how Marcel's narrative makes connections (I put a letter at the beginning of each distinct section):

(A) Swann now found equally intelligent anybody who was of his opinion, his old friend the Prince de Guermantes and my school-fellow Bloch, (B) whom previously he had avoided (C) and whom he now invited to luncheon. (D) Swann interested Bloch greatly by telling him that the Prince de Guermantes was a Dreyfusard. "We must ask him to sign our appeal for Picquart; a name like his would have a tremendous effect." But Swann, blending with his ardent conviction as an Israelite the diplomatic moderation of a man of the world, (E) whose habits he had too thoroughly acquired (Γ) to be able to shed them at this late hour, refused to allow Bloch to send the Prince a circular to sign, even on his own initiative. "He cannot do such a thing, we must not expect the impossible," Swann repeated. "There you have a charming man who has travelled thousands of miles to come over to our side. He can be very useful to us. If he were to sign your list, he would simply be compromising himself with his own people, would be made to suffer on our account, might even repent of his confidences and not confide in us again." Nor was this all, Swann refused his own signature. He felt that his name was too Hebraic not to create a bad effect. Besides, even if he approved of all the attempts to secure a fresh trial, he did not wish to be mixed up in any way in the antimilitarist campaign. He wore, (G) a thing he had never done previously, the decoration (H) he had won as a young militiaman, in '70, (*I*) and added a codicil to his will asking that, (*J*) contrary to his previous dispositions, (*K*) he might be buried with the military honours due to his rank as Chevalier of the Legion of Honour. A request which assembled round the church of Combray a whole squadron of (*L*) those troopers over whose fate Françoise used to weep in days gone by, when she envisaged (*M*) the prospect of a war. (*N*) In short, Swann refused to sign Bloch's circular, with the result that, if he passed in the eyes of many people as a fanatical Dreyfusard, my friend found him lukewarm, infected with Nationalism, and a militarist.

(*O*) Swann left me without shaking hands so as not to be forced into a general leave-taking.[12]

We have thus recognized here (once more, extremely crudely and for purely demonstrative purposes) fifteen narrative sections, distributed among nine temporal positions. These positions are the following, in chronological order: (1) the war of 1870; (2) Marcel's childhood in Combray; (3) a time before the Guermantes soirée; (4) the Guermantes soirée, which we can place in 1898; (5) the invitation to Bloch (necessarily later than this soirée, from which Bloch is absent); (6) the Swann-Bloch luncheon; (7) the addition of the codicil; (8) Swann's funeral; (9) the war whose prospect Françoise envisaged and which, strictly speaking, occupies no definite position, since it is purely hypothetical, but which—in order to place it in time and simplify things—we may identify with the war of 1914–18. The formula of positions is then the following:

$$A4\text{–}B3\text{–}C5\text{–}D6\text{–}E3\text{–}F6\text{–}G3\text{–}H1\text{–}I7\text{–}J3\text{–}K8\text{–}L2\text{–}M9\text{–}N6\text{–}O4$$

If we compare the temporal structure of this fragment to that of the preceding one, we notice, besides the greater number of positions, a much more complex hierarchical interlocking, since, for example, *M* depends on *L*, which depends on *K*, which depends on *I*, which depends on the large prolepsis *D–N*. Moreover, certain anachronies, like *B* and *C*, are juxtaposed without an explicit return to the base position: they are thus at the same level of subordination and are simply coordinate with each other. Finally,

[12] RH II, 82-83/P II, 712–713.

the transition from C5 to D6 does not produce a true prolepsis since we never come back to position 5; it therefore constitutes a simple ellipsis of the time that passed between 5 (the invitation) and 6 (the luncheon); the ellipsis, or leap forward without any return, is obviously not an anachrony but a simple acceleration of the narrative, which we will study in the chapter on duration: it certainly has to do with *time*, but not time approached as *order*, which is all that interests us here; we will thus mark the transition from C to D not with a bracket but simply with a hyphen to indicate sheer succession. This, then, is the complete formula:

$$A4[B3][C5 -D6(E3)F6(G3)(H1)(I7<J3><K8(L2<M9>)>)N6]O4$$

We will now leave the micronarrative level behind to examine the main articulations of the temporal structure of the *Recherche*. Needless to say, an analysis at this level cannot consider the details that belong to another scale, and therefore proceeds by means of very crude simplification: here we pass from the microstructure to the macrostructure.

The first temporal section of the *Recherche*, which occupies the first five pages of the book, evokes a moment that is impossible to date with precision but that takes place fairly late in the hero's life,[13] at the time when, going to bed early and suffering from insomnia, he spent a large part of his nights recalling his past. This first time in the narrative order is therefore far from being first in the diegetic order. Anticipating the analysis to follow, let us assign it at once to position 5 in the story. Thus: A5.

The second section (I, 7–33) is the account given by the narrator—but plainly inspired by the memories of the sleepless hero (who fulfills here the function of what Marcel Muller calls the *intermediary subject*)[14]—of a very limited but very important episode in his childhood in Combray: the famous scene that he

---

[13] As a matter of fact, one of the rooms evoked is that at Tansonville, where Marcel slept only during the visit recounted at the end of *La Fugitive* and the beginning of the *Temps retrouvé*. The period of the insomnias, necessarily later than that visit, could coincide with one and/or the other of the cures in a clinic which follow, and which frame the episode of Paris at war (1916).

[14] Muller, *Les Voix narratives*, Part I, chap. 2, and passim. I will return to the distinction between hero and narrator in the last chapter.

names "the drama of [his] going to bed," in the course of which his mother, prevented by Swann's visit from bestowing on him her ritual goodnight kiss, will finally—decisive "first concession"—yield to his pleas and spend the night with him: B2.

The third section (I, 33–34) brings us very briefly back to position 5, that of the insomnias: C5. The fourth probably also takes place somewhere within that period, since it brings about a modification in the content of the insomnias:[15] it is the episode of the madeleine (I, 34–36), in the course of which the hero finds a whole side of his childhood restored to him, a side of his childhood ("of Combray, save what was comprised in the theatre and the drama of my going to bed there") that until then had remained buried (and preserved) in apparent oblivion: D5'. Thus a fifth section follows, a second return to Combray but much vaster than the first in its temporal range since this time it covers (not without ellipses) the whole of the childhood in Combray. *Combray II* (I, 37–142) will thus be for us E2', contemporaneous with B2 but largely overflowing it, the way C5 overflows and includes D5'.

The sixth section (I, 143) returns to position 5 (insomnias): thus F5. This position again serves as a springboard for a new memory-elicited analepsis, whose place is the earliest of all since it antedates the hero's birth: *Un amour de Swann* (I, 144–292) is the seventh section, G1.

The eighth section is a very brief return (I, 293) to the position of the insomnias, thus H5. Again this position opens an analepsis, one that this time is aborted, although its function as advance notice or pointer is obvious to the attentive reader: the evocation in a half-page (still I, 293) of Marcel's room at Balbec is the ninth section, I4. Immediately coordinated with this, only now without a perceptible return to the transfer point of the insomnias, is the narrative (this, too, retrospective with respect to the starting point) of the dreams of traveling that the hero had in Paris, several years before his stay in Balbec; the tenth section will thus be J3: Parisian adolescence, love with Gilberte, partici-

---

[15] After the madeleine, the "total" Combray will be integrated into the insomniac's memories.

pation in Mme. Swann's circle, then, after an ellipsis, first stay at Balbec, return to Paris, entry into the milieu of the Guermantes, etc.: henceforth the movement is established, and the narrative, in its major articulations, for the most part becomes regular and conforms to chronological order—so much so that, at our level of analysis, we may take section *J*3 to extend to all the rest (and the end) of the *Recherche*.

The formula for this beginning is, then, according to our previous conventions:

$$A5[B2]C5[D5'(E2')]F5[G1]H5[I4][J3...$$

Thus, the *Recherche du temps perdu* is launched with a vast movement of coming-and-going from one key, strategically dominant position, obviously position 5 (insomnias) and its variant 5' (madeleine)—positions of the "intermediary subject," who is insomniac or beneficiary of the miracle of involuntary memory. His recollections control the whole of the narrative, giving point 5-5' the function of a sort of indispensable transfer point or—if one may say so—of a *dispatching* narrative: in order to pass from *Combray I* to *Combray II*, from *Combray II* to *Un amour de Swann*, from *Un amour de Swann* to Balbec, it is always necessary to come back to that position, which is central even though excentric (because later). Its control does not loosen until the transition from Balbec to Paris, even though this latter section (*J*3), inasmuch as it is coordinated with the preceding section, is also subordinated to the remembering activity of the intermediary subject, and so it too is analeptic. The difference—certainly essential—between this analepsis and all the preceding ones is that this one remains *open*, and its extent merges with almost the whole of the *Recherche* which means, among other things, that this analepsis will rejoin and pass beyond its own memory-created starting point without mentioning that point and seemingly without noticing it, swallowing it up in one of its ellipses. We will come back to this particular characteristic later. At the moment, let us only note this zigzag movement, this initial—and as it were initiatory, or propitiatory—stammering: 5-2-5-5'-2'-5-1-5-4-3..., itself already contained, like all the rest, in the embryonic cell of the first five pages, which lead us from room to room, from period to period, from Paris to Combray, from Doncières to Balbec, from Venice to Tansonville. Not a motionless shifting back and forth, however, despite its repeated returns, since, thanks to it, a pinpointed *Combray I* is succeeded by a more spacious *Combray II*, by an *Amour de Swann* that is earlier but has an already irreversible movement, by a *Noms de pays: le nom*, where finally the narrative definitively sets in motion and adopts its pace.

These complexly structured openings, mimicking, as it were, the unavoidable *difficulty of beginning* the better to exorcise it, are seemingly part of the earliest and most lasting narrative tradition: we have already noted the sidewise movement at the start of the *Iliad*, and must recall here that onto the convention of the beginning *in medias res* was added or superimposed, for the entire classical period, the convention of narrative embeddings (X tells that Y tells that . . .)—embeddings which are still at work (and we will return to this later) in *Jean Santeuil*, and which allow the narrator time to *position his voice*. The particular characteristic of the exordium of the *Recherche* is obviously its multiplication of memory-created instances, and consequently its multiplication *of beginnings*, among which each (except the last) can seem afterward like an introductory prologue. First beginning (absolute beginning): "For a long time I used to go to bed early . . . " Second beginning (ostensible beginning of the autobiography), five pages later: "At Combray, as every afternoon ended . . . " Third beginning (appearance on stage of involuntary memory), twenty-six pages later: "And so it was that, for a long time afterwards, when I lay awake at night and revived old memories of Combray . . . " Fourth beginning (resumption after the madeleine, real beginning of the autobiography), four pages later: "Combray at a distance, from a twenty-mile radius . . . " Fifth beginning, one hundred and seven pages later: *ab ovo*, Swann in love (an *exemplary* novella if there ever was one, archetype of all the Proustian loves), conjoint (and hidden) births of Marcel and Gilberte ("We will confess," Stendhal would say here, "that, following the example of many serious authors, we have begun the story of our hero a year before his birth." Is not Swann to Marcel, mutatis mutandis and, I hope, with nothing untoward in mind, what Lieutenant Robert is to Fabrice del Dongo?)[16]—fifth beginning, thus: "To admit you to the 'little nucleus,' the 'little group,' and 'little clan' at the Verdurins'... " Sixth beginning, one hundred and forty-nine pages later: "Among the rooms which used most commonly to take shape in my mind during my long nights of sleeplessness..." immediately followed by a seventh and thus, as it should be, a final beginning: "And yet nothing could have differed more utterly, either, from the real Balbec than that other Balbec of which I had often dreamed... " This time, the movement is launched: after this it will never stop.

Reach, Extent

I have said that, in its main articulations, the continuation of the *Recherche* was arranged in conformity with chronological order; but this general course does not exclude the presence of a great many anachronies in small points: analepses and prolepses, certainly, but also other forms that are more complex or more subtle, perhaps more specific to Proustian narrative, and that in any case are remote from both "real" chronology and classical narrative temporality. Before taking up the analysis of these anachronies, let us make clear that we are concerned here only with temporal analysis, and furthermore temporal analysis limited solely to questions of order: for the time being we are setting aside questions of speed and frequency and a fortiori characteristics of mood and voice, which can affect anachronies as they can affect any other kind of narrative segment. In particular, we will disregard an essential distinction between, on the one hand, the anachronies that the narrative takes direct responsibility for, and that thus stay at the same narrative level as their surroundings (example, lines 7–12 of the *Iliad* or the second chapter of *César Birotteau*), and, on the other hand, the anachronies that one of the characters of the first narrative takes

---

[16] But is not Swann's role in the bedtime scene symbolically *paternal*? After all, it is he who deprives the child of its mother's presence. The legal father, on the contrary, appears here with an unpardonable laxity, a bantering and suspect willingness to oblige: "Go with the boy." What can we conclude from this bundle?

on, and that thus appear at a second narrative level (example, Books IX–XII of the *Odyssey* [Ulysses' speech], or Raphael de Valentin's autobiography in the second part of *La Peau de chagrin*). Obviously we will again meet this question (which is not specific to anachronies although it concerns them in the highest degree) in the chapter on narrative voice.

An anachrony can reach into the past or the future, either more or less far from the "present" moment (that is, from the moment in the story when the narrative was interrupted to make room for the anachrony): this temporal distance we will name the anachrony's *reach*. The anachrony itself can also cover a duration of story that is more or less long: we will call this its *extent*. Thus when Homer, in Book XIX of the *Odyssey*, evokes the circumstances long ago in which Ulysses, while an adolescent, received the wound whose scar he still bears when Euryclea is preparing to wash his feet, this analepsis (filling lines 394–466) has a reach of several decades and an extent of a few days. So defined, the status of anachronies seems to be merely a question of more or less, a matter of measurement particular to each occasion, a timekeeper's work lacking theoretical interest. It is, however, possible (and, I claim, useful) to categorize— without too much emphasis—the characteristics of reach and extent with respect to the ways in which they are connected to certain "higher" moments in the narrative. This categorization applies in basically the same way to the two main classes of anachronies; but for convenience of exposition and to avoid the risk of becoming too abstract, we will first handle analepses exclusively, and broaden our procedure afterward.

Analepses

Every anachrony constitutes, with respect to the narrative into which it is inserted—onto which it is grafted—a narrative that is temporally second, subordinate to the first in a sort of narrative syntax that we met in the analysis we undertook above of a very short fragment from *Jean Santeuil*. We will henceforth call the temporal level of narrative with respect to which anachrony is defined as such, "first narrative." Of course—and this we have already verified—the embeddings can be more complex, and an anachrony can assume the role of first narrative with respect to another that it carries; and more generally, with respect to an anachrony the totality of the context can be taken as first narrative.

The narrative of Ulysses' wound deals with an episode that is quite obviously earlier than the temporal point of departure of the "first narrative" of the *Odyssey*, even if, according to this principle, we allow "first narrative" to include the retrospective tale Ulysses tells the Phaeacians, which goes back as far as the fall of Troy. We can thus describe as *external* this analepsis whose entire extent remains external to the extent of the first narrative. We can do the same, for example, with the second chapter of *César Birotteau*, whose story, as the title clearly indicates ("Les Antécédents de César Birotteau"), takes place earlier than the drama opened by the nocturnal scene of the first chapter. Inversely, we will describe as *internal* analepsis the sixth chapter of *Madame Bovary*, dealing with Emma's years in the convent, which are obviously later than Charles's entrance at school, which is the novel's starting point; or similarly, the beginning of the *Souffrances de l'inventeur*, which, after the narrative of the Parisian adventures of Lucien de Rubempré, serves to acquaint the reader with David Séchard's life in Angoulême during that period.[17] We can also imagine, and occasionally we come across, *mixed* analepses, whose reach goes back to a point earlier and whose extent arrives at a point later than the beginning of the first narrative: so it is with the story of Des Grieux in *Manon Lescaut*, which begins several years before the first meeting with the Man of Quality and continues up to the time of the second meeting, which is also the time of the narrating.

This distinction is not as useless as it might seem at first sight. In effect, external analepses and internal analepses (or the internal part of mixed analepses) function for purposes of narrative analysis in totally different ways, at least on one point that seems to me essential. External analepses, by the very fact that they are external, never at any moment risk interfering with the

---

[17] Balzac, *Illusions perdues*, Garnier ed., pp. 550–643.

NO EXTERNAL ANALEPSIS IN FAIx
SINCE IT BEGINS LITERALLY AT THE
BEGINING OF TIME!

first narrative, for their only function is to fill out the first narrative by enlightening the reader on one or another "antecedent."
This is obviously the case with some of the examples already
mentioned, and it is also, and just as typically, the case with
Un amour de Swann in the *Recherche du temps perdu*. The case is
otherwise with internal analepses: since their temporal field is
contained within the temporal field of the first narrative, they
present an obvious risk of redundancy or collision. We must
therefore examine these problems of interference more closely.

We will set aside at once the internal analepses that I propose
to call *heterodiegetic*,[18] that is, analepses dealing with a story line
(and thus with a diegetic content) different from the content (or
contents) of the first narrative. Such analepses deal, classically,
either with a character recently introduced whose "antecedents"
the narrator wants to shed light on, like Flaubert for Emma in
the chapter we referred to earlier; or they deal with a character
who has been out of sight for some time and whose recent past
we must catch up with, as is the case for David at the beginning
of the *Souffrances de l'inventeur*. These are, perhaps, the most
traditional functions of analepsis, and obviously the temporal
coinciding here does not entail real narrative interference. So it
is, for instance, when, at the Prince de Faffenheim's entrance
into the Villeparisis drawing room, a retrospective digression of
several pages informs us of the reasons for this appearance, that
is, the vicissitudes of the Prince's candidacy for the Academy of
Moral Sciences;[19] or when, reencountering Gilberte Swann who
has become Mlle. de Forcheville, Marcel has the reasons for this
change in name explained to him.[20] Swann's marriage, the mar-
riages of Saint-Loup and "the Cambremer boy," the death of
Bergotte[21] thus overtake the main line of the story—which is
Marcel's autobiography—after the event, without in any way
disturbing the prerogative of the first narrative.

[18] G. Genette, *Figures II* (Paris, 1969), p. 202.
[19] RH I, 899-904/P II, 257-263.
[20] RH II, 786-792/P III, 574-582.
[21] RH I, 358-361/P I, 467-471; RH II, 849-856/P III, 664-673; RH II, 506-510/P III, 182-188.

Very different is the situation of internal *homodiegetic* analepses, that is, internal analepses that deal with the same line of action as the first narrative. Here the risk of interference is obvious, and even apparently unavoidable. In fact, now we must once again differentiate two categories.

The first, which I will call *completing* analepses, or "returns," comprises the retrospective sections that fill in, after the event, an earlier gap in the narrative (the narrative is thus organized by temporary omissions and more or less belated reparations, according to a narrative logic that is partially independent of the passing of time). These earlier gaps can be ellipses pure and simple, that is, breaks in the temporal continuity. Thus, Marcel's stay in Paris in 1914 is recounted on the occasion of another Parisian stay, this one in 1916, partially filling in the ellipsis of several "long years" the hero spent in a clinic;[22] the meeting in Uncle Adolphe's apartment with the Lady in pink[23] opens, in the middle of the Combray narrative, a door onto the Parisian side of Marcel's childhood—a side totally concealed, except for this, until the third part of *Swann*. It is obviously in temporal gaps of this kind that we must hypothetically place certain events in Marcel's life known to us only by brief retrospective allusions: a trip to Germany with his grandmother earlier than the first trip to Balbec, a stay in the Alps earlier than the episode of Doncières, a trip to Holland earlier than the Guermantes dinner, or again—appreciably more difficult to locate, given the length of military service during that period—the years in the military parenthetically evoked during the final stroll with Charlus.[24]

But there is another type of gap, of a less strictly temporal kind, created not by the elision of a diachronic section but by the

---

[22] RH II, 900–913/P III, 737–755; cf. RH II, 889/P III, 723.

[23] RH I, 55–60/P I, 72–80.

[24] RH I, 544/P I, 718; RH I, 773/P II, 83; RH I, 1090/P II, 523; RH II, 954/P III, 808. Supposing, of course, that we take these items of retrospective information wholly seriously, which is the law of narrative analysis. The critic, however, for his part can just as well take such allusions to be authorial lapses; or perhaps Proust's biography is momentarily projected onto Marcel's.

omission of one of the constituent elements of a situation in a
period that the narrative does generally cover. An example: the
fact of recounting his childhood while systematically concealing
the existence of one of the members of his family (which Proust
would be doing vis-à-vis his brother Robert if we took the *Recherche* for a genuine autobiography). Here the narrative does
not skip over a moment of time, as in an ellipsis, but it *sidesteps* a
given element. This kind of lateral ellipsis we will call, conform-
ing to etymology and not excessively straining rhetorical usage,
a *paralipsis.* [25] Like temporal ellipsis, paralipsis obviously lends
itself very nicely to retrospective filling-in. For instance Swann's
death, or more precisely its effect on Marcel (for the death itself
could be considered external to the autobiography of the hero,
and thus heterodiegetic), was not recounted in its place; yet in
principle there is no room for a temporal ellipsis between
Swann's last appearance (at the Guermantes soirée) and the day
of the Charlus-Verdurin concert when the retrospective news of
his death slips in;[26] so we must assume that this very important
event in Marcel's affective life ("The death of Swann had been a
crushing blow to me at the time") was omitted laterally, in
paralipsis. An even more clear-cut example: the end of Marcel's
passion for the Duchesse de Guermantes, thanks to the quasi-
miraculous intervention of his mother, is the subject of a retrospective narrative with no specific date ("There had been a day
when");[27] but since his ailing grandmother is involved in this
scene, we must obviously place it before the second chapter of
Guermantes II (I, 965); but we must also, of course, place it after I,
861–862, where we see that Oriane has not yet "ceased to interest
[him]." Yet there is no identifiable temporal ellipsis; Marcel has
therefore omitted to report to us in its place this nonetheless extremely important aspect of his inner life. But the most remarkable

[25] The rhetoricians' paralipsis is, rather, a false omission, otherwise called
preterition. Here, paralipsis as a narrative trope is contrasted to ellipsis the way
put it aside is contrasted to *leave it where it is.* We will meet paralipsis again later as
an item of *mood.*
[26] RH II, 518/P III, 199–201. Unless we take as ellipsis the iterative handling of
the first months of joint life with Albertine at the beginning of the *Prisonnière.*
[27] RH I, 983/P II, 371.

case—although it is rarely picked up by critics, perhaps because they refuse to take it seriously—is the mysterious "girl-cousin" about whom we learn, when Marcel gives Aunt Léonie's sofa to a go-between, that with her on this same sofa he experienced "for the first time the sweets of love";[28] and this happened nowhere else but at Combray, and at a fairly early date, since he makes clear that the scene of the "initiation"[29] took place "one hour when my Aunt Léonie had gotten up," and we know in another connection that in her final years Léonie no longer left her room.[30] Let us set aside the probable thematic value of this belated confidence, and let us even admit that the omission of the event from the narrative of *Combray* is a purely temporal ellipsis: the omission of the *character* from the family tableau perhaps for that reason comes even closer to being censorship. This little cousin on the sofa will thus be for us—to each age its own pleasures—analepsis on paralipsis.

Up to now we have examined the (retroactive) localization of analepses as if they always involved a unique event to be placed at one single point in past history. In fact, certain retrospections, although dealing with individual events, can refer to iterative ellipses,[31] that is, ellipses dealing not with a single portion of elapsed time but with several portions taken as if they were alike and to some extent repetitive. Thus, the meeting with the Lady in pink can refer us to any day in the winter months when Marcel and his parents were living in Paris, in any year before the quarrel with Uncle Adolphe: an individual event, certainly,

---

[28] RH I, 440/P I, 578.

[29] "Girl-cousin (a little one). My initiator: I, 578 [P/RH I, 440]," imperturbably and precisely notes the Clarac and Ferré index of the names of the characters.

[30] It is true that she has two adjoining rooms, and goes into one while the other is being aired out (RH I, 37–38/P I, 49). But if that were the situation, the scene becomes extremely hazardous. On the other hand, the relationship is not clear between this "sofa" and the bed described on p. 38 (RH I/P I, 50), with its flowered quilt having a "nondescript, resinous, dull, indigestible, and fruity smell" where Marcel when very young, "with an unconfessed gluttony," always returned to "bury" himself. Let us leave this problem to the specialists, and remember that in the "Confession d'une Jeune Fille" of *Les Plaisirs et les jours* the "initiation" involves the fourteen-year-old heroine and a "cousin, a boy of fifteen . . . already very depraved" (Pléiade, p. 87; *Pleasures and Regrets*, trans. Louise Varèse [New York, 1948], p. 34).

[31] About the iterative in general we will speak in Chapter 3.

but for us its localization is on the order of the species or the class (a winter) and not of the individual (a given winter). It is the same a fortiori when the event recounted by the analepsis is itself iterative in nature. Thus, in the *Jeunes Filles en fleurs*, the day of the first appearance of the "little band" ends with a dinner at Rivebelle that is not the first; for the narrator, this dinner is the opportunity for a look back at the preceding series, a look back written mainly in the imperfect tense for repeated action and telling of all the previous dinners in the account of a single one:[32] clearly the ellipsis which this retrospection fills in must itself be iterative. Similarly, the analepsis that ends the *Jeunes Filles*, a final glance at Balbec after the return to Paris,[33] in a synthetic way bears on the whole series of naps that Marcel, on the doctor's order, had to take every morning until noon during his entire stay, while his young friends were strolling along the sunny jetty and the morning concert blared under his windows; it thus allows this part of the *Recherche* to end not with the greyness of a sad return home but with the glorious pause—the golden stop—of a changeless summer sun.

With the second type of (internal) homodiegetic analepses, which we will name precisely *repeating* analepses, or "recalls," we no longer escape redundancy, for in these the narrative openly, sometimes explicitly, retraces its own path. Of course, these recalling analepses can rarely reach very large textual dimensions; rather, they are the narrative's allusions to its own past, what Lämmert calls *Rückgriffe*, or "retroceptions."[34] But their importance in narrative economy, especially with Proust, amply compensates for their limited narrative scope.

We must obviously set among these recalls the three reminiscences owed to involuntary memory during the Guermantes matinée, all of which (contrary to that of the madeleine) refer to an earlier time in the narrative: the stay in Venice, the train's stop in front of a row of trees, the first morning by the sea at

[32] RH I, 609–617/P I, 808–823.
[33] RH I, 713–714/P I, 953–955.
[34] Eberhart Lämmert, *Bauformen des Erzählens* (Stuttgart, 1955), Part II.

Balbec.[35] These are recalls in the purest form, deliberately chosen or devised because of their casual and commonplace character. But at the same time they suggest a comparison between present and past, a comparison comforting for once, since the moment of reminiscence is always euphoric, even if it revives a past that in itself was painful: "I recognized that what seemed to me now so delightful was that same row of trees which I had found tedious both to observe and to describe."[36] The comparison between two situations that are similar and also different often motivates as well recalls in which involuntary memory does not play a role: for instance when the Duc de Guermantes's words about the Princesse de Parme ("she thinks you're charming") remind the hero—and give the narrator the opportunity to remind us—of those identical words of Mme. de Villeparisis about another "highness," the Princesse de Luxembourg.[37] Here the accent is on analogy. The accent is on contrast, on the other hand, when Saint-Loup introduces his Egeria Rachel to Marcel, who immediately recognizes her as the little prostitute from earlier times, she "who, but a few years since, . . . used to say to the procuress: 'To-morrow evening, then, if you want me for anyone, you will send round, won't you?'"[38] This sentence in effect reproduces almost verbatim what "Rachel when from the Lord" said in the *Jeunes Filles en fleurs:* "That's settled then; I shall be free to-morrow, if you have anyone you won't forget to send for me."[39] The variant in *Guermantes* is, so to speak, already foreseen in these terms: "She would simply vary her formula, saying indifferently: 'If you want me' or 'If you want anybody.'" In this case the recall has an evidently obsessive precision and puts the two sections in direct communication—whence the interpolation in the second section of the paragraph

---

[35] RH II, 997–999/P III, 866–869; cf. RH II, 820–840/P III, 623–655, RH II, 988/P III, 855, and RH I, 510–511/P I, 672–674.

[36] RH II, 998/P III, 868. Let us remember that the feeling of boredom before the row of trees had been for Marcel the sign of an abortive literary vocation, and thus of the failure of his life.

[37] RH I, 1022/P II, 425; cf. RH I, 531/P I, 700.

[38] RH I, 827/P II, 158.

[39] RH I, 439/P I, 577.

about Rachel's past conduct, which seems as if snatched from the text of the first section. A striking example of migration, or, if one wishes, of narrative scattering.

Again a comparison, in *La Prisonnière*, between the cowardice Marcel shows toward Albertine and his courage earlier in front of Gilberte, when he had "still enough strength left to give her up."[40] This return retroactively confers on the past episode a meaning that in its own time it did not yet have. Indeed, this is the most persistent function of recalls in the *Recherche*, to modify the meaning of past occurrences after the event, either by making significant what was not so originally or by refuting a first interpretation and replacing it with a new one.

The first modality is signaled very precisely by the narrator himself when he writes about the incident of the syringas: "At the actual moment, I saw nothing in all this that was not perfectly natural, at the most a little confused, but in any case *unimportant*," and again: "incident the cruel *significance* of which entirely escaped me and did not enter my mind until long afterwards."[41] That significance will be delivered up by Andrée after Albertine's death,[42] and this case of deferred interpretation yields us an almost perfect example of double narrative, first from the (naive) viewpoint of Marcel, then later from the (enlightened) viewpoint of Andrée and Albertine, when the clue, now finally supplied, dissipates every kind of "confusion." With much greater fullness, the late meeting with Mlle. de Saint-Loup,[43] daughter of Gilberte and Robert, will give Marcel the opportunity for a general "replay" of the main episodes of his existence, episodes which until then were lost to insignificance because of their dispersion and are now suddenly reassembled, now made significant by being bound all together amongst themselves, because all are bound now to the existence of this child who was born Swann and Guermantes,

---

[40] RH II, 622/P III, 344.
[41] RH II, 415–416/P III, 54–55: returning home with the syringas, Marcel bumps into Andrée who, making a pretext of some allergy, prevents him from going in right away. In fact, that day she had been in a sinful situation with Albertine.
[42] RH II, 803–804/P III, 600–601.
[43] RH II, 1125–1126/P III, 1029–1030.

granddaughter of the Lady in pink, grandniece of Charlus, evoker of both the "two ways" of Combray but also of Balbec, the Champs-Elysées, La Raspelière, Oriane, Legrandin, Morel, Jupien . . . : chance, contingency, arbitrariness now suddenly wiped out, his life's portrait now suddenly "captured" in the web of a structure and the cohesiveness of a meaning.

This principle of deferred or postponed significance[44] obviously fits perfectly into the mechanism of *enigma,* analyzed by Barthes in *S/Z;* and that so sophisticated a work as the *Recherche* should use this mechanism perhaps surprises those who place this work at the antipodes from popular novels—which it no doubt is in its significance and aesthetic value, but not always in its techniques. There is something of "it was Milady" in the *Recherche,* even if only in the humorous form of "it was my old friend Bloch" in the *Jeunes Filles,* when the thundering anti-semite emerges from his tent.[45] The reader will wait more than a thousand pages before learning, at the same time as the hero (if he has not already guessed on his own), the identity of the Lady in pink.[46] After the publication of his article in *Le Figaro,* Marcel receives a letter of congratulations signed "Sanilon," written in a colloquial and charming style: "I was desolate at my inability to discover who had written to me"; he will know later, and we will know with him, that it was Théodore, the ex-grocer's assistant and choirman of Combray.[47] Entering the Duc de Guermantes's library, Marcel passes a little, provincial, timid, and shabby bourgeois: it was the Duc de Bouillon![48] A tall woman makes overtures to him on the street: she will turn out to be Mme. d'Orvilliers![49] In the little train of La Raspelière, a large common woman with a massive face is reading the *Revue des deux mondes:* she will turn out to be Princess Cherbatoff![50] Some time after Albertine's death, a blond girl glimpsed in the Bois,

[44] See Jean-Yves Tadié, *Proust et le roman* (Paris, 1971), p. 124.
[45] RH I, 558–559/P I, 738.
[46] RH I, 907/P II, 267.
[47] RH II, 798 and 874/P III, 591 and 701.
[48] RH I, 1125 and II, 61/P II, 573 and 681.
[49] RH I, 985 and II, 88/P II, 373 and 721.
[50] RH II, 184 and 208/P II, 858 and 892.

then on the street, casts his way a glance that inflames him: met again in the Guermantes drawing room, she will turn out to be Gilberte![51] The technique is used so often, it so obviously forms background and norm, that for contrast or deviation one can sometimes play on its exceptional absence or zero degree. In the little train of La Raspelière there is a glorious girl with dark eyes, magnolia skin, bold manners, a voice quick, cool, and jocular: "'I should so much like to see her again,' I exclaimed. 'Don't worry, one always sees people again,' replied Albertine. In this particular instance, she was wrong; I never saw again, nor did I ever identify, the pretty girl with the cigarette."[52]

But the most typical use of the recall in Proust is without doubt when an event that at the time of its occurrence has already been provided with a meaning, has this first interpretation replaced afterward by another (not necessarily better) one. This technique is obviously one of the most efficient methods for circulating meaning in the novel and for achieving the perpetual "reversal from pro to con" that characterizes the Proustian apprenticeship to truth. Saint-Loup, in Doncières, meeting Marcel on the street, apparently does not recognize him and greets him coldly as if he were a soldier: later we will learn that he had recognized him but wished not to stop.[53] The grandmother, at Balbec, insists with an irritating futility that Saint-Loup photograph her with her beautiful hat on: she knew she was dying and wanted to leave her grandson a memento that would not show her looking poorly.[54] Mlle. Vinteuil's friend, the profaner of Montjouvain, devoted herself devoutly at the same period to recreating note by note the indecipherable rough drafts of the septet,[55] etc. We know the lengthy series of revelations and confessions by which the retrospective or even posthumous image of Odette, Gilberte, Albertine, or Saint-Loup dissolves and reforms: thus, the young man who accompanied Gilberte one particular evening on the Champs-Elysées "was Léa in male

[51] RH II, 777 and 786/P III, 563 and 574.
[52] RH II, 202/P II, 883.
[53] RH I, 813 and 841/P II, 138 and 176.
[54] RH I, 593 and II, 127–128/P I, 786 and II, 776.
[55] RH I, 123–127 and II, 562/P I, 160–165 and III, 261.

attire";[56] on the day of the walk in the suburban village and the slap on the journalist's cheek, Rachel was for Saint-Loup only a "screen," and at Balbec he secluded himself with the elevator boy of the Grand Hotel;[57] the evening of the cattleyas, Odette was coming from Forcheville's;[58] and there is the whole series of belated adjustments of Albertine's relationships with Andrée, Morel, and various young girls of Balbec and elsewhere;[59] but on the other hand, and by an even crueller irony, the sinful liaison between Albertine and Mlle. Vinteuil's friend, the reluctant admission of which crystallized Marcel's passion, was pure invention: "I stupidly thought that I might make myself seem interesting to you by inventing the story that I had known the girls quite well"[60]—the aim is achieved, but by another route (jealousy, and not artistic snobbishness), and with what outcome we know.

These revelations of the erotic habits of the male friend or the loved woman are obviously capital. I would be tempted to find even more capital ("capitalissime," in Proustian language)— because it touches the very foundation of the hero's *Weltanschauung* (the universe of Combray, the opposition of the two ways, "deepest layer of my mental soil"[61])—the series of reinterpretations for which the late stay at Tansonville will be the occasion and Gilberte de Saint-Loup the unwitting medium. I have already tried elsewhere[62] to show the importance, on various levels, of the "verification"—which is a refutation—that Gilberte inflicts on Marcel's system of thought when she reveals to him not only that the sources of the Vivonne (which he imagined like "something as extraterrestrial as the Gates of Hell") were only "a sort of rectangular basin in which bubbles rose to the surface," but also that Guermantes and Méséglise are not so removed from each other, so "irreconcilable," as he had be-

[56]RH I, 474 and II, 868/P I, 623 and III, 695.
[57] RH I, 825–844 and II, 859/P I, 155–180 and III, 681.
[58] RH I, 177 and 284/P I, 231 and 371.
[59] RH II, 744–745/P III, 515; RH II, 751/P III, 525; RH II, 802–803/P III, 599–601.
[60] RH II, 370 and 617–618/P II, 1120 and III, 337.
[61] RH I, 141/P I, 184.
[62] *Figures* (Paris, 1966), p. 60, and *Figures II*, p. 242.

lieved, since in a single walk one can "go to Guermantes, taking the road by Méséglise." The other side of those "new revelations of existence" is this stupefying information that at the time of the steep path at Tansonville and the flowering hawthorns Gilberte was in love with him, and the unusual gesture she had directed at him then was in fact too explicit an advance.[63] Marcel understands then that he had understood nothing, and— supreme truth—"that the true Gilberte—the true Albertine— were perhaps those who had at the first moment yielded themselves in their facial expression, one behind the hedge of pink hawthorn, the other upon the beach," and that he had thus, through incomprehension—through excess of reflection— "missed the boat" at that first moment.

With the misunderstood gesture of Gilberte, once again the whole profound geography of Combray is reshaped. Gilberte, it turns out, had wanted to take Marcel with her (and other neighborhood scamps, including Théodore and his sister— future chambermaid of Baroness Putbus and the very symbol of erotic fascination) to the ruins of the donjon of Roussainville-le-Pin: this same phallic donjon, a vertical "confidant," on the horizon, of Marcel's solitary pleasures in the little room smelling of orrisroot and of his roaming frenzies in the countryside of Méséglise.[64] But he did not then suspect that the donjon was even more: the real place—proffered, accessible and not recognized, "in reality, and so close at hand"[65]—of forbidden pleasures. Roussainville, and by metonymy the whole Méséglise way,[66] are already the Cities of the Plain, "a promised [and] accursed land."[67] "Roussainville, within whose walls I had

---

[63] RH I, 108 and II, 866/P I, 141 and III, 694.

[64] RH I, 10 and 121/P I, 12 and 158.

[65] RH II, 868/P III, 697.

[66] That the Méséglise way incarnates sexuality this sentence clearly shows: "The things for which at that time I so feverishly longed, she had been ready, if only I had had the sense to understand and to meet her again, to let me taste in my boyhood. More completely even than I had supposed, Gilberte had been in those days truly part of the 'Méséglise way'" (RH II, 868/P III, 697).

[67] Roussainville under the thunderstorm is obviously (like Paris, later under the enemy's fire) Sodom and Gomorrah under the thunderbolt from heaven: "Before our eyes, in the distance, a promised or an accursed land, Roussainville, within whose walls I had never penetrated, Roussainville was now, when the rain had ceased for us, still being chastised, like a village in the Old Testament,

never penetrated": what missed opportunity, what regret! Or what denial? Yes, as Bardèche says, Combray's geography, apparently so innocent, is "a countryside which, like many others, requires deciphering."[68] But this deciphering, along with others, is already at work in the *Temps retrouvé*, and it arises from a subtle dialectic between the "innocent" narrative and its retrospective "verification": such in part are the function and importance of Proustian analepses.

We have seen how the determination of *reach* allowed us to divide analepses into two classes, external and internal, depending on whether the point to which they reach is located outside or inside the temporal field of the first narrative. The mixed class—not, after all, much resorted to—is in fact determined by a characteristic of *extent*, since this class consists of external analepses prolonged to rejoin and pass beyond the starting point of the first narrative. Extent, once more, controls the distinction we are now going to talk about as, returning to the two examples from the *Odyssey* that we have already met, we now compare them.

The first is the episode of Ulysses' wound. As we have already noted, its extent is much less than its reach, much less even than the distance separating the moment of the wound from the starting point of the *Odyssey* (the fall of Troy). After having recounted the hunt on Parnassus, the battle against the wild boar, the wound, the healing, the return to Ithaca, the narrative interrupts its retrospective digression point-blank and, skipping over several decades, comes back to the present scene.[69] The "return

---

by all the innumerable spears and arrows of the storm, which beat down obliquely upon the dwellings of its inhabitants, or else had already received the forgiveness of the Almighty, Who had restored to it the light of His sun, which fell upon it in rays of uneven length, like the rays of a monstrance upon the altar" (RH I, 116–117/P I, 152). We will note the presence of the verb "beat down upon," a muffled redoubling of the link that unites this scene—ahead of time—to the episode of *M. de Charlus during the war*, the flagellation functioning both as "vice" ("sin") and as punishment.

[68] Maurice Bardèche, *Marcel Proust romancier* (Paris, 1971), I, 269.

[69] Let us remember that this passage, which some people challenge without much evidence and despite Plato's testimony (*Republic*, I, 334 b), has been the subject of a commentary by Auerbach (*Mimesis*, trans. Willard Trask [1953; rpt. Garden City, N.Y., 1957], chap. 1).

to the past" is thus followed by a leap forward (in other words, an ellipsis), which leaves a whole long portion of the hero's life in darkness. The analepsis here is as it were pinpointed, recounting a moment from the past that remains isolated in its remoteness, and not seeking to join that moment to the present by covering an intervening period which is not relevant to the epic (since the subject of the *Odyssey,* as Aristotle observed, is not Ulysses' life but only his return from Troy). I will name this type of retrospection, which ends on an ellipsis without rejoining the first narrative, simply *partial* analepsis.

The second example is Ulysses' narration before the Phaeacians. This time, in contrast, having gone back as far as the point where Fame to some degree lost sight of him—in other words, to the fall of Troy—Ulysses brings his tale along until it rejoins the first narrative, covering the entire period extending from the fall of Troy to his arrival on Calypso's island: *complete* analepsis, this time, which joins the first narrative without any gap between the two sections of the story.

There is no point in dwelling here on the obvious differences in function between these two types of analepsis. The first serves solely to bring the reader an isolated piece of information, necessary for an understanding of a specific moment of the action. The second, tied to the practice of beginning *in medias res,* aims at retrieving the whole of the narrative's "antecedents." It generally forms an important part of the narrative, and sometimes, as in *La Duchesse de Langeais* or *The Death of Ivan Ilych,* even presents the chief part of it, with the first narrative functioning as the denouement in advance.

Until now we have looked from this point of view only at external analepses, which we decreed complete inasmuch as they rejoin the first narrative at its temporal starting point. But a "mixed" analepsis like Des Grieux's narrative can be said to be complete in a totally different sense since, as we have already noted, it rejoins the first narrative not at that one's beginning but at the very point (the meeting in Calais) when the first was interrupted to give up its place to the second: in other words, the extent of the analepsis is rigorously equal to its reach, and the narrative movement completes a perfect round trip. It is likewise in this sense that we can speak of complete internal

analepses, as in *Les Souffrances de l'inventeur,* where the retrospective narrative is brought up to the moment when David's
and Lucien's destinies again meet.

By definition, partial analepses pose no problem of joining or
narrative juncture: the analeptic tale plainly interrupts itself on
an ellipsis, and the first narrative picks up right where it had
stopped—picks up either implicitly and as if nothing had sus-
pended it, as in the *Odyssey* ("Now the old woman took the
scarred limb and passed her hands down it, and knew it by the
touch..."), or else explicitly, taking note of the interruption
and, as Balzac likes to do, emphasizing the explanatory function
that was already pointed out at the beginning of the analepsis by
the famous "this is why" or one of its variants. Thus, the big
return to the past in *La Duchesse de Langeais,* introduced by a
most explicit formulation ("Now here is the adventure that had
brought about the respective situations of the two characters in
that scene"), has an ending not less openly acknowledged: "The
feelings that stirred the two lovers when they met each other
again at the gate of the Carmelites and in the presence of a
Mother Superior should now be understood in all their intensity, and the violence aroused in both of them will no doubt
explain the denouement of this adventure."[70] Proust, who de-
rided the Balzacian "this is why" in *Contre Sainte-Beuve,* was not
above imitating it at least once in the *Recherche.*[71] He is equally
capable of resumptions of the same type—like this one that follows the account of the negotiations about the Academy between Faffenheim and Norpois: "Thus it was that Prince von
Faffenheim had been led to call upon Mme. de Villeparisis"[72]—
or of resumptions at least explicit enough for the transition to
be perceptible at once: "And now, on my second return to
Paris,..." or "as I turned over in my mind this recent meeting
with Saint-Loup... "[73] But most often his resumption is far
more discreet: the evocation of Swann's marriage, brought on

[70] Garnier, pp. 214 and 341.
[71] *Contre Saint-Beuve,* Pléiade ed., p. 271 (*Marcel Proust on Art and Literature, 1896–1919,* trans. S. T. Warner [New York, 1958], p. 173), and *Recherche* RH I, 159/P I, 208.
[72] RH I, 904/P II, 263.
[73] RH II, 913/P III, 755 and RH II, 919/P III, 762.

by one of Norpois's answers in the course of a dinner, is abruptly cut off by a return to the present conversation ("I began next to speak of the Comte de Paris...''), as is the evocation later on of Swann's death, inserted between two of Brichot's sentences with no transition ("'No,' Brichot went on...").[74] Sometimes the resumption is so elliptical that on a first reading one experiences some difficulty discovering just where the temporal leap takes place. Thus, when the performance of Vinteuil's sonata at the Verdurins' reminds Swann of an earlier performance, the analepsis, although introduced in the Balzacian way that we have spoken of ("this is why"), ends, by contrast, with no other mark of return than a simple paragraph break: "And so, at last, he ceased to think of it. / But tonight, at Mme. Verdurin's, scarcely had the little pianist begun to play when... " In the same way, during the Villeparisis matinée, when Mme. Swann's arrival reminds Marcel of a recent visit by Morel, the first narrative connects to the analepsis in a particularly offhand manner: "I, as I gave him my hand, was thinking of Mme. Swann and saying to myself with amazement, so far apart, so different were they in my memory, that I should have henceforth to identify her with the 'Lady in pink.' / M. de Charlus was not long in taking his place by the side of Mme. Swann."[75]

As we see, for the attentive reader the elliptical character of these resumptions, at the end of partial analepses, simply underlines by asyndeton the temporal rupture. With completing analepses the reverse difficulty obtains, resulting not from the gap between analeptic narrative and first narrative but, on the contrary, from their necessary junction. This junction could hardly be without some degree of overlapping and thus an appearance of awkwardness, unless the narrator has the skill to extract from this awkwardness a sort of playful charm. Here, in *César Birotteau*, is an instance of overlapping that is not taken charge of—perhaps not noticed by the novelist himself. The (analeptic) second chapter ends thus: "A few moments later, Constance and César were snoring peacefully"; the third chap-

74 RH I, 361/P I, 471 and RH II, 520/P III, 201.
75 RH I, 162/P I, 211 and RH I, 907/P II, 267.

ter begins in these terms: "As he was going to sleep, César was afraid that the next day his wife would make some peremptory objections, and he set himself to get up very early in order to settle everything": we see that here the resumption is not without a touch of incoherence. The linking up in *Les Souffrances de l'inventeur* is more successful, because here the tapestry worker has been able to extract a decorative element from the difficulty itself. Here is the opening of the analepsis: "While the venerable churchman climbs the ramps of Angoulême, it is not useless to explain the network of interests into which he was going to set foot. / After Lucien's departure, David Séchard . . . " Here is how the first narrative resumes, more than one hundred pages further on: "At the moment when the old curé of Marsac was climbing the ramps of Angoulême to go inform Eve of the condition her brother was in, David had been hidden for eleven days only two doors from where the worthy priest had just come out."[76] This play between the time of the story and the time of the narrating (to tell of David's misfortunes "while" the curé of Marsac climbs the staircase) will be discussed on its own account in the chapter on voice; we see how it converts into humor what was a burden.

The typical behavior of Proustian narrative seems to consist, quite to the contrary, of *eluding* the juncture, either by dissimulating the end of the analepsis in the sort of temporal dispersion that iterative narrative procures (this is the case with two retrospections concerning Gilberte in *La Fugitive*, one about her adoption by Forcheville, the other about her marriage to Saint-Loup),[77] or else by pretending to be unaware that the point in the story where the analepsis closes had already been reached by the narrative. Thus, in *Combray*, Marcel begins by mentioning "the interruption which a visit from Swann once made, and the commentary which he then supplied to the course of my reading, which had brought me to the work of an author quite new to me, called Bergotte"; he then goes into the past to tell how he had discovered that author; six pages further

---

[76] Garnier, pp. 550 and 643.
[77] RH II, 792/P III, 582 and RH II, 856/P III, 676.

on, again picking up the thread of his narrative, he makes the linkage in these terms, as if he had not already named Swann and called attention to his visit: "One Sunday, however, while I was reading in the garden, I was interrupted by Swann, who had come to call upon my parents.—'What are you reading? May I look? Why, it's Bergotte!' "[78] Whether trick, oversight, or offhandedness, the narrative thus avoids *acknowledging* its own footprints. But the boldest avoidance (even if the boldness is pure negligence) consists of forgetting the analeptic character of a section of narrative and prolonging that section more or less indefinitely on its own account, paying no attention to the point where it rejoins the first narrative. That is what happens in the episode—famous for other reasons—of the grandmother's death. It opens with an obviously analeptic beginning: "I went upstairs, and found my grandmother not so well. For some time past, without knowing exactly what was wrong, she had been complaining of her health." Then the narrative that has been opened in the retrospective mood continues uninterruptedly on up to the death, without ever acknowledging and signaling the moment (although indeed necessarily come to and passed beyond) when Marcel, returning from Mme. de Villeparisis's, had found his grandmother "not so well." We can never, therefore, either locate the grandmother's death exactly in relation to the Villeparisis matinée, or decide where the analepsis ends and the first narrative resumes.[79] The case is obviously the same, but on a very much broader scale, with the analepsis opened in *Noms de pays: le pays*. We have already seen that this analepsis will continue to the last line of the *Recherche* without paying its respects in passing to the moment of the late insomnias, although these were its source in his memory and almost its narrative matrix: another retrospection that is more than complete, with an extent much greater than its reach, and which at an undetermined point in its career is covertly transformed into an anticipation. In his own way—without proclaiming it and probably even without perceiving it—Proust here unsettles the most basic

[78] RH I, 68 and 74/P I, 90 and 97.
[79] RH I, 928–964/P II, 298–345.

norms of narration, and anticipates the most disconcerting proceedings of the modern novel.

Prolepses

Anticipation, or temporal prolepsis, is clearly much less frequent than the inverse figure, at least in the Western narrative tradition—although each of the three great early epics, the *Iliad*, the *Odyssey*, and the *Aeneid*, begins with a sort of anticipatory summary that to a certain extent justifies the formula Todorov applied to Homeric narrative: "plot of predestination."[80] The concern with narrative suspense that is characteristic of the "classical" conception of the novel ("classical" in the broad sense, and whose center of gravity is, rather, in the nineteenth century) does not easily come to terms with such a practice. Neither, moreover, does the traditional fiction of a narrator who must appear more or less to discover the story at the same time that he tells it. Thus we will find very few prolepses in a Balzac, a Dickens, or a Tolstoy, even if the common practice, as we have already seen, of beginning *in medias res* (or yet, I may venture to say, *in ultimas res*), sometimes gives the illusion of it. It goes without saying that a certain load of "predestination" hangs over the main part of the narrative in *Manon Lescaut* (where we know, even before Des Grieux opens his story, that it ends with a deportation), or a fortiori in *The Death of Ivan Ilych*, which begins with its epilogue.

The "first-person" narrative lends itself better than any other to anticipation, by the very fact of its avowedly retrospective character, which authorizes the narrator to allude to the future and in particular to his present situation, for these to some extent form part of his role. Robinson Crusoe can tell us almost at the beginning that the lecture his father gave to turn him aside from nautical adventures was "truly prophetic," even though at the time he had no idea of it, and Rousseau, with the episode of the combs, does not fail to vouch for not only his past innocence but also the vigor of his retrospective indignation: "In writing

---

[80] Tzvetan Todorov, *The Poetics of Prose* (Ithaca, N.Y., and London, 1977), p. 65.

this I feel my pulse quicken yet."[81] Nonetheless, the *Recherche du temps perdu* uses prolepsis to an extent probably unequaled in the whole history of narrative, even autobiographical narrative,[82] and is thus privileged territory for the study of this type of narrative anachrony.

Here again, we can easily distinguish *internal* and *external* prolepses. The limit of the temporal field of the first narrative is clearly marked by the last nonproleptic scene, that is, for the *Recherche* (if we draw into the "first narrative" that enormous anachrony which begins on the Champs-Elysées and never ends), without any possible doubt, the Guermantes matinée. Now, it is well known that a certain number of episodes in the *Recherche* take place at a point later in the story than this matinée[83] (most, moreover, are told as digressions during this same scene): for us these will thus be external prolepses. They function most often as epilogues, serving to continue one or another line of action on to its logical conclusion, even if that conclusion takes place later than the day on which the hero decides to leave the world and withdraw into his work: quick allusion to Charlus's death; again an allusion (although more detailed, with a highly symbolic reach), to the marriage of Mlle. de Saint-Loup ("this daughter, whose name and fortune gave her mother the right to hope that she would crown the whole work of social ascent of Swann and his wife by marrying a royal prince, happening to be entirely without snobbery, chose for her husband an obscure man of letters. Thus it came about that the family sank once more, below even the level from which it had started its ascent");[84] final appearance of Odette, "showing signs of senility," nearly three years after the Guermantes

---

[81] Rousseau, *Confessions*, Pléiade ed., p. 20.

[82] The *Recherche* contains more than twenty proleptic sections of significant length, not counting simple allusions in the course of a sentence. The analepses of like definition are not more numerous, but it is true that they take up, by their extent, the quasi-totality of the text, and that it is atop that first retrospective layer that analepses and prolepses of the second degree are set.

[83] See Tadié, *Proust et le roman*, p. 376.

[84] RH II, 950/P III, 804 and RH II, 1124/P III, 1028.

matinée;[85] Marcel's future experience as a writer, with his anguish in the face of death and the encroachments of social life, the first reactions of readers, the first misapprehensions, etc.[86] The latest of these anticipations is the one, especially improvised in 1913 for that purpose, which closes the *Côté de chez Swann*. That tableau of the Bois de Boulogne "today," in direct contrast to the one from the years of adolescence, is obviously very close to the moment of narrating, since that last walk took place, Marcel tells us, "this year," "one of those mornings early in November," or so far as we can tell less than two months from this moment.[87]

One further step, therefore, and here we are in the narrator's present. Prolepses of this type, quite numerous in the *Recherche*, almost all correspond to the Rousseauistic model evoked above: they are testimonies to the intensity of the present memory, and to some extent authenticate the narrative of the past. For example, apropos of Albertine: "Thus it is, calling a halt, her eyes sparkling beneath her polo-cap, that I see her again to-day, outlined against the screen which the sea spreads out behind her"; apropos of the church in Combray: "And so even to-day, in any large provincial town, or in a quarter of Paris which I do not know well, if a passer-by who is putting me on the right road shews me from afar, as a point to aim at, some belfry of a hospital, or a convent steeple . . . "; apropos of the Baptistery of Saint Mark's: "A time came for me when, remembering the Baptistery . . . "; the end of the Guermantes soirée: "I can see all that departing crowd now, I can see, if I be not mistaken in placing him upon that staircase, . . . the Prince de Sagan."[88] And especially, of course, apropos of the scene of his going to bed,

[85] RH II, 1063/P III, 951–952.

[86] RH II, 1133–1136/P III, 1039–1043.

[87] RH I, 321–325/P I, 421–427. I will come back later to the difficulties raised by this passage, written in 1913 but fictively (diegetically) contemporaneous with the final narrating, and therefore later than the war.

[88] RH I, 624/P I, 829; RH I, 50/P I, 67; RH [omitted in the English translation]/P III, 646; RH II, 87/P II, 720; cf. RH I, 127/P I, 165 (on the village of Combray), RH I, 141–142/P I, 185 (on the Guermantes countryside), RH I, 142/P I, 186 (on the "two ways"), RH I, 487/P I, 641 (on Mme. Swann), RH II, 202/P II, 883 (on the young woman from the train of La Raspelière), RH II, 822/P III, 625 (on Venice), etc.

that poignant testimonial, already commented on in *Mimesis*, which we cannot refrain from quoting here in its entirety—a perfect illustration of what Auerbach calls "the symbolic omnitemporality" of the "remembering consciousness," but a perfect example also of fusion, quasi-miraculous fusion, between the event recounted and the narrating instance, which is both late (final) and "omnitemporal":

> Many years have passed since that night. The wall of the staircase, up which I had watched the light of his candle gradually climb, was long ago demolished. And in myself, too, many things have perished which, I imagined, would last for ever, and new structures have arisen, giving birth to new sorrows and new joys which in those days I could not have foreseen, just as now the old are difficult of comprehension. It is a long time, too, since my father has been able to tell Mamma to "Go with the child." Never again will such hours be possible for me. But of late I have been increasingly able to catch, if I listen attentively, the sound of the sobs which I had the strength to control in my father's presence, and which broke out only when I found myself alone with Mamma. Actually, their echo has never ceased: it is only because life is now growing more and more quiet round about me that I hear them afresh, like those convent bells which are so effectively drowned during the day by the noises of the streets that one would suppose them to have been stopped for ever, until they sound out again through the silent evening air.[89]

To the extent that they bring the narrating instance itself directly into play, these anticipations in the present constitute not only data of narrative temporality but also data of *voice:* we will meet them later under that heading.

---

[89] RH I, 28/P I, 37. Auerbach's commentary, *Mimesis*, p. 481. Here we cannot avoid thinking of Rousseau: "Nearly thirty years have passed since I left Bossey, without my recalling to mind my stay there with any connected and pleasurable recollections; but, now that I have passed the prime of life and am approaching old age, I feel these same recollections springing up again while others disappear; they stamp themselves upon my memory with features, the charm and strength of which increase daily, as if, feeling life already slipping away, I were endeavoring to grasp it again by its commencement" (*Confessions*, Pléiade, p. 21; New York: Modern Library, 1945, p. 20).

Internal prolepses present the same kind of problem that analepses of the same type do: the problem of interference, of possible useless duplication between the first narrative and the narrative taken on by the proleptic section. Here again we will disregard heterodiegetic prolepses, for which this risk is nil, whether the anticipation is internal or external;[90] and, among homodiegetic prolepses, we will again differentiate between those that fill in ahead of time a later blank (completing prolepses), and those that—still ahead of time—double, however slightly, a narrative section to come (repeating prolepses).

Examples of completing prolepses are the quick evocation, in *Combray*, of Marcel's future years in school; the last scene between his father and Legrandin; the evocation, apropos of the scene of the cattleyas, of the sequel of the erotic relations between Swann and Odette; the anticipatory descriptions of the changing scene of the sea at Balbec; the advance notice, in the middle of the first dinner at the Guermantes', of the long series of like dinners, etc.[91] All these anticipations offset future ellipses or paralipses. More subtle is the situation of the last scene in *Guermantes* (the visit by Swann and Marcel to the Duchess) which is, we know,[92] reversed with the first in *Sodome* (the

[90] Here is a list of the main ones, in their order of succession in the text: RH II, 24/P II, 630, during the Jupien-Charlus meeting: sequel of the relations between the two men, advantages Jupien derives from Charlus's goodwill, Françoise's esteem for the moral qualities of the two inverts; RH II, 101–102/P II, 739–741, on the return from the Guermantes soirée: the Duke's later conversion to Dreyfusism; RH II, 529–530/P III, 214–216, before the Verdurin concert: Charlus's later discovery of Morel's connections with Léa; RH II, 604–605/P III, 322–324, at the end of the concert: Charlus's illness and forgetting his grudge against the Verdurins; RH II, 932–934/P III, 779–781, during the walk with Charlus: sequel of his relations with Morel, who loved a woman. We see that all of them have the function of anticipating a paradoxical evolution, one of those unlooked-for reversals that Proustian narrative delights in.

[91] RH I, 56/P I, 74; RH I, 99–102/P I, 129–133; RH I, 178–180/P I, 233–234; RH I, 510–511 and 605–608/P I, 673 and 802–806; RH I, 1082–1083/P II, 512–514; cf. RH I, 772/P II, 82–83 (on the room in Doncières), RH II, 950/P III, 804 (the meeting with Morel, two years after the walk with Charlus), RH II, 875–876/P III, 703–704 (the meeting with Saint-Loup in society), etc.

[92] "Now this wait on the staircase was to have for me consequences so considerable, and to reveal to me a picture no longer Turneresque but ethical, of so great importance, that it is preferable to postpone the account of it for a little while by interposing first that of my visit to the Guermantes when I knew that they had come home" (RH I, 1125/P II, 573).

Charlus-Jupien "conjunction"), so that we must consider the first as a prolepsis filling in the ellipsis opened, by this very anticipation, between *Sodome I* and *Sodome II*, and the second as an analepsis filling in the ellipsis opened in *Guermantes* by its own delaying—a rearrangement of interpolations that is obviously motivated by the narrator's desire to have done with the properly worldly aspect of the "Guermantes way" before approaching what he calls the "moral landscape" of Sodom and Gomorrah.

Perhaps one will have noticed here the presence of iterative prolepses, which, like analepses of the same kind, refer us to the question of narrative *frequency*. Without discussing that question here on its own account, I will simply note the characteristic attitude, which consists, on the occasion of a *first time* (first kiss of Swann and Odette, first sight of the sea at Balbec, first evening at the hotel in Doncières, first dinner with the Guermantes), of envisaging in advance the whole series of occurrences that the first one inaugurates. We will see in the next chapter that most of the typical big scenes of the *Recherche* concern an initiation of this kind ("débuts" of Swann at the Verdurins', of Marcel at Mme. de Villeparisis's, at the Duchess's, at the Princess's); the first meeting is obviously the best opportunity to describe a scene or a milieu, and moreover it serves as a paradigm of the others that follow. The generalizing prolepses more or less make clear this paradigmatic function by opening out a view onto the later series: "window in which I was, henceforward, to plant myself every morning. . . . " They are thus, like any anticipation, a mark of narrative impatience. But they have also, it seems to me, an inverse weight that is perhaps more specifically Proustian and that betokens rather a sentiment of nostalgia for what Vladimir Jankélévitch once called the "primultimateness" of the first time: that is, the fact that the first time, to the very extent to which one experiences its inaugural value intensely, is at the same time always (already) a last time—if only because it is forever the last to have been the first, and after it, inevitably, the sway of repetition and habit begins. Before kissing her for the first time, Swann holds Odette's face for a moment "at a little distance between his hands": this, the

narrator says, is to give his mind time to catch up and be witness
to the fulfillment of the dream it had cherished for so long. But
there is another reason:

> Perhaps, moreover, Swann himself was fixing upon these features
> of an Odette not yet possessed, not even kissed by him, on whom
> he was looking now *for the last time*, that comprehensive gaze with
> which, on the day of his departure, a traveller strives to bear away
> with him in memory the view of a country to which he may never
> return.[93]

To possess Odette, to kiss Albertine for the first time, is to set
eyes for the last time upon the Odette not yet possessed, the
Albertine not yet kissed: so true is it that in Proust the event—
any event—is only the transition, evanescent and *irretrievable* (in
the Virgilian sense), from one habit to another.

Repeating prolepses, like analepses of the same type and for
reasons equally obvious, scarcely occur except as brief allusions:
they refer in advance to an event that will be told in full in its
place. As repeating analepses fulfill a function of recall with
respect to the addressee of the narrative, so repeating prolepses
play a role of advance notice, and I will designate them by this
term as well. The canonical formula for them is generally a "we
will see" or "one will see later," and the paradigm or prototype
is this notice apropos of the scene of the sacrilege at
Montjouvain: "We shall see, in due course, that for quite
another reason, the memory of this impression was to play an
important part in my life." An allusion, of course, to the
jealousy that the (false) revelation of relations between Albertine
and Mlle. Vinteuil will provoke in Marcel.[94] The role these advance notices play in the organization and what Barthes calls the

---

[93] RH I, 179/P I, 233. (My emphasis.)
[94] RH I, 122/P I, 159 and RH II, 366/P II, 1114. But we must remember that
when he wrote this sentence before 1913 Proust had not yet "invented" the
character of Albertine, who will be worked out between 1914 and 1917. Clearly,
however, he has in mind for the scene of Montjouvain a "fallout" of this order,
which became specified only afterward: an advance notice, thus, doubly prophetic.

"weaving" of the narrative is fairly obvious, through the expectation that they create in the reader's mind—an expectation that can be fulfilled immediately, in the case of those advance notices with a very short reach or a nearby resolution, which, for example, at the end of a chapter disclose the subject of the following chapter by adumbrating it, as happens frequently in *Madame Bovary*.[95] The more unbroken construction of the *Recherche* in general excludes this kind of effect, but whoever remembers the end of Part II, chapter 4, in *Bovary* ("She did not know that when the gutters of a house are plugged up, the rain forms pools on the roof; and so she continued to feel secure, when suddenly she discovered a crack in the wall") will have no trouble recognizing this model of metaphorized presentation in the opening sentence of the last scene of the *Temps retrouvé:*

> But it is sometimes just at the moment when we think that everything is lost that the intimation arrives which may save us; one knocks at all the doors which lead nowhere, and then one stumbles without knowing it on the only door through which one can enter—which one might have sought in vain for a hundred years—and it opens of its own accord.[96]

But most often the advance notice has a considerably longer reach. We know that Proust prized the cohesiveness and the architecture of his work, and that he suffered at seeing so many effects of distant symmetry and "telescopic" correspondences misunderstood. The separated publication of the various volumes could not but aggravate the misunderstanding, and it is certain that long-distance advance notices, as for the scene at Montjouvain, were supposed to serve to reduce misunderstanding by giving a provisional justification to episodes whose presence could otherwise seem adventitious and gratuitous. Here are some further occurrences of this, in the order in which they come: "As for Professor Cottard, *we shall meet him again, . . .*

---

[95] I, chap. 3; II, chap. 4; II, chap. 5; II, chap. 10; II, chap. 13; III, chap. 2.
[96] RH II, 997/P III, 866. Cf., this time without metaphor, the anticipated summaries of the Verdurin dinner (RH I, 193/P I, 251) or of the Sainte-Euverte soirée (RH I, 247/P I, 322).

much later in the course of our story, with the 'Mistress,' Mme. Verdurin, in her country house La Raspelière"; "*we shall see* how this sole social ambition that [Swann] had entertained for his wife and daughter was precisely that one the realisation of which proved to be forbidden him by a veto so absolute that Swann died in the belief that the Duchess would never possibly come to know them. *We shall see also* that, on the contrary, the Duchesse de Guermantes did associate with Odette and Gilberte after the death of Swann"; "That I was one day to experience a grief as profound as that of my mother, *we shall find* in the course of this narrative" (this grief is obviously the one that Albertine's flight and death will provoke); "[Charlus] had recovered [his health], only to fall later into the condition in which *we shall see him* on the day of an afternoon party given by the Princesse de Guermantes."[97]

We will not confuse these advance notices, which by definition are explicit, with what we should instead call mere *advance mentions*,[98] simple markers without anticipation, even an allusive anticipation, which will acquire their significance only later on and which belong to the completely classic art of "preparation" (for example, having a character appear at the beginning who will really step in only very much later, like the Marquis de la Môle in the third chapter of *Le Rouge et le noir*). We can consider as such the first appearance of Charlus and Gilberte at Tansonville, of Odette as the Lady in pink, or the first mention of Mme. de Villeparisis on the fifteenth page of *Swann*, or again, more obviously functional, the description of the bank at Montjouvain, "on a level with [the] drawing-room, upstairs, and only a few feet away from its window," which prepares for Marcel's situation during the profanation scene;[99] or, more ironically, the idea Marcel rejects of mentioning before M. de Crécy

[97] RH I, 332 and II, 190 ff./P I, 433 and II, 866 ff.; RH I, 361 and II, 786 ff./P I, 471 and III, 575 ff.; RH II, 122 and II, 669 ff./P II, 768 and III, 415 ff.; RH II, 951 and II, 992/P III, 805 and III, 859. (My emphasis.)

[98] Cf. Raymonde Debray-Genette, "Les Figures du récit dans *Un coeur simple*," *Poétique*, 3 (1970).

[99] RH I, 108–109/P I, 141; RH I, 57/P I, 76; RH I, 15/P I, 20; RH I, 86 and 122/P I, 113 and 159.

what he believes to be Odette's former "code name," which
prepares for the subsequent revelation (by Charlus) of the au-
thenticity of this name and of the real relationship between the
two characters.[100] The difference between advance notice and
advance mention is clearly discernible in the way in which Proust
prepares, in several stages, for Albertine's entrance. The first
reference, in the course of a conversation at the Swanns': Albertine is named as niece of the Bontemps, and deemed "the quain-
test spectacle" by Gilberte—simple advance mention. The second reference—another advance mention—by Mme. Bontemps
herself, who describes her niece as having "impudence," as
being a "little wretch, . . . as cunning as a monkey": she has
publicly reminded a minister's wife that the latter's father was a
scullion; this description will be explicitly recalled very much
later, after Albertine's death, and held up as the "insignificant
seed [which] would develop and would one day overshadow
the whole of my life." The third reference—this time a genuine
advance notice:

> There was a scene at home because I did not accompany my father
> to an official dinner at which the Bontemps were to be present
> with their niece Albertine, a young girl still hardly more than a
> child. So it is that the different periods of our life overlap one
> another. We scornfully decline, because of one whom we love and
> who will some day be of so little account, to see another who is of
> no account today, with whom we shall be in love tomorrow, with
> whom we might, perhaps, had we consented to see her now, have
> fallen in love a little earlier and who would thus have put a term to
> our present sufferings, bringing others, it is true, in their place.[101]

Unlike the advance notice, the advance mention is thus in general, at its place in the text, only an "insignificant seed," and
even an imperceptible one, whose importance as a seed will not
be recognized until later, and retrospectively.[102] But we must

[100] RH II, 345 and 589/P II, 1085 and III, 301.
[101] RH I, 391/P I, 512; RH I, 455/P I, 598, cf. RH II, 1027/P III, 904; RH I, 476/P I,
626.
[102] "The 'soul' of any function is, as it were, its seedlike quality, which enables
the function to inseminate the narrative with an element that will later come to
maturity" (Roland Barthes, "An Introduction to the Structural Analysis of Narrative," *NLH*, 6 [Winter 1975], 244).

consider the possible (or rather the variable) narrative *competence* of the reader, arising from practice, which enables him both to decipher more and more quickly the narrative code in general or the code appropriate to a particular genre or a particular work, and also to identify the "seeds" when they appear. Thus, no reader of *Ivan Ilych* (helped, it is true, by the presentation of the denouement in advance, and by the very title) can fail to identify Ivan's fall against the French-window fastener as the instrument of destiny, as the beginning of the death struggle. Moreover, this very competence is what the author relies on to fool the reader by sometimes offering him false advance mentions, or *snares*[103]—well known to connoisseurs of detective stories. Once the reader has acquired this second-degree competence of being able to detect and thus to outmaneuver the snare, the author is then free to offer him *false snares* (that are genuine advance mentions), and so on. Proustian believability, of course—based, as Jean-Pierre Richard puts it, on the "logic of inconsistency"[104] plays on (particularly in what concerns homosexuality and its subtle variant, heterosexuality) this complex system of frustrated expectations, disappointed suspicions, surprises looked forward to and finally all the more surprising in being looked forward to and occurring nonetheless—by virtue of this principle for all purposes, that "The laborious process of causation . . . sooner or later will bring about every possible effect, including (consequently) those which one had believed to be most nearly impossible":[105] a warning to connoisseurs of "psychological laws" and realistic *motivations*.

Still, before leaving narrative prolepses there is a word to say about their extent, and the distinction possible here too between partial and complete prolepses if one is willing to grant completeness to anticipations prolonged in the time of the story up to the "denouement" (for internal prolepses) or up to the narrating moment itself (for external or mixed prolepses). I find hardly any examples of completeness, and it seems that in fact all prolepses are of the *partial* type, often interrupted in as abrupt a

[103] See Roland Barthes, *S/Z* (New York, 1974), p. 32.
[104] Jean-Pierre Richard, "Proust et l'objet herméneutique," *Poétique*, 13 (1973).
[105] RH I, 361/P I, 471.

way as they were begun. Marks of prolepsis: "*to anticipate* for a moment, since I am still finishing my letter to Gilberte . . . "; "*interrupting for a few moments* our narrative, which shall be resumed immediately after the closure of this *parenthesis* . . . "; "*to anticipate a little* for I am still at Tansonville . . . "; "the next day, *to anticipate* . . . "; "*I take a leap* of many years . . . "[106] Marks of the end of prolepsis and return to the first narrative: "*To return to* this first evening at the Princesse de Guermantes's . . . "; "but it *is time to rejoin* the Baron as he advances with Brichot and myself towards the Verdurins' door . . . "; "*to go backwards*, to the Verdurin soirée . . . "; "But I must *return to my narrative* . . . "; "*But we have anticipated, and let us now go back three years*, to the afternoon party which is being given by the Princesse de Guermantes . . . "[107] We see that Proust does not always retreat from the burden of explicitness.

The importance of "anachronic" narrative in the *Recherche du temps perdu* is obviously connected to the retrospectively synthetic character of Proustian narrative, which is totally present in the narrator's mind at every moment. Ever since the day when the narrator in a trance perceived the unifying significance of his story, he never ceases to hold all of its threads simultaneously, to apprehend simultaneously all of its places and all of its moments, to be capable of establishing a multitude of "telescopic" relationships amongst them: a ubiquity that is spatial but also temporal, an "omnitemporality" perfectly illustrated by the passage in the *Temps retrouvé* where the hero, in the presence of Mlle. de Saint-Loup, reconstitutes in a flash the "network of [entangled] memories" that his life has become, and that will become the fabric of his work.[108]

But the very ideas of retrospection or anticipation, which ground the narrative categories of analepsis and prolepsis in

[106] RH II, 101/P II, 739; RH II, 529/P III, 214; RH II, 875/P III, 703; RH II, 932/P III, 779; RH II, 950/P III, 803. (My emphasis.)
[107] RH II, 85/P II, 716; RH II, 530/P III, 216; RH II, 952/P III, 806; RH II, 1064/P III, 952. (My emphasis.) Of course, these signs of the organization of the narrative are in themselves marks of the instance of narrating, which we will meet again as such in the chapter on voice.
[108] RH II, 1126/P III, 1030.

"psychology," take for granted a perfectly clear temporal consciousness and unambiguous relationships among present, past, and future. Only because the exposition required it, and at the cost of excessive schematization, have I until now postulated this to have always been so. In fact, the very frequency of interpolations and their reciprocal entanglement often embroil matters in such a way as to leave the "simple" reader, and even the most determined analyst, sometimes with no way out. To conclude this chapter we shall examine some of these ambiguous structures, which bring us to the threshold of *achrony* pure and simple.

Toward Achrony

Since our first microanalyses we have met examples of complex anachronies: second-degree prolepses in the section taken from *Sodome et Gomorrhe* (anticipation of Swann's death on anticipation of his luncheon with Bloch), analepses on prolepses (retrospection of Françoise at Combray on that same anticipation of Swann's funeral), and prolepses on analepses (twice in the excerpt from *Jean Santeuil*, recalls of past plans). Such second or third-degree effects are likewise frequent in the *Recherche* at the level of large or medium-sized narrative structures, even without taking into account that first degree of anachrony which the quasi-totality of the narrative is.

The typical situation evoked in our fragment of *Jean Santeuil* (memories of anticipations) has taken root in the *Recherche* in the two characters born by fission from the original hero. The return to Swann's marriage, in the *Jeunes Filles*, includes a retrospective evocation of the plans of worldly ambition for his daughter and his (future) wife:

> But when Swann in his daydreams saw Odette as already his wife he invariably formed a picture of the moment in which he would take her—her, and above all her daughter—to call upon the Princesse des Laumes (who was shortly . . . to become Duchesse de Guermantes). . . . His heart would soften as he invented—uttering their actual words to himself—all the things that the Duchess would say of him to Odette, and Odette to the Duchess. . . . He enacted to himself the scene of this introduction with the same precision in each of its imaginary details that people shew when

they consider how they would spend, supposing they were to
win it, a lottery prize the amount of which they have arbitrarily
determined.[109]

This "waking dream" is proleptic insofar as Swann entertains it
before his marriage, analeptic insofar as Marcel recalls it after
that marriage, and the two movements come together to cancel
each other out, in this way perfectly superimposing the fantasy
on its cruel refutation by the facts, since here is Swann married
for several years to an Odette still unwelcome in the Guermantes salon. It is true that he married Odette when he no
longer loved her, and that "the creature that, in [him], had so
longed to live, had so despaired of living all its life in company
with Odette, . . . that creature was extinct." So here now face to
face in ironic contradiction are the earlier resolutions and the
present realities: resolution to elucidate some day the mysterious relations between Odette and Forcheville, replaced by a
total lack of curiosity:

> Formerly, while his sufferings were still keen, he had vowed that,
> as soon as he should have ceased to love Odette, and so to be
> afraid either of vexing her or of making her believe that he loved
> her more than he did, he would afford himself the satisfaction of
> elucidating with her, simply from his love of truth and as a histori-
> cal point, whether or not she had had Forcheville in her room that
> day when he had rung her bell and rapped on her window with-
> out being let in, and she had written to Forcheville that it was an
> uncle of hers who had called. But this so interesting problem, of
> which he was waiting to attempt the solution only until his
> jealousy should have subsided, had precisely lost all interest in
> Swann's eyes when he had ceased to be jealous.

Resolution to express some day the indifference that lay ahead,
replaced by the circumspection of real indifference:

> But whereas at that other time he had made a vow that if ever he
> ceased to love her whom he did not then imagine to be his future
> wife, he would implacably exhibit to her an indifference that

[109] RH I, 360–361/P I, 470.

would at length be sincere, so as to avenge his pride that had so long been trampled upon by her—of those reprisals which he might now enforce without risk . . ., of those reprisals he took no more thought; with his love had vanished the desire to shew that he was in love no longer.

The contrast, via the past, between anticipated present and real present, in Marcel when he is finally "cured" of his passion for Gilberte: "I had no desire now to see her, not even that desire to shew her that I did not wish to see her which, every day, when I was in love with her, I vowed to myself that I would flaunt before her, when I should be in love with her no longer." Or, with slightly different psychological significance, when Marcel again, now Gilberte's "chum" and an intimate in the Swann dining room, in order to measure the progress he has made, tries in vain to recover the feeling he had earlier of how inaccessible this "inconceivable place" was—not without attributing to Swann himself analogous thoughts about his life with Odette, that once "unhoped-for paradise" not to be imagined without turmoil but now a prosaic and totally charmless reality.[110] What one had planned does not occur; what one had not dared to hope for materializes, but only at the moment when one no longer desires it. In both cases the present superimposes itself on the previous future whose place it has taken: a retrospective refutation of a mistaken anticipation.

An inverse movement—a recall that is anticipated, a detour no longer by the past but by the future—occurs each time the narrator explains in advance how he will later, after the event, be informed of a present incident (or of its significance). So, for example, in telling of a scene between M. and Mme. Verdurin, he specifies that it will be reported to him by Cottard "a few years later." The seesawing speeds up in this indication in *Combray:* "Many years later we discovered that, if we had been fed on asparagus day after day throughout that whole season, it was because the smell of the plants gave the poor kitchen-maid, who

[110] RH I, 361/P I, 471; RH I, 399–400/P I, 523; RH I, 401/P I, 525; RH II, 83/P II, 713; RH I, 410/P I, 537–538.

had to prepare them, such violent attacks of asthma that she was finally obliged to leave my aunt's service."[111] It becomes almost instantaneous in this sentence from *La Prisonnière:* "I learned that a death had occurred that day which distressed me greatly, that of Bergotte"—so elliptical, so discreetly misshaped that the reader at first thinks he has read: "I learned that day that a death had occurred."[112] There is the same zigzag round trip when the narrator introduces a present, or even a past event through the anticipation of the memory he will have of it later, as we have already seen for the final pages of the *Jeunes Filles en fleurs,* which carry us forward to the first weeks at Balbec through the future memories of Marcel in Paris; similarly, when Marcel sells Aunt Léonie's sofa to a go-between, we learn that only "very much later" will he remember having, very much earlier, used that sofa with the enigmatic cousin we have already spoken of: analepsis on paralipsis we called it then, a formula we must now complete by adding *via prolepsis.* These narrative contortions would doubtless be enough to bring down upon the hypothetical young lady the suspicious, albeit kindly, glance of the hermeneut.

Another effect of double structure is that a first anachrony may invert—necessarily inverts—the relationship between a second anachrony and the order of arrangement of the events in the text. Thus, the analeptic status of *Un amour de Swann* has the effect that an anticipation (in the time of the story) is able to refer to an event already covered by the narrative: when the narrator compares the vesper anguish of Swann deprived of Odette to the anguish he himself will suffer "some years later" on the nights when this same Swann will come to dine at Combray, this diegetic *advance notice* is at the same time a narrative *recall* for the reader, since he has already read the narrative of that scene some one hundred and ninety pages "earlier"; inversely and for the same reason, the reference to Swann's earlier anguish, in the narrative of Combray, is for the reader an advance

[111] RH II, 607/P III, 326; RH I, 95/P I, 124.

[112] RH II, 506/P III, 182. The Clarac-Ferré résumé (P III, 1155) conveys it thusly: "I learn that day of the death of Bergotte."

notice of the forthcoming narrative of *Un amour de Swann*. [113] The specific formula of such double anachronies would thus be something like this: "It would happen later, as we have already seen," or: "It had already happened, as we will see later." Retrospective advance notices? Anticipatory recalls? When later is earlier, and earlier later, defining the direction of movement becomes a delicate task.

These proleptic analepses and analeptic prolepses are so many complex anachronies, and they somewhat disturb our reassuring ideas about retrospection and anticipation. Let us again recall the existence of open analepses (analepses whose conclusion cannot be localized), which therefore necessarily entails the existence of temporally indefinite narrative sections. But we also find in the *Recherche* some events not provided with any temporal reference whatsoever, events that we cannot place at all in relation to the events surrounding them. To be unplaceable they need only be attached not to some other event (which would require the narrative to define them as being earlier or later) but to the (atemporal) commentarial discourse that accompanies them—and we know what place that has in this work. In the course of the Guermantes dinner, apropos of Mme. de Varambon's obstinacy in relating Marcel by marriage to Admiral Jurien de la Gravière (and thus, by extension, apropos of the so frequently made analogous errors in society), the narrator evokes the error of a friend of the Guermantes' who was recommending himself to Marcel by making use of the name of a cousin, Mme. de Chaussegros, a person totally unknown to the narrator: one can assume that this anecdote, which implies a certain progress in Marcel's social career, occurs later than the Guermantes dinner, but nothing permits us to affirm this. After the scene of the missed introduction to Albertine, in the *Jeunes Filles en fleurs*, the narrator offers some reflections on the subjectivity of the feeling of love, then illustrates this theory with the example of a drawing master who had never known the color of the hair of a mistress he had passionately loved and who had left

[113] RH I, 228 and 23–24/P I, 297 and 30–31.

him a daughter ("I never saw her except with a hat on").[114] Here, no inference from the content can help the analyst define the status of an anachrony deprived of every temporal connection, which is an event we must ultimately take to be dateless and ageless: to be an achrony.

Now, it is not only such isolated events that express the narrative's capacity to disengage its arrangement from all dependence, even inverse dependence, on the chronological sequence of the story it tells. The *Recherche* presents, at least in two places, genuine *achronic structures*. At the end of *Sodome*, the itinerary of the "Transatlantic" and its sequence of stops (Doncières, Maineville, Grattevast, Hermenonville) gives rise to a short narrative sequence[115] whose order of succession (Morel's misadventure at the brothel in Maineville—meeting with M. de Crécy at Grattevast) owes nothing to the temporal connection between the two events composing it and everything to the fact (itself, however, diachronic, but not a diachrony of the events recounted) that the little train goes first to Maineville, then to Grattevast, and that these stations evoke in the narrator's mind, in that order, anecdotes connected to them.[116] As J. P. Houston has rightly noted in his study of temporal structures in the *Recherche*,[117] this "geographic" ordering does no more than repeat and make clear the ordering—more implicit but more important in every respect—of the last forty pages of *Combray*. There the narrative order is governed by the opposition Méséglise way/ Guermantes way, and by the sites' increasing distance from the family home in the course of an atemporal and synthetic walk.[118] First appearance of Gilberte; farewell to the hawthorns; meeting with Swann and Vinteuil; Léonie's death; profanation

---

[114] RH I, 1072/P II, 498; RH I, 645/P I, 858–859.

[115] RH II, 338–346/P II, 1075–1086.

[116] "I confine myself at present, as the train halts and the porter calls out 'Doncières,' 'Grattevast,' 'Maineville,' etc., to noting down the particular memory that the watering-place or garrison town recalls to me" (RH II, 339/P II, 1076).

[117] J. P. Houston, "Temporal Patterns in *A.L.R.T.P.*," *French Studies*, 16 (1962), 33–45.

[118] The greater part of this sequence belongs for this reason in the category of the iterative. For the moment I am disregarding that aspect in order to examine only the order of succession of the singular events.

scene at the Vinteuils'; appearance of the Duchess at church; sight of the steeples of Martinville—this succession has no connection to the temporal order of the events composing it, or only a partially coincidental connection. The succession depends essentially on the location of the sites (Tansonville—Méséglise plain—Montjouvain—return to Combray—Guermantes way) and thus on a very different temporality: on the opposition between the days of the walk to Méséglise and the days of the walk toward Guermantes and, within each of these two series, on the approximate order of the "stations" of the walk. Only by naively confusing the narrative's syntagmatic order with the story's temporal order does one imagine, as hurried readers do, that the meeting with the Duchess or the episode of the steeples comes later than the scene at Montjouvain. The truth is that the narrator had the clearest of reasons for grouping together, in defiance of all chronology, events connected by spatial proximity, by climatic identity (the walks to Méséglise always take place in bad weather, those to Guermantes in good weather), or by thematic kinship (the Méséglise way represents the erotic-affective side of the world of childhood, that of Guermantes its aesthetic side); he thus made clear, more than anyone had done before him and better than they had, narrative's capacity for *temporal autonomy*. [119]

But it would be utterly vain to think of drawing definitive conclusions merely from an analysis of anachronies, which illustrate simply one of the constitutive features of narrative temporality. It is fairly obvious, for example, that distortions of speed contribute to emancipation from narrative temporality quite as much as transgressions of chronological order do. These are the subject of our next chapter.

[119] Having christened the anachronies by retrospection and anticipation *analepses* and *prolepses*, we could give the name *syllepses* (the fact of taking together)—*temporal* or other—to those anachronic groupings governed by one or another kinship (spatial, temporal, or other). Geographical syllepsis, for example, is the principle of narrative grouping in voyage narratives that are embellished by anecdotes, such as the *Mémoires d'un touriste* or *Le Rhin*. Thematic syllepsis governs in the classical episodic novel with its numerous insertions of "stories," justified by relations of analogy or contrast. We will meet the notion of syllepsis again apropos of iterative narrative, which is another variety of it.

2 Duration

Anisochronies

At the beginning of the last chapter I recalled what difficulties the very idea of "time of the narrative" runs up against in written literature. It is obviously apropos of duration that these difficulties are so strongly felt, for the data of order, or of frequency, can be transposed with no problem from the temporal plane of the story to the spatial plane of the text: to say that episode A comes "after" episode B in the syntagmatic arrangement of a narrative text or that episode C is told "twice" is to make statements that have an obvious meaning and that can be clearly compared with other assertions such as "event A is earlier than event B in the story's time" or "event C happens only once." Here, therefore, comparison between the two planes is legitimate and relevant. On the other hand, comparing the "duration" of a narrative to that of the story it tells is a trickier operation, for the simple reason that no one can measure the duration of a narrative. What we spontaneously call such can be nothing more, as we have already said, than the time needed for reading; but it is too obvious that reading time varies according to particular circumstances, and that, unlike what happens in movies, or even in music, nothing here allows us to determine a "normal" speed of execution.

The reference point, or degree zero, which in matters of order was the concurrence between diegetic sequence and narrative sequence, and which here would be rigorous isochrony between narrative and story, is now therefore absent—even if it be true, as Jean Ricardou notes, that a scene with dialogue (supposing it unadulterated by any intervention of the narrator and without any ellipsis) gives us "a *sort* of equality between the narrative section and the fictive section."[1] It is I who emphasize "sort," in order to insist on the unrigorous, and especially unrigorously temporal, nature of this equality. All that we can affirm of such a narrative (or dramatic) section is that it reports everything that was said, either really or fictively, without adding anything to it; but it does not restore the speed with which those words were pronounced or the possible dead spaces in the conversation. In no way, therefore, can it play the role of temporal indicator; it would play that role only if its indications could serve to measure the "narrative duration" of the differently paced sections surrounding it. Thus a scene with dialogue has only a kind of *conventional* equality between narrative time and story time, and later we will utilize it in this way in a typology of the traditional forms of narrative duration, but it cannot serve us as reference point for a rigorous comparison of real durations.

We must thus give up the idea of measuring variations in duration with respect to an inaccessible, because unverifiable, equality of duration between narrative and story. But the isochronism of a narrative may also be defined—like that of a pendulum, for example—not relatively, by comparing its duration to that of the story it tells, but in a way that is more or less absolute and autonomous, as *steadiness in speed*. By "speed" we mean the relationship between a temporal dimension and a spatial dimension (so many meters per second, so many seconds per meter): the speed of a narrative will be defined by the relationship between a duration (that of the story, measured in seconds, minutes, hours, days, months, and years) and a length

[1] Jean Ricardou, *Problèmes du nouveau roman* (Paris, 1967), p. 164. Ricardou contrasts *narrating* to *fiction* in the sense in which I contrast *narrative* (and sometimes *narrating*) to *story* (or *diegesis*): "narrating is the manner of telling, fiction is what is told" (p. 11).

(that of the text, measured in lines and in pages).[2] The isochronous narrative, our hypothetical reference zero, would thus be here a narrative with unchanging speed, without accelerations or slowdowns, where the relationship duration-of-story/length-of-narrative would remain always steady. It is doubtless unnecessary to specify that such a narrative does not exist, and cannot exist except as a laboratory experiment: at any level of aesthetic elaboration at all, it is hard to imagine the existence of a narrative that would admit of no variation in speed—and even this banal observation is somewhat important: a narrative can do without anachronies, but not without *anisochronies*, or, if one prefers (as one probably does), effects of *rhythm*.

Detailed analysis of these effects would be both wearying and devoid of all real rigor, since diegetic time is almost never indicated (or inferable) with the precision that would be necessary. The analysis is relevant, therefore, only at the macroscopic level, that of large narrative units, granting that the measurement for each unit covers only a statistical approximation.[3]

If we want to draw up a picture of these variations for the *Recherche du temps perdu*, we must decide at the very beginning what to consider as large narrative articulations, and then, to measure their story time, we must have at our disposal an approximately clear and coherent internal chronology. If the first datum is fairly easy to establish, the second is not.

So far as narrative articulations are concerned, we must observe first that they do not coincide with the work's visible divisions into parts and chapters supplied with titles and numbers.[4] If for our demarcating criterion, however, we adopt the

---

[2] This procedure is proposed by Gunther Müller, "Erzählzeit," and Roland Barthes, "Le Discours de l'histoire," *Information sur les sciences sociales*, August 1967.

[3] Metz (pp. 119 ff.) calls this "the large syntagmatic category" of narrative.

[4] We know, besides, that only external constraint is responsible for the existing break between *Swann* and the *Jeunes Filles en fleurs*. The relations between external divisions (parts, chapters, etc.) and internal narrative articulations have not—up until now, in general and to my knowledge—generated all the attention they deserve. These relations, however, are what mainly determine the rhythm of a narrative.

presence of an important temporal and/or spatial break, we can establish the separation without too much hesitation, as follows (I give some of these units titles—purely indicative ones—of my own making):

(1) I, 3–142, leaving out the memory-elicited analepses studied in the preceding chapter, is the unit devoted to the childhood in Combray: we, like Proust himself, will obviously name it *Combray.*

(2) After a temporal and spatial break, *Un amour de Swann,* I, 144–292.

(3) After a temporal break, the unit devoted to the Parisian adolescence and dominated by love with Gilberte and the discovery of Swann's milieu, occupying the third part of *Du côté de chez Swann* ("Noms de pays: le nom") and the first part of the *Jeunes Filles en fleurs* ("Autour de Mme. Swann"), I, 293–487: we will name it *Gilberte.*

(4) After a break that is both temporal (two years) and spatial (the movement from Paris to Balbec), the episode of the first stay at Balbec, corresponding to the second part of the *Jeunes Filles* ("Noms de pays: le pays"), I, 488–714: *Balbec I.*

(5) After a spatial break (return to Paris), we will take as one and the same unit everything coming between the two visits to Balbec, occurring almost entirely in Paris (with the exception of a short visit to Doncières) and in the Guermantes milieu, thus the complete *Côté de Guermantes* (I, 719–1141) and the beginning of *Sodome et Gomorrhe* (II, 3–109): *Guermantes.*

(6) The second visit to Balbec, after a new spatial break, in other words, all the rest of *Sodome et Gomorrhe,* II, 110–378: we will christen this unit *Balbec II.*

(7) After a new change of place (return to Paris), the story of Albertine's confinement, flight, and death, up to II, 820, in other words, the entire *Prisonnière* and most of *La Fugitive,* up to the departure for Venice: *Albertine.*

(8) II, 821–856, the visit to Venice and the trip back: *Venice.*

(9) II, 856–889, straddling *La Fugitive* and *Le Temps retrouvé,* the stay at *Tansonville.*

(10) After a break that is both temporal (stay in a clinic) and spatial (return to Paris), II, 890–987: *The War.*

(11) After a final temporal break (again a stay in a clinic),

comes the final narrative unit, II, 988–1140,[5] the *Matinée Guermantes*.[6]

With respect to chronology, the task is slightly more delicate, since in its details the chronology of the *Recherche* is neither clear nor coherent. We have no need here to join in an already old and apparently insoluble debate, whose chief documents are three articles by Willy Hachez and the books by Hans Robert Jauss and Georges Daniel, which readers can refer to for a detailed account of the discussion.[7] Let us recall only the two main difficulties: on the one hand, the impossibility of connecting the external chronology of *Un amour de Swann* (references to historical events requiring the episode to be dated near 1882–1884) to the general chronology of the *Recherche* (putting this same episode about 1877–1878);[8] on the other hand, the disagreement between the external chronology of the episodes *Balbec II* and *Albertine* (references to historical events that took place between 1906 and 1913) and the general internal chronology (which puts them back between 1900 and 1902).[9] So we cannot establish an

[5] [Translator's note.] The corresponding Pléiade page numbers are: (1) I, 3–186; (2) I, 188–382; (3) I, 383–641; (4) I, 642–955; (5) II, 9–751; (6) II, 751–1131; (7) III, 9–623; (8) III, 623–675; (9) III, 675–723; (10) III 723–854; (11) III, 854–1048. Omitted in the English translation are P III, 673–676.

[6] We see that the only two times when narrative articulations and external divisions coincide are the two ends of visit to Balbec (the end of *Jeunes Filles* and the end of *Sodome*); we can add the times when articulations and subdivisions coincide: the end of "Combray," the end of "Amour de Swann," and the end of "Autour de Mme. Swann." All the rest is overlapping. But of course my carving up is not sacrosanct, and it lays claim to a value that is no more than operational.

[7] Willy Hachez, "La Chronologie et l'âge des personnages de *A.L.R.T.P.*, *"Bulletin de la société des amis de Marcel Proust*, 6 (1956); "Retouches à une chronologie," *BSAMP*, 11 (1961); "Fiches biographiques de personnages de Proust," *BSAMP*, 15 (1965). H. R. Jauss, *Zeit und Erinnerung in A.L.R.T.P.* (Heidelberg, 1955). Georges Daniel, *Temps et mystification dans A.L.R.T.P.* (Paris, 1963).

[8] Added to this chronological disagreement is the one resulting from the absence in *Un amour de Swann* of any mention (and of any likelihood) of Gilberte's birth, which is nonetheless required by the general chronology.

[9] We know that these two contradictions result from external circumstances: the separate writing of *Un amour de Swann*, integrated after the fact into the whole, and the late projection onto the character of Albertine of facts linked to the relations between Proust and Alfred Agostinelli. [Translator's note: Agostinelli was a young man for whom Proust developed an extremely deep affection in 1913. In 1914 he died in the crash of the plane he was learning to fly, an event Genette refers to on p. 99.]

approximately coherent chronology except by eliminating these two external series and adhering to the main series, whose two fundamental guide marks are, for *Guermantes*, autumn 1897–spring 1899 (because of the Dreyfus affair) and, for *The War*, naturally 1916. Given these reference points, we establish an almost homogeneous series, but it still has a few partial obscurities. These are due, in particular, to: (a) the blurred nature of the chronology of *Combray* and its poorly defined relationship to the chronology of *Gilberte*; (b) the obscurity of the chronology of *Gilberte*, not allowing us to ascertain whether one or two years pass between the two "New Years" mentioned;[10] (c) the indeterminate length of the two stays in a clinic.[11] I will make short work of these uncertainties by establishing a purely indicative chronology, since our purpose is only to form an overall idea of the major rhythms of the Proustian narrative. Our chronological *hypothesis*, within the limits of exactitude we have thus settled on, is therefore as follows:

Un amour de Swann: 1877–1878
(Births of Marcel and Gilberte: 1878)
Combray: 1883–1892
Gilberte: 1892–spring 1895
Balbec I: summer 1897
Guermantes: autumn 1897–summer 1899
Balbec II: summer 1900
Albertine: autumn 1900–beginning 1902

[10] RH I, 372 and 462/P I, 486 and 608.

[11] The length of the first, between *Tansonville* and *The War* (RH II, 890/P III, 723), is not specified by the text ("the *long years* which I spent far from Paris receiving treatment in a sanatorium, until there came a time, at the beginning of 1916, when it could no longer get medical staff"), but it is fairly precisely determined by the context: the *terminus ab quo* is 1902 or 1903, and the *terminus ad quem* is the explicit date of 1916, with the two-month trip to Paris in 1914 (RH II, 900–919/P III, 737–762) being only an interlude within that stay. The length of the second (between *The War* and *Matinée Guermantes*, RH II, 988/P III, 854), which can begin in 1916, is equally indefinite; but the phrase used ("many years passed") prevents us from taking it to be very much briefer than the first, and forces us to put the second return, and therefore the Guermantes matinée (and a fortiori the moment of the narrating, which comes later by three years at least) *after* 1922, the date of Proust's death—which is an inconvenience only if one claims to identify the hero with the author. That wish is obviously what obliges Hachez (1965, p. 290) to shorten the second stay to three years at the most, in defiance of the text.

Venice: spring 1902
Tansonville: 1903?
The War: 1914 and 1916
Matinée Guermantes: about 1925

According to this hypothesis, and some other temporal data of secondary importance, the main variations of speed in the narrative work out approximately like this:

Combray: 140 pages for about ten years.
Un amour de Swann: 150 pages for some two years.
Gilberte: 200 pages for about two years.
(Here, ellipsis of two years.)
Balbec I: 225 pages for three or four months.
Guermantes: 525 pages for two and one-half years. But we must specify that this sequence itself contains very wide variations, since 80 pages tell about the Villeparisis reception, which must last two or three hours; 110 pages tell about the dinner at the Duchesse de Guermantes's, lasting almost the same length of time; and 65 pages tell about the Princess's soirée: in other words, almost half the sequence is for fewer than ten hours of fashionable gatherings.
Balbec II: 270 pages for nearly six months, 80 of which are for a soirée at La Raspelière.
Albertine: 440 pages for some eighteen months, 215 of which are devoted to only two days, and 95 of these are for the Charlus-Verdurin musical soirée alone.
Venice: 35 pages for some weeks.
(Indefinite ellipsis: at least some weeks.)
Tansonville: 30 pages for "some days."
(Ellipsis of about twelve years.)
The War: 100 pages for some weeks, the main part of which is for a single evening (stroll in Paris and Jupien's male brothel).
(Ellipsis of "many years.")
Matinée Guermantes: 150 pages for two or three hours.

It seems to me, from this very sketchy list, that we can draw at least two conclusions. First, the range of variations, going from 150 pages for three hours to three lines for twelve years, viz. (very roughly), from a page for one minute to a page for one century. Next, the internal evolution of the narrative in proportion as it advances toward its end, an evolution that we can summarily describe by saying that we observe on the one hand a gradual slowing down of the narrative, through the growing importance of very long scenes covering a very short time of story; and on the other hand, in a sense compensating for this slowing down, a more and more massive presence of ellipses. We can easily synthesize these two aspects with the following phrase: the *increasing discontinuity* of the narrative. The Proustian narrative tends to become more and more discontinuous, syncopated, built of enormous scenes separated by immense gaps, and thus it tends to deviate more and more from the hypothetical "norm" of narrative isochrony. Let us remember that we are not by any means dealing here with an evolution over time that would refer us to a psychological transformation in the author, since the *Recherche* was not by any means written in the order in which it is arranged today. On the other hand, it is true that Proust, who we well know tended unceasingly to inflate his text with additions, had more time to increase the later volumes than the earlier ones; the bulkiness of the later scenes thus partakes of that well-known imbalance that the publication delay imposed by the war brought about in the *Recherche*. But circumstances, if they explain the "stuffing" with details, cannot account for the overall composition. It certainly seems that Proust wanted, and wanted from the beginning, this ever more abrupt rhythm, with a Beethovenian massiveness and brutality, which contrasts so sharply with the almost imperceptible fluidity of the early parts, as if to compare the temporal texture of the older events with that of the more recent ones—as if the narrator's memory, while the facts draw nearer, were becoming both more selective and more enormously enlarging.

This change in rhythm cannot be accurately defined and interpreted until we connect it to other temporal treatments that we will study in the next chapter. But from now on we can and should examine more closely how the more or less infinite diversity of narrative speeds is in fact distributed and organized. Theoretically, indeed, there exists a continuous gradation from the infinite speed of ellipsis, where a nonexistent section of narrative corresponds to some duration of story, on up to the absolute slowness of descriptive pause, where some section of narrative discourse corresponds to a nonexistent diegetic duration.[12] In fact, it turns out that narrative tradition, and in particular the novel's tradition, has reduced that liberty, or at any rate has regulated it by effecting a selection from all the possibilities: it has selected four basic relationships that have become—in the course of an evolution that the (as yet unborn) *history of literature* will some day start to study—the canonical forms of novel *tempo*, a little bit the way the classical tradition in music singled out, from the infinitude of possible speeds of execution, some canonical movements (*andante, allegro, presto*, etc.) whose relationships of succession and alternation governed structures like those of the sonata, the symphony, or the concerto for some two centuries. These four basic forms of narrative movement, that we will hereafter call the four narrative *movements*, are the two extremes that I have just mentioned (*ellipsis* and descriptive *pause*), and two intermediaries: *scene*, most often in dialogue, which, as we have already observed, realizes conventionally the equality of time between narrative and story; and what English-language critics call *summary*[13]—a form with variable tempo (whereas the tempo of the other three is fixed, at least in principle), which with great flexibility of pace covers the entire range included between scene and ellipsis. We could schematize the temporal values of these four movements fairly well with the following formulas, with ST designating story time and NT the pseudo-time, or conventional time, of the narrative:

---

[12] This formulation can occasion two misunderstandings that I wish to dissipate at once. (1) The fact that a section of discourse corresponds to no duration in the story does not in itself characterize description: it may also characterize those commentarial excursuses in the present tense which, ever since Blin and Brombert, we have generally called *author's intrusions or interventions*, and which we will meet again in the last chapter. But what is distinctive about these excursuses is that they are not strictly speaking narrative. Descriptions, on the other hand, as constituents of the spatio-temporal universe of the story, are *diegetic*, and thus when we deal with them we are involved with the *narrative* discourse. (2) Every description is not necessarily a pause in the narrative, which we will observe in Proust himself. So we are not concerned here with description, but with *descriptive pause*, which is therefore not to be confused either with every pause or with every description.

[13] [Translator's note.] I have omitted from the text a brief statement on French terminology.

pause: $NT = n$, $ST = 0$. Thus: $NT \infty > ST$ [14]
scene: $NT = ST$
summary: $NT < ST$
ellipsis: $NT = 0$, $ST = n$. Thus: $NT < \infty \; ST$.

A plain reading of this chart reveals an asymmetry, which is the absence of a form with variable tempo symmetrical to the summary and whose formula would be $NT > ST$. This would obviously be a sort of scene in slow motion, and we think immediately of the long Proustian scenes, the reading of which often seems to take longer, much longer, than the diegetic time that such scenes are supposed to be covering. But, as we shall see, big scenes in novels, and especially in Proust, are extended mainly by extranarrative elements or interrupted by descriptive pauses, but are not exactly slowed down. And needless to say, pure dialogue cannot be slowed down. So there remains detailed narration of acts or events told about more slowly than they were performed or undergone. The thing is undoubtedly feasible as a deliberate experiment,[15] but we are not dealing there with a canonical form, or even a form really actualized in literary tradition. The canonical forms are indeed restricted, in fact, to the four movements I have enumerated.

Summary

Now, if we examine from this point of view the narrative pacing of the *Recherche*, what we are first compelled to note is the almost total absence of summary in the form it had during the whole previous history of the novel: that is, the narration in a few paragraphs or a few pages of several days, months, or

---

[14] This sign $\infty >$ (infinitely greater), as well as the inverse one $< \infty$ (infinitely less), are not, I am told, mathematically orthodox. I am retaining them, however, because they seem to me, in this context and for anyone of good will, as transparent a means as there is to designate an idea that is itself mathematically suspect, but very clear here.

[15] This is somewhat the circumstance with *L'Agrandissement* by Claude Mauriac (1963), which devotes some two hundred pages to a period of two minutes. But there again, the lengthening of the text does not arise from a real expansion of the time period, but from various insertions (memory-elicited analepses, etc.).

years of existence, without details of action or speech. Borges quotes an example of this, taken from *Don Quixote*, which seems to me fairly typical:

> In the end it seemed to [Lothario] necessary to take full advantage of the opportunity which Anselmo's absence gave him, and to intensify the siege of the fortress. So he assailed her self-love with praise of her beauty; for there is nothing which reduces and levels the embattled towers of a beautiful woman's vanity so quickly as this same vanity posted upon the tongue of flattery. In fact, he most industriously mined the rock of her integrity with such charges that Camilla would have fallen even if she had been made of brass. Lothario wept, beseeched, promised, flattered and swore, with such ardour and with such signs of real feeling, that he overcame Camilla's chastity and achieved the triumph which he least expected and most desired.[16]

"Chapters like [this one]," comments Borges, "form the overwhelming majority of world literature, and not the most unworthy." He is thinking here, however, less of relations of speed as such than of the contrast between classical *abstraction* (here, despite the metaphors or perhaps because of them) and "modern" *expressivity*. If one has one's eye more on the contrast between scene and summary,[17] one obviously cannot maintain that texts of this type "form the immense majority of world literature," for the simple reason that the very brevity of summary gives it almost everywhere an obvious quantitative inferiority to descriptive and dramatic chapters, and that therefore summary probably occupies a limited place in the whole corpus

---

[16] Cervantes, *The Adventures of Don Quixote*, Part I, chap. 34, trans. J. M. Cohen (Harmondsworth: Penguin, 1950), p. 300; quoted in J. L. Borges, *Discussions* (Paris, 1966), pp. 51–52. The comparison with a more flippant (but motivated) summary on an analogous subject, in Fielding, is unavoidable: "Not to tire the Reader, by leading him thro' every Scene of this Courtship, (which, tho', in the Opinion of a certain great Author, it is the pleasantest Scene of Life to the Actor, is, perhaps, as dull and tiresome as any whatever to the Audience) the Captain made his Advances in Form, the Citadel was defended in Form, and at length, in proper Form, surrendered at Discretion" (Henry Fielding, *Tom Jones*, Book I, chap. 11 [New York: Norton Critical Editions, 1973], p. 52).

[17] See Percy Lubbock, *The Craft of Fiction* (London, 1921).

of narrative, even of classical narrative. On the other hand, it is obvious that summary remained, up to the end of the nineteenth century, the most usual transition between two scenes, the "background" against which scenes stand out, and thus the connective tissue par excellence of novelistic narrative, whose fundamental rhythm is defined by the alternation of summary and scene. We must add that most retrospective sections, and particularly in what we have called complete analepses, belong to this type of narration, of which the second chapter of *Birotteau* gives an example as typical as it is admirable:

> A cotter, Jacques Birotteau by name, living near Chinon, took unto himself a wife, a domestic servant in the house of a lady, who employed him in her vineyard. Three sons were born to them; his wife died at the birth of the third, and the poor fellow did not long survive her. Then the mistress, out of affection for her maid, adopted the oldest of the cotter's boys; she brought him up with her own son, and placed him in a seminary. This François Birotteau took orders, and during the Revolution led the wandering life of priests who would not take the oath, hiding from those who hunted them down like wild beasts, lucky to meet with no worse fate than the guillotine.[18]

Nothing of the kind in Proust. With him, narrative cutting is never accomplished by this sort of acceleration, even in the anachronies, which in the *Recherche* are almost always genuine scenes, earlier or later, and not offhand glances at past or future. In Proust cutting either arises from a quite different kind of synthesis, which we will study more closely in the next chapter

---

[18] Garnier, p. 30; *César Birotteau, Béatrix, and Other Stories*, trans. E. Marriage and J. Waring (Philadelphia, 1899), p. 22. After Lubbock, the functional relationship between summary and analepsis was clearly indicated by Phyllis Bentley: "One of the most important and frequent uses of the summary is to convey rapidly a sketch of *past* life. The novelist, having excited our interest in his characters by telling a scene to us, suddenly whizzes his pageant back, then forward, giving us a rapid summary of their past history, a retrospect" ("Use of Summary," from *Some Observations on the Art of Narrative*, 1947; rpt. in Philip Stevick, ed., *The Theory of the Novel* [New York, 1967], p. 49).

under the name of iterative narrative,[19] or else it pushes acceleration so far as to cross the limits separating summary from ellipsis pure and simple. An example is the way in which the narrative sums up Marcel's years of retirement that precede and follow his return to Paris during the war.[20] The confusion between acceleration and ellipsis is, moreover, all but obvious in Proust's famous commentary on a page of the *Education sentimentale:*

> Here there is an implied "silence" of vast duration,[21] and suddenly, without the hint of a transition,[22] time ceases to be a matter of mere successive quarters of an hour, and appears to us in the guise of years and decades, . . . this extraordinary change of tempo, for which nothing in the preceding lines has prepared us.[23]

Now, Proust has just introduced that passage with these words: "The finest thing, to my mind, in the whole of *Education sentimentale,* is to be found, not in words at all, but in a passage where there comes a sudden moment of silence," and he will go on as follows: "in Balzac, . . . the change of tempo has an active and documentary character." So we do not know whether his

---

[19] Which the classical novel, by no means ignorant of it, integrated into summary; example, *Birotteau* (Garnier, pp. 31–32; Marriage and Waring, pp. 23–24): "He used to cry sometimes when the day was over and he thought of Touraine, where the peasant works leisurely and the mason takes his time about laying a stone, and toil is judiciously tempered by idleness; but he usually fell asleep before he reached the point of thinking of running away, for his morning's round of work awaited him, and he did his duty with the instinctive obedience of a yard dog."

[20] RH II, 890/P III, 723: "These ideas, tending on the one hand to diminish, and on the other to increase, my regret that I had no gift for literature, were entirely absent from my mind during the long years—in which I had in any case completely renounced the project of writing—which I spent far from Paris receiving treatment in a sanatorium, until there came a time, at the beginning of 1916, when it could no longer get medical staff"; and RH II, 988/P III, 854: "The new sanatorium to which I withdrew was no more successful in curing me than the first one, and many years passed before I came away."

[21] It is the change of chapter between ". . . and Frédéric, gaping, recognized Sénéchal" (III, chap. 5) and "He traveled . . . " (III, chap. 6).

[22] As if the change of chapter were not, precisely, a transition. But probably Proust, who is quoting from memory, forgot this detail.

[23] *Essais et articles,* Pléiade, p. 595; "About Flaubert's Style," in *Marcel Proust: A Selection from His Miscellaneous Writings,* trans. Gerard Hopkins (London, 1948), pp. 234–235.

admiration here is for the *sudden silence*, that is, the ellipsis separating the two chapters, or for the *change of tempo*, that is, the
summary in the opening lines of chapter 6. No doubt the truth
is that the distinction matters little to him, so true is it that, ad-
dicted to a kind of narrative "all or nothingness," he himself can
accelerate only (according to his own expression) "wildly,"[24]
even at the risk of (let us dedicate this metaphor from mechanics
to the spirit of the unfortunate Agostinelli) *lifting off.*[25]

Pause

A second negative finding concerns descriptive pauses. Proust
is customarily viewed as a novelist lavish in descriptions, and
no doubt he owes that reputation to an acquaintance with his
work that is apt to be from anthologies, where apparent digressions like the hawthorns at Tansonville, the seascapes of
Elstir, the Princess's fountain, etc., are inevitably isolated. In
fact, the clear descriptive passages are, relative to the scope of
the work, neither very numerous (there are scarcely more than
about thirty) nor very long (most do not exceed four pages): the
proportion is probably lower than in some of Balzac's novels. In
addition, a large number of these descriptions (undoubtedly
more than a third)[26] are the iterative type, that is, they are not
connected to a particular moment in the story but to a series of
analogous moments, and consequently cannot in any way contribute to slowing down the narrative but, indeed, the reverse:
for example, Léonie's room, the church at Combray, the "views

[24] "And to make [Time's] flight perceptible novelists are obliged, by wildly
accelerating the beat of the pendulum, to transport the reader in a couple of
minutes over ten, or twenty, or even thirty years" (RH I, 369/P I, 482).

[25] The *Contre Sainte-Beuve* contains this very allusive criticism of the Balzacian
use of summaries: "There are his recapitulations where, without allowing a
moment's breathing-space, he tells us everything we ought to know" (Pléiade,
p. 271; *Marcel Proust on Art*, p. 173).

[26] These figures might seem vague; but it would be absurd to look for precision
apropos of a corpus whose boundaries are themselves very uncertain, since
obviously pure description (purified of any narration) and pure narration
(purified of any description) do not exist, and since the counting of "descriptive
passages" necessarily omits thousands of sentences, portions of sentences, or
descriptive words set among scenes where narrative is dominant. On this matter, see my *Figures II*, pp. 56–61.

of the sea" at Balbec, the hotel in Doncières, the scenery of
Venice,[27] so many pages all synthesizing several occurrences of
the same sight into one single descriptive section. But most important is this: even when the object described has been met
only once (like the trees at Hudimesnil),[28] or when the description concerns only a single one of its appearances (generally the
first, as with the church at Balbec, the Guermantes fountain, the
sea at La Raspelière),[29] that description never brings about a
pause in the narrative, a suspension of the story or of (according
to the traditional term) the "action." In effect, Proustian narrative never comes to a standstill at an object or a sight unless that
halt corresponds to a contemplative pause by the hero himself
(Swann in *Un amour de Swann*, Marcel everywhere else), and
thus the descriptive piece never evades the temporality of the
story.

Of course, such treatment of description is not in itself an
innovation; and, for example, when the narrative in *Astrée* describes at length the pictures displayed in Céladon's room at the
château d'Isoure, we can assume that that description more or
less accompanies Céladon's gaze as he discovers these pictures
on waking up.[30] But we know that the Balzacian novel, on the
contrary, established a typically extratemporal descriptive canon
(furthermore, more in conformity with the model of epic *ec-
phrasis*),[31] a canon where the narrator, forsaking the course of
the story (or, as in *Le Père Goriot* or *La Recherche de l'absolu*,
before arriving there), makes it his business, in his own name
and solely for the information of his reader, to describe a scene
that at this point in the story no one, strictly speaking, is looking
at. For example, as the sentence in the *Vieille Fille* that opens the
scene at the Cormon townhouse certainly indicates: "Now,
however, it will be necessary to enter the household of that
elderly spinster toward whom so many interests converge, and

[27] RH I, 37–38/P I, 49–50; RH I, 45–51/P I, 59–67; RH I, 510–511/P I, 672–673; RH
I, 605–608/P I, 802–806; RH I, 784–785/P II, 98–99; RH II, 821–823/P III, 623–625.
[28] RH I, 543–545/P I, 717–719.
[29] RH I, 500–502/P I, 658–660; RH II, 43/P II, 656–657; RH II, 212/P II, 897.
[30] Honoré d'Urfé, *Astrée*, Vaganay ed., I. 40–43.
[31] Except for the shield of Achilles (*Iliad*, Book XVIII), described, as we know,
at the time of its construction by Hephaistus.

within whose walls the actors in this Scene are to meet this very evening."[32] This "entering" is obviously the doing of the narrator and reader alone, who are going to wander over the house and the garden while the real "actors in this Scene" continue to attend to their business elsewhere, or rather wait to go back to their business until the narrative agrees to return to them and restore them to life.[33]

We know that Stendhal always avoided that canon by pulverizing the descriptions, and by almost systematically integrating what he allowed to remain of them to the level of his characters' actions—or daydreams. But Stendhal's position, here as elsewhere, remains marginal and has no direct influence. If we wish to find in the modern novel a model or a precursor of Proustian description, we should much rather think of Flaubert. Not that the Balzacian type is completely foreign to him: see the scene of Yonville that begins the second part of *Bovary*. But most of the time, and even in descriptive passages of a certain extent, the general movement of the text[34] is governed by the step or the gaze of one (or several) character(s), and the unfolding of that movement corresponds exactly to the length of the trip (Emma's inspection of the house at Tostes, Frédéric's and Rosanette's walk in the forest)[35] or of the motionless contemplation (sight of the garden at Tostes, gallery with colored panes of glass at la Vaubyessard, view of Rouen).[36]

---

[32] Garnier, p. 67; *The Old Maid*, trans. W. Walton (Washington, D.C., 1898), p 61.

[33] Gautier will use this technique to the point of a flippancy that "bares" it, as the Formalists would say: "The Marquise inhabited a separate suite, which the Marquis did not enter unless he was announced. We will commit this impropriety that authors of all times have allowed themselves, and without saying a word to the buttons who would have forewarned the lodger, we will penetrate into the bedroom, sure of disturbing no one. The writer of a novel naturally wears on his finger the ring of Gyges, which makes him invisible" (*Le Capitaine Fracasse*, Garnier ed., p. 103). Later we will again meet this trope, the *metalepsis*, with which the narrator pretends to enter (with or without his reader) into the diegetic universe.

[34] Setting aside certain *descriptive intrusions* of the narrator, generally in the present tense, very brief, and as if unintentional: see my *Figures*, pp. 223–243.

[35] *Bovary*, Garnier ed. (edited by Gothot-Mersch), pp. 32–34; *L'Education*, edited by Dumesnil, II, 154–160.

[36] *Bovary*, Pommier-Leleu version, pp. 196–197 and 216; Garnier, pp. 268–269. The latter is iterative as well.

Proustian narrative seems to have turned this principle of concurrence into a rule. We know what characteristic habit of the author himself is reflected in the hero's capacity to come to a stop for long minutes before an object (hawthorns at Tansonville, pond at Montjouvain, trees at Hudimesnil, apple trees in bloom, views of the sea, etc.)—an object whose power to fascinate derives from the presence of a secret not disclosed, a message still illegible but insistent, a rough sketch and veiled promise of the ultimate revelation. The duration of these contemplative halts is generally such that it is in no danger of being exceeded by the duration of the reading (even a very slow reading) of the text that "tells of" them. So it is, for example, with the gallery of the Elstir paintings at the Duc de Guermantes's, the evocation of which takes up less than four pages[37] and which itself—Marcel notices after the event—has delayed him for three quarters of an hour, during which time the famished Duke leads some respectful guests, including the Princesse de Parme, in being patient. In fact, Proustian "description" is less a description of the object contemplated than it is a narrative and analysis of the perceptual activity of the character contemplating: of his impressions, progressive discoveries, shifts in distance and perspective, errors and corrections, enthusiasms or disappointments, etc. A contemplation highly active in truth, and containing "a whole story." This story is what Proustian description recounts. Suppose we reread, for example, the few pages devoted to Elstir's seascapes at Balbec.[38] We will see how jammed they are with terms designating not what the painting of Elstir *is*, but the "optical illusions" that it "recreates," and the false impressions it arouses and dissipates in turn: *seem, appear, give the impression, as if, you felt, you would have said, you thought, you understood, you saw reappear, they went racing over sunlit fields*, etc. Aesthetic activity here is not repose at all, but this characteristic is not due only to the sleight-of-hand "metaphors" of the impressionist painter. The same *labor* of perception, the same struggle or play with appearances, occurs again in the presence

37 RH I, 1017–1020/P II, 419–422.
38 RH I, 629–632/P I, 836–840.

of the slightest object or landscape. Here is the (very) young Marcel grappling with Aunt Léonie's handful of dried lime-flowers: *"as though a painter,"* "the leaves . . . *assumed [the ap-pearance] . . . of the most incongruous things imaginable,"* "A thousand trifling little details . . . gave me . . . the pleasure of *finding that these were indeed real lime-blossoms,"* "I *recognized,"* "the rosy . . . glow *shewed me* that these were petals which," etc.:[39] a whole precocious education in the art of seeing, of going beyond false appearances, of discerning true identities, giving this description (which, furthermore, is iterative) a story dura-tion that is packed full. There is the same labor of perception in front of Hubert Robert's fountain, the description of which I reprint in its entirety, merely emphasizing the terms that mark the duration of the scene and the activity of the hero, who is hidden here by a falsely generalizing impersonal pronoun (a little like Brichot's "one") that multiplies his presence without abolishing it:

In a clearing surrounded by fine trees several of which were as old as itself, set in a place apart, *one could see it in the distance,* slender, immobile, stiffened, allowing the breeze to stir only the lighter fall of its pale and quivering plume. The eighteenth century had re-fined the elegance of its lines, but, by fixing the style of the jet, *seemed* to have arrested its life; *at this distance one had the impression* of a work of art *rather than the sensation* of water. The moist cloud itself that was *perpetually* gathering at its crest preserved the character of the period like those that in the sky assemble round the palaces of Versailles. But *from a closer view one realised* that, while it respected, like the stones of an ancient palace, the design traced for it beforehand, it was *a constantly changing stream of water* that, springing upwards and seeking to obey the architect's tra-ditional orders, performed them to the letter only by *seeming* to infringe them, its thousand separate bursts succeeding only *at a distance in giving the impression* of a single flow. This was in reality as *often* interrupted as the scattering of the fall, whereas *from a distance it had appeared to me* unyielding, solid, unbroken in its continuity. *From a little nearer, one saw* that this continuity, *appar-ently* complete, was assured, at every point in the ascent of the jet,

[39] RH I, 39/P I, 51.

wherever it must otherwise have been broken, by the entering into line, by the lateral incorporation of a parallel jet which mounted higher than the first and was itself, at an altitude greater but *already* a strain upon its endurance, relieved by a third. *Seen close at hand*, drops without strength fell back from the column of water crossing on their way their climbing sisters and, *at times*, torn, caught in an eddy of the night air, disturbed by this *ceaseless* flow, floated awhile *before* being drowned in the basin. They teased with their *hesitations*, with their *passage* in the opposite direction, and blurred with their soft vapour the vertical tension of that stem, bearing aloft an oblong cloud composed of a thousand tiny drops, but *apparently* painted in an unchanging, golden brown which rose, unbreakable, constant, urgent, swift, to mingle with the clouds in the sky. Unfortunately, a gust of wind was enough to scatter it obliquely on the ground; *at times* indeed a single jet, disobeying its orders, swerved and, had they not kept a respectful distance, would have drenched to their skins the incautious crowd of gazers.[40]

We meet this situation again, developed much more extensively, in the course of the Guermantes matinée. Its first twenty-five pages at least [41] are based on this activity of recognizing and identifying, an activity forced on the hero by the aging of an entire "society." At first glance these twenty-five pages are purely descriptive: the sight of the Guermantes salon after a ten-year absence. In fact, we are definitely dealing instead with a narrative: how the hero, passing from one to another (or from some to others), must each time make the effort—sometimes a fruitless one—to recognize, in this little old man, the Duc de Châtellerault; under his beard, M. d'Argencourt; the Prince d'Agrigente, dignified by age; the young count of———, as an old colonel; Bloch, as poppa Bloch, etc.— revealing at each encounter "the mental effort that made [him] hesitate between three or four people," and that other "mental effort," the even more disturbing one of identification itself:

[40] RH II, 43/P II, 656.
[41] We are dealing here with the first twenty-five pages of the reception as such (RH II, 1039–1064/P III, 920–952), once Marcel has entered the salon, after the meditation in the library (RH II, 997–1039/P III, 866–920).

For to "recognize" someone, and, *a fortiori*, having failed to recognize someone to learn his identity, is to predicate two contradictory things of a single subject, it is to admit that what was here, the person whom one remembers, no longer exists, and also that what is now here is a person whom one did not know to exist; and to do this we have to apprehend a mystery almost as disturbing as that of death, of which it is, indeed, as it were the preface and the harbinger.[42]

A painful substitution, like the one he must effect at the church of Balbec, of the real for the imaginary: "my mind . . . was astonished to see the statue which it had carved a thousand times, reduced now to its own apparent form in stone," a work of art "transformed, as was the church itself, into a little old woman in stone whose height I could measure and count her wrinkles."[43] A euphoric superimposition, by contrast: the one setting up a comparison between the memory of Combray and the scenery of Venice, "impressions analogous . . . but transposed into a wholly different and far richer key."[44] Finally a difficult, almost acrobatic juxtaposition: the pieces of the "countryside at sunrise" perceived alternately through the two opposite window panes of the railroad car between Paris and Balbec, and requiring the hero to be "running from one window to the other to reassemble, to collect on a single canvas the intermittent, antipodean fragments of [his] fine, scarlet, ever-changing morning, and to obtain a comprehensive view of it and a continuous picture."[45]

So we see that in Proust contemplation is neither an instantaneous flash (like recollection) nor a moment of passive and restful ecstasy; it is an activity—intense, intellectual, and often physical—and the telling of it is, after all is said and done, a narrative just like any other. What we are compelled to conclude, therefore, is that description, in Proust, becomes absorbed into narration, and that the second canonical type of

---

[42] RH II, 1054/P III, 939.
[43] RH I, 501–502/P I, 659–660.
[44] RH II, 821/P III, 623.
[45] RH I, 497/P I, 654–655.

movement—the descriptive pause—does not exist in Proust, for the obvious reason that with him description is everything *except* a pause in the narrative.

Ellipsis

Absence of summary, absence of descriptive pause—on the roster of Proustian narrative, then, only two of the traditional movements still exist: scene and ellipsis. Before examining the temporal pacing and the function of scene in Proust, we will say a few words about ellipsis. Obviously we are dealing here only with ellipsis as such, or *temporal* ellipsis, leaving aside those lateral omissions for which we have reserved the name *paralipsis*.

From the temporal point of view, the analysis of ellipses comes down to considering the story time elided, and here the first question is to know whether that duration is indicated (*definite* ellipses) or not indicated (*indefinite* ellipses). Thus, between the end of *Gilberte* and the beginning of *Balbec* a two-year ellipsis occurs that is clearly definite: "I had arrived at a state almost of complete indifference to Gilberte when, *two years later*, I went with my grandmother to Balbec";[46] on the other hand, we remember, the two ellipses relating to the hero's sojourns in a clinic are (almost) equally indefinite ("long years," "many years"), and the analyst is reduced to sometimes difficult inferences.

From the formal point of view, we will distinguish:

(a) *Explicit* ellipses, like those I have just quoted. They arise either from an indication (definite or not) of the lapse of time they elide, which assimilates them to very quick summaries of the "some years passed" type (in this case the indication *constitutes* the ellipsis as textual section, which is then not totally equal to zero); or else from elision pure and simple (zero degree of the elliptical text) plus, when the narrative starts up again, an indication of the time elapsed, like the "two years later" quoted just above. This latter form is obviously more rigorously elliptical, although quite as explicit, and not necessarily shorter; but in this form the text expresses the perception of narrative void or gap

⁴⁶ RH I, 488/P I, 642.

more analogically, more "iconically" (in Peirce's or Jakobson's sense).[47] Both of these forms, in addition, can supplement the purely temporal indication with a piece of information having diegetic content, such as "some years *of happiness* passed," or "after some years *of happiness*." These *characterizing* ellipses are one of the resources of novelistic narration. In the *Chartreuse* Stendhal gives an example that is memorable, and moreover ingenuously contradictory, after the nocturnal reunion of Fabrice and Clélia: "Here, we ask for permission to pass over, *without saying a single word about it*, a space of three years.... After three years *of divine happiness* ... "[48] Let us add that a negative characterization is a characterization just like any other: an example is when Fielding, who with some exaggeration flatters himself on being the first to vary the rhythm of the narrative and to elide the dead spaces of the action,[49] leaps over twelve years in the life of Tom Jones, asserting that "nothing worthy of a Place in this History occurred within that Period."[50] We know how much Stendhal admired and imitated this flippant manner. In the *Recherche*, the two ellipses that frame the episode of the war are obviously characterizing ellipses, since we learn that Marcel spent those years in a clinic, being cared for without being cured, and without writing. But almost equally characterizing, although retrospectively, is the ellipsis opening *Balbec I*, for to say "I had arrived at a state almost of complete indifference to Gilberte when, two years later... " amounts to say-

---

[47] See Roman Jakobson, "Quest for the Essence of Language," *Diogenes*, 51 (Fall 1965), 21–37.

[48] Garnier, p. 474.

[49] See Book II, chap. 1, of *Tom Jones*, where he attacks the dull historians who "fill up as much Paper with the Detail of Months and Years in which nothing remarkable happened, as [they employ] upon those notable Æras when the greatest Scenes have been transacted on the human Stage," and whose books he compares "to a Stage-Coach, which performs constantly the same Course, empty as well as full." In opposition to this somewhat imaginary tradition, he boasts of inaugurating "a contrary Method," sparing nothing to "open [any extraordinary Scene] at large to our Reader," while on the contrary ignoring "whole Years [that] pass without producing any Thing worthy [of] Notice"—like the "[sagacious] Registers of [the Guild-hall] Lottery" who announce only the winning numbers (Norton Critical Edition, pp. 58–59).

[50] Book III, chap. 1 (Norton, p. 88).

ing, "for two years, I was detaching myself from Gilberte little by little."

→   (b) *Implicit* ellipses, that is, those whose very presence is not announced in the text and which the reader can infer only from some chronological lacuna or gap in narrative continuity. This is the case for the indefinite time elapsing between the end of the *Jeunes Filles en fleurs* and the beginning of *Guermantes*: we know Marcel had returned to Paris, to "[his] own room, the ceiling of which was low";[51] we meet him next in a new apartment attached to the Guermantes townhouse, which presumes the elision of at least a few days, and perhaps considerably more. It is also the case, and in a more puzzling way, for the few months following the grandmother's death.[52] This ellipsis is perfectly mute: we left the grandmother on her deathbed, most likely at the beginning of the summer; the narrative takes up again in these terms: "Albeit it was simply a Sunday in autumn . . . " The ellipsis is apparently definite, thanks to this indication of date, but it is very imprecisely so, and will soon become rather confused.[53] Above all it is not characterized, and it will remain not characterized: we will never, even retrospectively, know anything of what the hero's life has been during these few months. This is perhaps the most opaque silence in the entire *Recherche*, and, if we remember that the death of the grandmother is to a great extent a transposition of the death of the author's mother, this reticence is undoubtedly not devoid of significance.[54]

---

[51] RH I, 712/P I, 953.

[52] Between chapters 1 and 2 of *Guermantes II* (RH I, 964–965/P II, 345).

[53] "First it is an indefinite Sunday in autumn [RH I, 965/P II, 345] and soon it is the end of autumn [RH I, 994/P II, 385]. However, shortly thereafter [RH I, 999/P II, 392] Françoise says, 'It's the end of "Sectember" already. . . .' In any case, it is not a September atmosphere, but a November or even a December one that the restaurant is deep in where the narrator dines the day before the first invitation to the Duchesse de Guermantes's. And on leaving her reception, the narrator asks for his *snowboots*" (Daniel, *Temps et mystification*, pp. 92–93).

[54] Let us remember that Marcel himself has the habit of interpreting certain words "in the same way as . . . a sudden silence" (RH II, 439/P III, 88). The hermeneutics of narrative must also take on these sudden silences, by accounting for their "duration," their intensity, and naturally their *placement*.

(c) Finally, the most implicit form of ellipsis is the purely *hypothetical* ellipsis, impossible to localize, even sometimes ⟵ impossible to place in any spot at all, and revealed after the event by an analepsis such as those we already met in the preceding chapter:[55] trips to Germany, to the Alps, to Holland, military service. We are obviously there at the limits of the narrative's coherence, and for that very reason at the limits of the validity of temporal analysis. But the *designation of limits* is not the most trifling task of a method of analysis; and we may say in passing that perhaps the main justification for studying a work like the *Recherche du temps perdu* according to the traditional criteria of narrative is, on the contrary, to allow one to establish with precision the points on which such a work, deliberately or not, goes beyond such criteria.

Scene

If we consider the fact that ellipses, whatever their number and power of elision may be, represent a practically nonexistent portion of text, we must surely come to the conclusion that the whole of Proust's narrative text can be defined as *scene*, taking that term in the temporal sense in which we are defining it here and setting aside for the moment the iterative nature of some of those scenes.[56] Thus the traditional alternation summary/scene is at an end. Later we will see it replaced by another alternation, but now we must note a change in function which in any case modifies the structural role of the scene.

In novelistic narrative as it functioned before the *Recherche*, the contrast of tempo between detailed scene and summary almost always reflected a contrast of content between dramatic and nondramatic, the strong periods of the action coinciding with the most intense moments of the narrative while the weak periods were summed up with large strokes and as if from a great distance, according to the principle that we have seen set forth by Fielding. The real rhythm of the novelistic canon, still

[55] P. 51.
[56] On the dominance of scene, see Tadié, *Proust et le roman*, pp. 387 ff.

very perceptible in *Bovary*, is thus the alternation of nondramatic summaries, functioning as waiting room and liaison, with dramatic scenes whose role in the action is decisive.[57]

One can still grant that status to some of the scenes in the *Recherche*, like the "drama of bedtime," the profanation at Montjouvain, the evening of the cattleyas, Charlus's deep anger at Marcel, the grandmother's death, Charlus's exclusion, and naturally (although there we are dealing with a completely internal "action") the ultimate revelation,[58] all of which mark irreversible stages in the fulfillment of a destiny. But clearly such is not the function of the longest and most typically Proustian scenes, those five enormous ones that all by themselves take up about 450 pages: the Villeparisis matinée, the Guermantes dinner, the soirée at the Princess's, the soirée at La Raspelière, the Guermantes matinée.[59] As we have already observed, each of these has inaugural importance: each marks the hero's entrance into a new place or milieu and stands for the entire series, which it opens, of similar scenes that will not be reported: other receptions at Mme. de Villeparisis's and in the Guermantes milieu, other dinners at Oriane's, other receptions at the Princess's, other soirées at La Raspelière. None of these inaugural social gatherings merits more attention than all the analogous ones that succeed it and that it represents except by being the first in each series, and as such arousing a curiosity that habit will immediately after begin to blunt.[60] So we are not dealing

[57] This assertion should obviously be taken with qualifications: for instance, in the *Souffrances de l'inventeur*, the most dramatic pages are perhaps those where Balzac sums up with the spareness of a military historian the procedural battles waged against David Séchard.

[58] RH I, 16–36/P I, 21–48; RH I, 122–127/P I, 159–165; RH I, 173–179/P I, 226–233; RH I, 1110–1119/P II, 552–565; RH I, 956–964/P II, 335–345; RH II, 537–606/P III, 226–324; RH II, 996–999/P III, 865–869.

[59] RH I, 846–920/P II, 183–284; RH I, 1016–1106/P II, 416–547; RH II, 27–89/P II, 633–722; RH II, 190–269/P II, 866–979; RH II, 997–1140/P III, 866–1048.

[60] The status of the final scene (the Guermantes matinée) is more complex because it involves as much (and even more) a farewell to the world as an initiation. But the theme of *discovery* is nonetheless present there, in the form, as we know, of a rediscovery, a recognition made difficult by the mask of aging and transformation—a reason for curiosity as powerful as, if not more so than, the reason animating the earlier scenes of entry into society.

here with dramatic scenes, but rather with *typical* or illustrative scenes, where action (even in the very broad sense one must give this term in the Proustian universe) is almost completely obliterated in favor of psychological and social characterization.[61]

This change of function entails a very appreciable modification in temporal texture: contrary to the earlier tradition, which made scene into a place of dramatic concentration almost entirely free of descriptive or discursive impedimenta, and free even more of anachronic interferences, the Proustian scene—as J. P. Houston has said[62]—plays in the novel a role of "temporal hearth" or magnetic pole for all sorts of supplementary information and incidents. It is almost always inflated, indeed encumbered with digressions of all kinds, retrospections, anticipations, iterative and descriptive parentheses, didactic interventions by the narrator, etc., all intended to collect in a syllepsis around the gathering-as-pretext a cluster of events and considerations able to give that gathering a fully paradigmatic importance. A very approximate breakdown bearing on the large scenes in question reveals fairly well the relative weight of these elements that are external to the gathering being told about but thematically essential to what Proust called his "supernourishment": in the Villeparisis matinée, twenty-five pages out of seventy-five; in the Guermantes dinner, forty-three out of ninety; in the Guermantes soirée, seventeen out of sixty-two; in the last Guermantes matinée, finally—the first forty-two pages of which are taken up with an almost indistinguishable mixture of internal monologue by the hero and speculative discourse by the narrator, and the remainder of which is handled (as we will see later) chiefly in an iterative mode—the proportion is reversed and it is the strictly narrative moments (barely forty pages out of one hundred and forty) that seem to emerge from a sort of

[61] B. G. Rogers (*Proust's Narrative Techniques* [Geneva, 1965], pp. 143 ff.) sees in the unfolding of the *Recherche* a gradual disappearance of dramatic scenes, which, according to him, are more numerous in the early parts. His main argument is that Albertine's death is not cause for a scene. Not a very convincing proof; the proportion hardly varies in the course of the work, and the relevant feature is much rather the steady predominance of nondramatic scenes.

[62] Houston, pp. 33–34.

descriptive-discursive magma very remote from the usual criteria of "scenic" temporality and even from all narrative temporality—like those melodic scraps that one perceives in the opening measures of "La Valse," through a mist of rhythm and harmony. But here the haziness is not inceptive, like Ravel's or like that of the opening pages of *Swann*, but the contrary: as if in this final scene the narrative wanted, at the end, to dissolve gradually and to enact the intentionally indistinct and subtly chaotic reflection of its own disappearing.

Thus we see that Proustian narrative does not leave any of the traditional narrative movements intact, and that the whole of the rhythmic system of novelistic narrative is thereby profoundly affected. But we still have one last modification left to understand, undoubtedly the most decisive one: its emergence and diffusion will give the narrative temporality of the *Recherche* a completely new cadence—a perfectly unprecedented rhythm.

3 Frequency

Singulative/Iterative

What I call *narrative frequency*, that is, the relations of frequency (or, more simply, of repetition) between the narrative and the diegesis, up to this time has been very little studied by critics and theoreticians of the novel. It is nonetheless one of the main aspects of narrative temporality, and one which, at the level of common speech, is well known to grammarians under the category precisely of *aspect*.

An event is not only capable of happening; it can also happen again, or be repeated: the sun rises every day. Of course, strictly speaking the *identity* of these multiple occurrences is debatable: "the sun" that "rises" every morning is not exactly the same from one day to another—any more than the "8:25 P.M. Geneva-to-Paris" train, dear to Ferdinand de Saussure, is made up each evening of the same cars hooked to the same locomotive.[1] The "repetition" is in fact a mental construction, which eliminates from each occurrence everything belonging to it that is peculiar to itself, in order to preserve only what it shares with all the others of the same class, which is an abstraction: "the sun," "the morning," "to rise." This is well known, and I recall it only to specify once and for all that what we will name here "identical events" or "recurrence of the same event" is a series of several similar events *considered only in terms of their resemblance*.

[1] Ferdinand de Saussure, *Course in General Linguistics*, trans. Wade Baskin (New York: McGraw-Hill, 1959), p. 108.

Symmetrically, a narrative statement is not only produced, it can be produced again, can be repeated one or more times in the same text: nothing prevents me from saying or writing, "Pierre came yesterday evening, Pierre came yesterday evening, Pierre came yesterday evening." Here again, the identity and therefore the repetition are facts of abstraction; materially (phonetically or graphically) or even ideally (linguistically) none of the occurrences is completely identical to the others, solely by virtue of their co-presence and their succession, which diversify these three statements into a first, a next, and a last. Here again one can refer to the famous pages of the *Cours de linguistique générale* on the "problem of identities." That is a further abstraction to take into consideration, and we will do so.

A system of relationships is established between these capacities for "repetition" on the part of both the narrated events (of the story) and the narrative statements (of the text)—a system of relationships that we can a priori reduce to four virtual types, simply from the multiplication of the two possibilities given on both sides: the event repeated or not, the statement repeated or not. Schematically, we can say that a narrative, whatever it is, may tell once what happened once, *n* times what happened *n* times, *n* times what happened once, once what happened *n* times. Let us linger a bit with these four types of relations of frequency.

Narrating once what happened once (or, if we want to abbreviate with a pseudo-mathematical formula: $1N/1S$). For example, a statement such as "Yesterday, I went to bed early." This form of narrative, where the singularness of the narrative statement corresponds to the singularness of the narrated event, is obviously far and away the most common—so common, and apparently considered so "normal," that it bears no name, at least in our language. However, to express specifically that we are dealing with only one possibility among others, I propose to give it a name. I will hereafter call it singulative narrative—a neologism that I hope is transparent, and that we will sometimes lighten by using the adjective "singular" in the same technical sense: a singulative or singular scene.

Narrating n times what happened n times (nN/nS). For example, the statement, "Monday, I went to bed early, Tuesday I went to bed early, Wednesday I went to bed early, etc." From the point of view we are interested in here, that is, relations of frequency between narrative and story, this anaphoric type is still in fact singulative and thus reduces to the previous type, since the repetitions of the narrative simply correspond—according to a connection that Jakobson would call iconic—to the repetitions of the story. The singulative is therefore defined not by the number of occurrences on both sides but by the equality of this number.[2]

Narrating n times what happened once (nN/1S). For example, a ⟵ statement like this one: "Yesterday I went to bed early, yesterday I went to bed early, yesterday I went to bed early, etc."[3] This form might seem purely hypothetical, an ill-formed offspring of the combinative mind, irrelevant to literature. Let us remember, however, that certain modern texts are based on narrative's capacity for repetition: we may remember, for instance, a recurrent episode like the death of the centipede in *La Jalousie*. On the other hand, the same event can be told several times not only with stylistic variations, as is generally the case in Robbe-Grillet, but also with variations in "point of view," as in *Rashomon* or *The Sound and the Fury*.[4] The epistolary novel of the eighteenth century was already familiar with contrasts of this type, and of course the "repeating" anachronies that we met in Chapter 1 (*advance notices* and *recalls*) belong to this narrative type, which they bring into existence more or less fleetingly. Let us also remember (and this is not as foreign to the function of literature as one might believe) that children love to be told the same story several times—indeed, several times in a row—or to reread the same book, and that this predilection is not entirely the prerogative of childhood: later we will examine in some

[2] That is, the formula *nN/nS* defines equally the first two types, granting that most often *n* = 1. To tell the truth, this grid does not take into account a fifth possible relationship (but one that to my knowledge we have no example of), where what happened several times would also be recounted several times, but a different (either greater or lesser) number of times: *nN/mS*.

[3] With or without stylistic variations, such as, "Yesterday I went to bed early, yesterday I went to bed before it was late, yesterday I put myself to bed early. . . ."

[4] We will come back to this question in the next chapter.

detail the scene of the "Saturday luncheon at Combray," which ends on a typical example of ritual narrative. This type of narrative, where the recurrences of the statement do not correspond to any recurrence of events, I will obviously call *repeating* narrative.

Finally, *narrating one time* (or rather: *at one time*) *what happened n times* ($1N/nS$). Let us go back to our second—singulative anaphoric—type: "Monday I went to bed early, Tuesday, etc." Plainly, when such repeating phenomena occur in the story, the narrative is not by any means condemned to reproduce them in its discourse as if it were incapable of the slightest effort to abstract and synthesize: in fact, and except for deliberate stylistic effect, a narrative—and even the most unpolished one—will in this case find a sylleptic[5] formulation such as "every day," or "the whole week," or "every day of the week I went to bed early." It is well known what variant of this phrase opens the *Recherche du temps perdu*. This type of narrative, where a single narrative utterance takes upon itself several occurrences together[6] of the same event (in other words, once again, several events considered only in terms of their analogy), we will call *iterative* narrative. We are dealing here with a linguistic proceeding that in its different forms[7] is completely common and probably universal or quasi-universal—one well known to grammarians, who have conferred its name upon it.[8] Literature's investment in it, on the other hand, does not seem to have provoked very intense interest so far.[9] It is, however, a completely traditional form: we can find examples of it as early as the Homeric epic, and throughout the history of the classical and modern novel.

But in the classical narrative and even up to Balzac, iterative sections are almost always functionally subordinate to singula-

[5] In the sense in which we defined narrative syllepsis earlier (p. 85).

[6] It is indeed a question of taking on *together*, synthetically, and not of recounting a single one of them which would stand for all the others, which is a *paradigmatic* use of singulative narrative: "I report the conversation at one of these meals, which may give an idea of the others" (RH II, 289/P II, 1006).

[7] For example, the "iterative" or "frequentative" form of the English verb, or the French imperfect tense for repeated action."

[8] In concurrence, then, with "frequentative."

[9] Let us mention, however, J. P. Houston's article, already referred to, and Wolfgang Raible's "Linguistik und Literaturkritik," *Linguistik und Didaktik*, 8 (1971).

tive scenes, for which the iterative sections provide a sort of informative frame or background, in a mode illustrated fairly well, for example, in *Eugénie Grandet,* by the preliminary scene of daily life in the Grandet family, a scene which serves only to prepare for the opening of the narrative as such: "In 1819, towards the beginning of the evening, in the middle of November, big Nanon lit the fire for the first time."[10] The classic function of iterative narrative is thus fairly close to that of description, with which, moreover, it maintains very close relations: the "moral portrait," for example, which is one of the varieties of the descriptive genre, operates most often (see La Bruyère) through accumulation of iterative traits. Like description, in the traditional novel the iterative narrative is *at the service* of the narrative "as such," which is the singulative narrative. The first novelist who undertook to liberate the iterative from this functional dependence is clearly Flaubert in *Madame Bovary,* where pages like those narrating Emma's life in the convent, her life at Tostes before and after the ball at La Vaubyessard, or her Thursdays at Rouen with Léon[11] take on a wholly unusual fullness and autonomy. But no novelistic work, apparently, has ever put the iterative to a use comparable—in textual scope, in thematic importance, in degree of technical elaboration—to Proust's use of it in the *Recherche du temps perdu.*

The first three main sections of the *Recherche*—that is, *Combray, Un amour de Swann,* and "*Gilberte*" (*Noms de pays: le nom* and *Autour de Madame Swann*)—can without exaggeration be considered essentially iterative. Other than some singulative scenes (which are, for that matter, dramatically very important, like Swann's visit, the meeting with the Lady in pink, the Legrandin episodes, the profanation at Montjouvain, the appearance of the Duchess at church, and the trip to the steeples at Martinville), the text of *Combray* narrates, in the French imperfect tense for repeated action, not what *happened* but what *used to happen* at Combray, regularly, ritually, every day, or every

---

[10] Garnier, p. 34.
[11] I, chap. 6; I, chap. 7; I, chap. 9; III, chap. 5.

Sunday, or every Saturday, etc. The narrative of Swann's and Odette's love is also carried on, for the most part, in this mode of custom and repetition (major exceptions: the two Verdurin soirées, the scene of the cattleyas, the Sainte-Euverte concert), just like the love between Marcel and Gilberte (notable singulative scenes: Berma, the dinner with Bergotte). An approximate count (precision here would not be pertinent) reveals something like 86 iterative to 52 singulative pages in *Combray*, 68 to 77 in *Un amour de Swann*, 109 to 85 in *Gilberte*, or about 265 iterative to 215 singulative pages for the whole of these three sections. Only with the first visit to Balbec is the predominance of the singulative established (or *reestablished*, if we think of what the proportion was in the traditional narrative).[12] Yet we note, up to the end, numerous iterative sections, like the rides at Balbec with Mme. de Villeparisis in the *Jeunes Filles en fleurs*; the hero's maneuvers, at the beginning of *Guermantes*, to meet the Duchess every morning; the sights of Doncières; the trips in the little train of La Raspelière; life with Albertine in Paris; the outings in Venice.[13]

And we must note the presence of iterative passages within singulative scenes: for example, at the beginning of the dinner at the Duchess's, the long parenthesis devoted to the wit of the Guermantes.[14] In this case, the temporal field covered by the iterative section obviously extends well beyond the temporal field of the scene it is inserted into: the iterative to some extent opens a window onto the external period. So we will describe parentheses of this type as *generalizing iterations*, or *external iterations*. Another, much less classical type of move to the iterative within a singular scene is partly to treat the duration of the scene itself in an iterative form, whereupon the scene is then synthesized by a sort of paradigmatic classification of the events com-

---

[12] We would have to have a gigantic set of statistics to establish this proportion accurately; but probably the iterative's share would not reach anything near ten per cent.

[13] RH I, 534–548/P I, 704–723; RH I, 755–756/P II, 58–59; RH I, 782–785/P II, 96–100; RH II, 308–364/P II, 1034–1112; RH II, 383–434/P III, 9–81; RH II, 820–825/P III, 623–630.

[14] RH I, 1031–1063/P II, 438–483.

posing it. A very clear example of such a treatment, even though it extends over a necessarily very short period of time, is this passage about the meeting between Charlus and Jupien, in which we see the Baron raise his eyes "every now and then" and dart an attentive look at the tailor: "*each time* that M. de Charlus looked at Jupien, he took care that his glance should be accompanied by a spoken word. . . . Thus, *every other minute*, the same question seemed to be being intensely put to Jupien." The iterative nature of the action is confirmed here by the indication of frequency, with a wholly hyperbolic precision.[15] We find the same effect again, on a much vaster scale, in the final scene of the *Temps retrouvé*, which is treated almost continuously in the iterative mode. What governs the composition of the text here is not the diachronic unfolding of the reception at the Princess's, in the succession of events filling it up, but rather the enumeration of a certain number of classes of occurrences, each of which synthesizes several events that are in fact scattered throughout the "matinée."

> In some of the guests I recognized after a while . . . And yet, in complete contrast with these, I had the surprise of talking to men and women who had . . . Some men walked with a limp . . . Certain faces . . . seemed to be muttering a last prayer . . . the white hair of these women . . . profoundly disquieted me . . . Some of the old men . . . There were men in the room whom I knew to be related . . . the [women] who were either too beautiful or too ugly . . . Others too, both men and women . . . Even in the case of the men . . . More than one of the men and women . . . Sometimes . . . But with other people . . . [16]

I will call this second type *internal* or *synthesizing iteration*, in the sense that the iterative syllepsis extends not over a wider period of time but over the period of time of the scene itself.

[15] RH II, 6/P II, 605. Without an indication of frequency, but in just as hyperbolic a way, cf. RH I, 827/P II, 157: while Saint-Loup went to get Rachel, Marcel "strolled up and down the road," past the gardens; for these few minutes, "If I raised my head I could see, *now and then*, girls sitting in the windows."
[16] RH II, 1052–1083/P III, 936–976.

A single scene, furthermore, can contain both types of syllepsis. In the course of that same Guermantes matinée, Marcel evokes in an external iteration the amatory relationship between the Duke and Odette: "he was always in her house... he spent his days and his evenings with Mme. de Forcheville... he permitted her to receive friends.... At moments... the lady in pink would interrupt him with a sprightly sally.... It must be added that Odette was unfaithful to M. de Guermantes...."[17] The iterative here obviously synthesizes several months or even several years of relations between Odette and Basin, and thus a period of time very much longer than that of the Guermantes matinée. But it also happens that the two types of iteration blend to the point that the reader can no longer differentiate them, or untangle them. For example, in the scene of the Guermantes dinner, near the top of page 1097, we will meet an unambiguous internal iteration: "I cannot, by the way, say how many times in the course of this evening I heard the word 'cousin' used." But the next sentence, still iterative, can already bear on a longer period of time: "On the one hand, M. de Guermantes, almost at every name that was mentioned [in the course of this dinner, certainly, but perhaps also in a more habitual way], exclaimed: 'But he's Oriane's cousin!'" The third sentence perhaps brings us back to the period of the scene: "On the other hand the word cousin was employed in a wholly different connexion... by the Turkish Ambassadress, who had come in after dinner." But the next is an iterative plainly external to the scene, since it goes on to give a sort of general portrait of the Ambassadress:

> Devoured by social ambition and endowed with a real power of assimilating knowledge, she would pick up with equal facility the story of the Retreat of the Ten Thousand or the details of sexual perversion among birds.... She was, incidentally, a dangerous person to listen to.... She was at this period little received in society

—so much so that when the narrative returns to the conversation between the Duke and the Ambassadress, we are not able to tell whether we are dealing with *this* conversation (in the course of *this* dinner) or with a wholly other one:

> She hoped to give herself a really fashionable air by quoting the most historic names of the little-known people who were her friends. At once M. de Guermantes, thinking that she was referring to people who frequently dined at his table, quivered with joy at finding himself once more in sight of a landmark and shouted the rallying-cry: "But he's Oriane's cousin!"

Likewise, one page further on, the iterative treatment that Proust imposes on the genealogical conversations between the Duke and M. de Beauserfeuil wipes out all demarcation between this first dinner at the Guermantes', subject of the present scene, and the whole of the series it inaugurates.

Thus in Proust the singulative scene itself is not immune to a sort of contamination by the iterative. The importance of this mode, or rather of this narrative *aspect*, is further accentuated by the very characteristic presence of what I will call the *pseudo-iterative*—that is, scenes presented, particularly by their wording in the imperfect, as iterative, whereas their richness and precision of detail ensure that no reader can seriously believe they occur and reoccur in that manner, several times, without any variation.[18] For example, consider certain long conversations between Léonie and Françoise (every Sunday at Combray!), between Swann and Odette, at Balbec with Mme. de Villeparisis, in Paris at Mme. Swann's, in the pantry between Françoise and "her" footman, or the scene of Oriane's pun, "Teaser Augustus."[19] In all these cases, and in some others as well, a singular scene has been converted almost arbitrarily, and without any modification except in the use of tenses, into an iterative scene. This is obviously a literary convention (I would readily say *narrative license,* as we speak of poetic license) that presumes a great obligingness on the part of the reader or, as Coleridge said, a "willing suspension of disbelief." This convention is, besides, of

---

18 Cf. Houston, p. 39.
19 RH I, 77–83/P I, 100–109; RH I, 186–187/P I, 243; RH I, 546–548/P I, 721–723; RH I, 453–456/P I, 596–599; RH I, 727–732/P II, 22–26; RH I, 1049–1051/P II, 464–467.

very long standing. I note an example at random in *Eugénie Grandet* (dialogue between Mme. Grandet and her husband) and another in *Lucien Leuwen* (conversation between Leuwen and Gauthier), but also in one of Cervantes' exemplary novels: for example, the monologue of old Carrizales in "The Jealous Extremaduran," which we are told was spoken "not once but a hundred times."[20] Every reader naturally interprets this as hyperbole, not only for its indication of number but also for its claim of exact identity among several soliloquies almost alike, of which this one presents a sort of sample. In short, in classical narrative the pseudo-iterative typically constitutes a *figure* of narrative rhetoric which is not required to be taken literally, but just the reverse. The narrative affirms literally "this happened every day," to be understood figuratively as "every day something of this kind happened, of which this is one realization among others."

It is obviously possible to treat in this way the several examples of pseudo-iteration noticed in Proust.[21] It seems to me, however, that their extent, especially when we compare it to the importance of the iterative in general, prohibits such a limitation. The convention of the pseudo-iterative does not function in Proust in the intentional and purely figurative mode it takes in the classical narrative. In Proustian narrative the characteristic and very marked tendency toward inflating the iterative is intended to be taken in its impossible literalness.

The best (although paradoxical) proof of this is perhaps given by the three or four times when Proust inadvertently lets a necessarily singulative passé simple slip into the middle of a scene presented as iterative—"'And it will come in the middle of my luncheon!' *she would murmur* [*ajouta-t-elle* à mi-voix] to herself. . . . At the mention of Vigny [Mme. de Villeparisis] *laughed* [se *mit* à rire]. . . . 'The Duchess must be connected with

---

[20] *Eugénie Grandet*, Garnier ed., pp. 205–206; *Lucien Leuwen*, Part I, chap. 7; Cervantes, "The Jealous Extremaduran," in *Exemplary Stories*, trans. C. A. Jones (Harmondsworth, England: Penguin, 1972), p. 149.
[21] See Pierre Guiraud, *Essais de stylistique* (Paris, 1971), p. 142.

all that lot,' *said* [*dit*] Françoise"[22]—or links an iterative scene
with a consequence that is singular by definition, as on the page
of the *Jeunes Filles en fleurs* where we learn from the mouth of
Mme. Cottard that at *euch* of Odette's "Wednesdays" the hero
had "made a complete conquest, first shot, of Mme. Verdurin,"
assuming that action to have a capability for repetition and re-
newal wholly contrary to its nature.[23] We can, no doubt, see in
these apparent blunders the traces of a first draft written in the
singulative, in which Proust supposedly forgot or neglected to
convert certain verbs; but it seems to me sounder to read these
slips as so many signs that the writer himself sometimes "lives"
such scenes with an intensity that makes him forget the distinction of aspects—and that excludes on his part the purposeful
attitude of the classical novelist using in full awareness a purely
conventional figure. These confusions, it seems to me, instead
reflect in Proust a sort of *intoxication with the iterative.*

It is tempting to connect this characteristic to what is supposedly one of the dominant features of Proustian psychology,
to wit, a very sharp sense of habit and repetition, a feeling of the
analogy between moments. But the iterative nature of the narrative is not always, as it is in *Combray*, based on the actually
repetitive and routine aspect of a provincial and petit-bourgeois
life like Aunt Léonie's: this motivation does not apply to the
Parisian milieu or the visits to Balbec and Venice. In fact, and
contrary to what one is often led to believe, the Proustian creature is as little sensitive to the individuality of moments as he is
spontaneously sensitive to the individuality of places. Moments
in Proust have a strong tendency to resemble and blend with

---

[22] RH I, 43/P I, 57; RH I, 547/P I, 722; RH I, 729/P II, 22. Another out-of-place
passé simple ("'I am sure . . . ,' *said* my aunt in a resigned tone [*dit* mollement
ma tante]") is present in the Clarac-Ferré edition (RH I, 79/P I, 104), as in the
NRF [Gallimard] edition of 1917, but the original (Grasset, 1913, p. 128) gave the
"correct" form: "*would say*" ["*disait*"]. This variant seems to have escaped Clarac
and Ferré, who do not call attention to it. The 1917 correction is hard to explain,
but the principle of *lectio difficilior* gives it precedence by the very reason of its
improbability.
[23] RH I, 462/P I, 608.

each other, and this capacity is obviously the very condition for experiencing "involuntary memory." This contrast between the "singularism" of his spatial sensitivity and the "iteratism" of his temporal sensitivity is well illustrated, for example, in the sentence from *Swann* where he speaks of the Guermantes landscape, a landscape "whose *individuality sometimes*, at night, in my dreams, binds me with a power that is almost fantastic":[24] individuality of place, indefinite, quasi-erratic ("sometimes") recursiveness of the moment. We find the same contrast again in this passage from *La Prisonnière*, where the singularity of a real morning is blotted out in favor of the "ideal morning" that it evokes and represents:

> Because I had refused to savour with my senses this particular morning, I enjoyed in imagination all the similar mornings, past or possible, or more precisely a certain type of morning of which all those of the same kind were but the intermittent apparition which I had at once recognised; for the keen air blew the book open of its own accord at the right page, and I found clearly set out before my eyes, so that I might follow it from my bed, the Gospel for the day. This ideal morning filled my mind full of a permanent reality, identical with all similar mornings, and infected me with . . . cheerfulness.[25]

But the mere fact of recurrence is not what defines the most rigorous form of iteration, the form that is apparently most satisfying to the spirit—or most soothing to Proustian sensibility. The repetition also has to be regular, has to obey a law of frequency, and this law has to be discernible and formulable, and therefore predictable in its effects. At the time of the first visit to Balbec, when he has not yet become the intimate of the "little band," Marcel contrasts these young girls, whose habits are still

[24] RH I, 142/P I, 185. (My emphasis.)
[25] RH II, 395/P III, 26. That these "identities" are a mental construction obviously does not escape Proust, who writes further on (RH II, 434/P III, 82): "But each day was for me a *different* country"; and apropos of the sea at Balbec: "For none of those Seas ever stayed with us longer than a day. On the morrow there would be another, which sometimes resembled its predecessor. But I *never* saw *the same one twice*" (RH I, 534/P I, 705. But "twice" perhaps means here "twice in a row").

unknown to him, with the little traffickers on the beach, with whom he is already familiar enough to know "where and at what time it will be possible to see them again." The young girls, on the contrary, are absent "certain days" that are apparently indefinite:

> not knowing the cause of their absence I sought to discover whether it was something *fixed* and regular, if they were to be seen only *every other day*, or *in certain states of the weather*, or if there were *days on which no one ever saw them*. I imagined myself already friends with them, and saying: "But you weren't there the other day?" "Weren't we? Oh, no, of course not; that was because it was a Saturday. On *Saturdays* we don't *ever* come, because . . . " If it were only as simple as that, to know that on black Saturday it was useless to torment oneself, that one might range the beach from end to end, sit down outside the pastry-cook's and pretend to be nibbling an *éclair*, poke into the curiosity shop, wait for bathing time, the concert, high tide, sunset, night, all without seeing the longed-for little band. But the *fatal day* did not, perhaps, come *once a week*. It did not, perhaps, of necessity fall on Saturdays. Perhaps certain *atmospheric conditions* influenced it or were entirely unconnected with it. How many observations, patient but not at all serene, must one accumulate of the movements, to all appearance irregular, of those unknown worlds before being able to be sure that one has not allowed oneself to be led astray by mere coincidence, that one's forecasts will not be proved wrong, before one elucidates the *certain laws*, acquired at the cost of so much painful experience, of that passionate astronomy.[26]

I have italicized here the most obvious marks of this anxious search for a law of recurrence. Certain ones—*once a week, every other day, in certain states of the weather*—we will recall a little later. For the moment, let us notice the most emphatic one, and perhaps superficially the most arbitrary one: *Saturdays*. It sends us back without any possible hesitation to a passage in *Swann* where the specific nature of Saturdays has already been expressed.[27] At Combray that is the day when, in order to leave Françoise time in the afternoon to go to the market at Roussain-

26 RH I, 625–626/P I, 831.
27 RH I, 84–85/P I, 110–111.

ville, lunch is put forward an hour. A "weekly exception" to custom, itself obviously a custom in the second degree, one of those variations that, "repeated at regular intervals and in identical form, did no more, really, than print a sort of uniform pattern upon the greater uniformity of [Léonie's] life," which she, and all her household with her, "clung to . . . as much as to the rest"—and all the more so since the regular "asymmetry" of Saturdays, unlike that of Sundays, is specific and original, peculiar to the hero's family and almost incomprehensible to others. Whence the "civic," "national," "patriotic," "chauvinist" nature of the event, and the atmosphere of ritual surrounding it. But most characteristic in this text, perhaps, is the idea (expressed by the narrator) that this custom, becoming "the favourite theme for conversations, for pleasantries, for anecdotes which can be embroidered . . . would have provided a nucleus, ready-made, for a legendary cycle, if any of us had had the epic mind"—the classic passage from ritual to explanatory or illustrative myth. The reader of the *Recherche* is well aware who, in that family, has "the epic mind" and will one day write the family's "legendary cycle," but the main point here is the spontaneously established link between narrative inspiration and repetitive event, that is, in one sense, the absence of event. We are present to some extent at the birth of a vocation, which is in fact that of iterative narrative. But that is not all: the ritual was once (or perhaps several times, but to a certainty only occasionally and not every Saturday) slightly violated (and thus confirmed) by the visit of a "barbarian" who, nonplussed to find the family at lunch so early, heard from the paterfamilias, guardian of tradition, the response: "You see, it's Saturday!" This irregular, perhaps singular, event is immediately integrated into the custom in the form of a tale by Françoise, a tale which will be repeated dutifully from then on, no doubt every Saturday, to the general satisfaction:

and then, to add to her own enjoyment, [she] would prolong the dialogue, inventing a further reply for the visitor to whom the word "Saturday" had conveyed nothing. And so far from our objecting to these interpolations, we would feel that the story was not yet long enough, and would rally her with: "Oh, but surely he said something else as well. There was more than that, the first time you told it."

My great-aunt herself would lay aside her work, and raise her head and look on at us over her glasses.

Such in fact is the first manifestation of the "epic" spirit. All that is left is for the narrator to treat that element of the Sabbath ritual like the others, that is, in the iterative mode, in order to "iteratize," as it were, the deviant event in its turn, in accord with this irresistible process: singular event—repetitive narrating—iterative narrative (of that narrating). Marcel tells (at) one time how Françoise told often what happened undoubtedly only once: or how to turn a unique event into the subject of an iterative narrative.[28]

Determination, Specification, Extension

Every iterative narrative is a synthetic narrating of the events that occur and reoccur in the course of an iterative *series* that is composed of a certain number of singular *units*. Take the series: Sundays in the summer of 1890. It is composed of a dozen real units. The series is defined, first, by its diachronic limits (between the end of June and the end of September in the year 1890), and then by the rhythm of recurrence of its constituent units: one day out of seven. We will term the first distinguishing characteristic *determination*, and the second *specification*. Finally, we will term the *diachronic extent* of each of the constituent units, and consequently of the constituted synthetic unit, *extension*: for instance, the account of a Sunday in summer covers a synthetic duration that could be twenty-four hours but can just as easily (as is the case in *Combray*) be limited to about ten hours, from getting up to going to bed.

[28] In an earlier version (*Contre Sainte-Beuve*, ed. Bernard de Fallois, pp. 106–107)—a version which, let us note in passing, is set in Paris, and in which the cause of the Sabbath asymmetry is therefore not the Roussainville market but a class given at the beginning of the afternoon by the hero's father—the commemoration of the incident is not narrative only; it is a mimetic ritual which consists of "bringing about the scene" (that is, its repetition) by "inviting on purpose" some barbarians.

⟶ *Determination.* The diachronic limits of a series can be left implicit, especially when we are dealing with a recurrence that in practice can be considered unlimited: if I say, "the sun rises every morning," it simply would be ridiculous to want to state precisely since when and until when. The events that novelistic-type narration is concerned with are obviously less permanent, so those series are generally defined by the indication of their beginning and their end. But this determination can very easily remain *indefinite,* as when Proust writes: "After *a certain year* we never saw [Mlle. Vinteuil] alone."[29] Sometimes it is definite, made so either by an absolute date ("When spring drew round, . . . I used often to see [Mme. Swann] entertaining her guests in her furs")[30] or (more often) by reference to a singular event. For example, the breach between Swann and the Verdurins puts an end to one series (meetings between Swann and Odette at the Verdurins') and at the same time inaugurates another (obstructions placed by the Verdurins in the way of Swann and Odette's affair): "And so that drawing-room which had brought Swann and Odette together became an obstacle in the way of their meeting. She no longer said to him, as she had said in the early days of their love . . . "[31]

⟶ *Specification.* It too can be indefinite, that is, indicated by an adverb of the type *sometimes, certain days, often,* etc. It can on the other hand be definite, either in an absolute way (this is *frequency* as such: *every day, every Sunday,* etc.) or else in a more relative and more irregular way, nonetheless expressing a very strict law of concomitance, like that presiding over the choice of walks at Combray: the Méséglise way *on days of unsettled weather,* the Guermantes way *on days of clear weather.*[32] Definite or not, these are simple specifications, or rather I have presented them as such. There also exist complex specifications, where two (or several) laws of recurrence are superimposed, which is always

[29] RH I, 113/P I, 147.
[30] RH I, 482/P I, 634.
[31] RH I, 221/P I, 289.
[32] RH I, 115/P I, 150 and RH I, 127/P I, 165.

possible when iterative units can be embedded in each other: for example, the simple specification *every month of May* and the simple specification *every Saturday*, which combine in the complex specification *every Saturday in the month of May*.[33] And we know that all the iterative specifications of *Combray* (every day, every Saturday, every Sunday, every day of good or bad weather) are themselves governed by the overarching specification *every year between Easter and October*—and also by the determination *during my years of childhood*. We can obviously produce much more complex definitions, such as, for example, "every hour on Sunday afternoons in the summer when it didn't rain, between my fifth and fifteenth years": this is approximately the law of recurrence governing the piece about the passing of the hours during the hero's reading in the garden.[34]

Extension. An iterative unit can have so slight a duration that it gives no hold for narrative expansion: for example, a statement such as "every evening I go to bed early" or "every morning my alarm goes off at seven o'clock." Such iterations are to some extent *pinpointed.* On the other hand, an iterative unit such as *sleepless night* or *Sunday at Combray* has enough extent to become the subject of an expanded narrative (five and forty-five pages, respectively, in the text of the *Recherche*). So it is here that the specific problems of iterative narrative appear. In effect, if in such a narrative one wanted to retain only the invariant features common to all the units of the series, one would be doomed to the diagrammatic barrenness of a fixed timetable, like "to bed at nine o'clock, an hour of reading, several hours of sleeplessness, sleep in the early morning," or "getting up at 9 o'clock, breakfast at 9:30, mass at 11, lunch at 1, reading from 2 to 5, etc."—an abstraction which is obviously due to the synthetic nature of the iterative but which is unable to satisfy either the narrator or the reader. That is when, to "concretize" the narrative, *internal determinations and specifications* of the iterative series step in, offering a means of diversification (a means, therefore, of variation).

---

[33] RH I, 85/P I, 112.
[34] RH I, 66/P I, 87–88.

In fact, as we have already glimpsed, determination does not mark only the outer limits of an iterative series; it can just as easily punctuate its stages, and divide it into subseries. For instance, I said that the breach between Swann and the Verdurins brought one series to an end and inaugurated another; but we could just as well say, moving to the higher unit, that this singular event determines, in the series "meetings between Swann and Odette," two subseries (before the breach/after the breach), each of which functions as a *variant* of the synthetic unit: meetings at the Verdurins'/meetings away from the Verdurins'. More plainly still, we can take as internal determination the interposition, into the series of Sunday afternoons at Combray, of the meeting with the Lady in pink at Uncle Adolphe's[35]—a meeting whose consequence will be the falling-out between Marcel's uncle and parents, and the shutting up of his "little sitting-room." Hence this simple variation: before the Lady in pink, Marcel's routine includes a stop in his uncle's little room; after the Lady in pink, this ritual disappears and the boy goes directly up to his bedroom.[36] Similarly, a visit from Swann[37] will determine a shift in the subject (or at least in the setting) of Marcel's amorous daydreams: before this visit, and under the influence of his earlier reading, they take place against a background of a wall gay with purple flowers, shaped like bunches of grapes, hanging over water; after this visit and Swann's disclosure of the amicable relations between Gilberte and Bergotte, these daydreams will stand out from "a wholly different background, the porch of a gothic cathedral" (like those Gilberte and Bergotte visit together). But previously these fantasies had been changed by a piece of information (from Dr. Percepied) about the flowers and spring waters of the Guermantes park:[38] the watery erotic region had been identified with Guermantes, and its heroine had taken on the features of the Duchess. So we have here an iterative series, *amorous daydreams*, subdivided by three singular events (reading, Percepied information, Swann information)

[35] RH I, 55–60/P I, 72–80.
[36] RH I, 61/P I, 80.
[37] RH I, 68–76/P I, 90–100.
[38] RH I, 132/P I, 172.

into four "determined" sections (before reading, between reading and Percepied, between Percepied and Swann, after Swann) that constitute the same number of variants (daydreams without a distinct setting/in a river setting/in the same setting identified with Guermantes and the Duchess/in a Gothic setting with Gilberte and Bergotte). But this series is dislocated, in the text of *Combray*, by the system of anachronies: the third section, whose chronological position is obvious, will not be mentioned until some sixty-four pages later, on the occasion of the walks by the Guermantes way. Analysis must therefore reconstitute it here, despite the actual order of the text, as an underlying and hidden structure.[39]

We should not, however, infer too quickly from this notion of internal determination that the interposition of a singular event always has the effect of "determining" the iterative series. As we will see later, the event can be simply an illustration, or on the contrary an exception without follow-up, producing no change. An example is the episode of the steeples of Martinville, after which the hero will resume as if nothing had happened ("I never thought again of this page")[40] his previous custom of carefree and (apparently) spiritually profitless walks. So we must differentiate, among singulative episodes interposed into an iterative section, between those which have a determinative function and those which do not.

Beside these definite internal determinations, we find indefinite ones, of a type we have already met: "starting from a certain year." The walks by the Guermantes way give an example that is remarkable in its conciseness and the apparent confusion of its writing: "And *then it happened that* [*Puis il arriva que*], going the 'Guermantes way,' *I passed occasionally* [*je passai parfois*] by a row of well-watered little gardens, over whose hedges rose clusters of dark blossoms. I would stop before them, hoping to gain

---

[39] Another series, only a few pages away—that of the daydreams of literary ambition—undergoes a modification of the same order after the Duchess's appearance in church: "How often, after that day, in the course of my walks along the 'Guermantes way,' and with what an intensified melancholy did I reflect on my lack of qualification for a literary career" (RH I, 137/P I, 178).

[40] RH I, 140/P I, 182.

some precious addition to my experience, for I seemed to . . . "⁴¹
We are indeed dealing with an internal determination: starting
from a certain date, the walks along the Vivonne include an
element which was lacking until then. The difficulty of the text is
due in part to the paradoxical presence of an iterative in the
passé simple ("I passed occasionally [je passai parfois]")—
paradoxical but perfectly grammatical, just like the iterative
passé composé of the opening sentence of the *Recherche*, which
could also just as well be written in the passé simple ('"*For a
long time I went to bed early [*Longtemps je me couchai de
bonne heure]"), but not in the imperfect, which does not have
enough syntactic autonomy to *begin* an iteration. The same pattern occurs elsewhere after a definite determination: "*Once we
had got to know [Une fois que nous connûmes]* this road, for a change
we *would return [revînmes]*—that is, if we had not taken it on the
outward journey—by another which ran through the woods of
Chantereine and Canteloup."⁴²

The variants obtained by internal determination are still, I
emphasize, iterative in kind: there are several reveries in a
Gothic setting, as there are several reveries in a river setting; but
the relationship they maintain is diachronic in kind, and therefore singulative, like the unique event that separates them: one
subseries comes *after* the other. Internal determination therefore
arises from singulative segments in an iterative series. *Internal
specification*, on the other hand, is a technique of purely iterative
diversification, since it consists simply of subdividing the recurrence to get two variants in a (necessarily iterative) relationship
of alternation. For example, the specification *every day* can be
divided into two halves that are not successive (as they are in
every day before/after such an event), but alternating, in the sub-
specification *one day out of two*. We have already met one form—
less rigorous, actually—of this principle in the opposition *good
weather/bad weather* that articulates the law of recurrence of the
walks at Combray (apparently *every afternoon except Sunday*). We
know that a considerable part of the text of *Combray* is composed

⁴¹ RH I, 132/P I, 172.
⁴² RH I, 545/P I, 720.

in accord with that internal specification, which governs the alternation *walks toward Méséglise/walks toward Guermantes:* "the habit we had of never going both ways on the same day, or in the course of the same walk, but the 'Méséglise way' one time and the 'Guermantes way' another"[43]—an alternation in the temporality of the story, which the arrangement of the narrative, as we have already seen,[44] is careful not to respect, devoting one segment (pages 103–127) to the Méséglise way, then another (pages 127–141) to the Guermantes way.[45] So much so that the totality of *Combray II* (after the detour via the madeleine) is arranged approximately according to these iterative specifications: (1) *every Sunday*, pages 37–103 (with a parenthetical *every Saturday*, pages 83–88); (2) *every* (week) *day of unsettled weather*, pages 103–127; (3) *every day of fine weather*, pages 127–141.[46]

There we were dealing with a definite specification. Other occurrences of this technique appear in the *Recherche*, but they are never exploited in so systematic a way.[47] Most often, in fact, the iterative narrative is articulated through indefinite specifications of the type *sometimes/sometimes*, which permits a very flexible system of variations and very elaborate diversification without ever leaving the iterative mode. For example, the literary anxieties of the hero during his walks to Guermantes are divided into two classes (*sometimes* . . . *but other times*) according to wheth-

---

[43] RH I, 104/P I, 135. The term *alternation*, and Proust's own expression (*one time* the Méséglise way and *another time* the Guermantes way), should not lead us to believe in so regular a succession, which would assume that the weather in Combray is fine strictly one day out of two; in fact, it seems that the walks of the Guermantes way are much rarer (see RH I, 102/P I, 133).

[44] Pp. 84–85.

[45] We are in fact dealing with a three-term specification (days of fine weather/ of unsettled weather/of bad weather), the third of which involves no narrative expansion: "If the weather was bad all morning, my family would abandon the idea of a walk, and I would remain at home" (RH I, 117/P I, 153).

[46] The composition of *Combray I*, if we set aside the memory-grounded opening of pp. 3–7 [RH I/P I, 3–9] and the transition (the madeleine) of pp. 33–36 [RH I/P I, 43–48], is governed by the succession of an iterative section (*every evening*, RH I, 7–17/P I, 9–21) and a singulative section (*the evening of Swann's visit*, RH I, 17–33/P I, 21–43).

[47] For example, Eulalie's dominical visits, sometimes with, sometimes without the Curé of Combray (RH I, 82/P I, 108).

er he reassures himself about his future by counting on the miraculous intervention of his father or whether he sees himself desperately alone facing the "nullity of [his] intellect."[48] The variations of the walks to Méséglise according to the degrees of "bad weather" fill, or rather engender, a text of three pages[49] composed according to this system: *often* (threatening weather)/ *at other times* (shower during the walk, shelter in the Roussainville wood)/*also often* (shelter under the portal of Saint-André-des Champs)/*sometimes* (weather so worsened that there is a return home). The system, moreover, is a little more complex than this enumeration paralleling the text indicates, for variants two and three are in fact subclasses of one same class: sudden shower. The real structure is thus:

1. Weather threatening but without sudden shower.
2. Sudden shower:
   a. shelter in the woods,
   b. shelter under the portal.
3. Weather definitely worsened.[50]

But the most characteristic example of constructing a text on the resources of internal specification alone is undoubtedly the portrait of Albertine that comes near the end of the *Jeunes Filles en fleurs*. Its theme is, as we know, the variety of Albertine's countenance, which symbolizes the mobile and elusive nature of the young girl, a "creature in flight" par excellence. But however changeful she may be, and even though Proust uses the expression "*each* of these Albertines," the description treats "each" of these variants not as an individual, but as a type, a class of

[48] RH I, 132–133/P I, 173–174.
[49] RH I, 115–117/P I, 150–153.
[50] Another complex system of internal specifications is the meetings (and nonmeetings) with Gilberte on the Champs-Elysées, a system articulated like this (RH I, 302/P I, 395):
   (1) days of Gilberte's presence
   (2) days of her absence
      (a) given notice of
         —for lessons
         —for a party
      (b) impromptu
      (c) impromptu but foreseeable (bad weather).

occurrences: *certain days / other days / other times / sometimes / often / most often / it might happen / at times, even* . . . : as much as a collection of faces, this portrait is a catalogue of frequentative locutions:

> So it was with Albertine as with her friends. *On certain days,* slim, with grey cheeks, a sullen air, a violet transparency falling obliquely from her such as we notice *sometimes* on the sea, she seemed to be feeling the sorrows of exile. *On other days* her face, more sleek, caught and glued my desires to its varnished surface and prevented them from going any farther; *unless* I caught a sudden glimpse of her from the side, for her dull cheeks, like white wax on the surface, were visibly pink beneath, which made me anxious to kiss them, to reach that different tint which thus avoided my touch. *At other times* happiness bathed her cheeks with a clarity so mobile that the skin, grown fluid and vague, gave passage to a sort of stealthy and subcutaneous gaze, which made it appear to be of another colour but not of another substance than her eyes; *sometimes,* instinctively, when one looked at her face punctuated with tiny brown marks among which floated what were simply two larger, bluer stains, it was like looking at the egg of a goldfinch—or *often* like an opalescent agate cut and polished in two places only, where, from the heart of the brown stone, shone like the transparent wings of a sky-blue butterfly her eyes, those features in which the flesh becomes a mirror and gives us the illusion that it allows us, more than through the other parts of the body, to approach the soul. But *most often* of all she shewed more colour, and was then more animated; *sometimes* the only pink thing in her white face was the tip of her nose, as finely pointed as that of a mischievous kitten with which one would have liked to stop and play; *sometimes* her cheeks were so glossy that one's glance slipped, as over the surface of a miniature, over their pink enamel, which was made to appear still more delicate, more private, by the enclosing though half-opened case of her black hair; or *it might happen that* the tint of her cheeks had deepened to the violet shade of the red cyclamen, and, *at times, even,* when she was flushed or feverish, with a suggestion of unhealthiness which lowered my desire to something more sensual and made her glance expressive of something more perverse and unwholesome, to the deep purple of certain roses, a red that was almost black; and *each of these Albertines* was different, as in every fresh appearance of the dancer whose colours, form, character, are transmuted

according to the innumerably varied play of a projected
limelight.[51]

Naturally, the two techniques (internal determination and
specification) can come into play together in the same section.
That is what happens in a very clear and felicitous way in the
paragraph that begins the section of *Combray* devoted to the
"two ways"—begins it by evoking through anticipation the returns home from the walk:

> We used *always* to return from our walks in good time to pay aunt
> Léonie a visit before dinner. *In the first weeks of our Combray holi-
> days*, when the days ended early, we would still be able to see, as
> we turned into the Rue du Saint-Esprit, a reflection of the western
> sky from the windows of the house and a band of purple at the
> foot of the Calvary, which was mirrored further on in the pond; a
> fiery glow which, *accompanied often* by a cold that burned and
> stung, would associate itself in my mind with the glow of the fire
> over which, at that very moment, was roasting the chicken that
> was to furnish me, in place of the poetic pleasure I had found in
> my walk, with the sensual pleasures of good feeding, warmth and
> rest. *But in summer*, when we came back to the house, the sun
> would not have set; and while we were upstairs paying our visit to
> aunt Léonie its rays, sinking until they touched and lay along her
> window-sill, would there be caught and held by the large inner
> curtains and the bands which tied them back to the wall, and split
> and scattered and filtered; and then, at last, would fall upon and
> inlay with tiny flakes of gold the lemonwood of her chest-of-
> drawers, illuminating the room in their passage with the same
> delicate, slanting, shadowed beams that fall among the boles of
> forest trees. But *on some days, though very rarely*, the chest-of-
> drawers would long since have shed its momentary adornments,
> there would no longer, as we turned into the Rue du Saint-Esprit,
> be any reflection from the western sky burning along the line of
> window-panes; the pond beneath the Calvary would have lost its
> fiery glow, *sometimes* indeed had changed already to an opalescent
> pallor, while a long ribbon of moonlight, bent and broken and
> broadened by every ripple upon the water's surface, would be
> lying across it, from end to end.[52]

[51] RH I, 708/P I, 946–947. (My emphasis.)
[52] RH I, 102/P I, 133.

The first sentence here lays down an absolute iterative principle, "We used *always* to return from our walks in good time";
opening within it is a diversification by internal determination,
spring/summer, [53] which governs the following two sentences; finally, an internal specification, which seems to bear on both of
the two preceding sections, introduces a third exceptional (but
not singulative) variant, "*on some days, though very rarely*" (these
are apparently the days of walking toward Guermantes). The
complete iterative system, then, is articulated according to the
diagram, which reveals, under the apparently even continuity of
the text, a more complex and more entangled hierarchical structure.

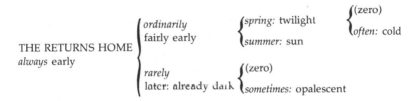

(One may perhaps find, and quite rightly, that such a
schematization does not account for the "beauty" of this page;
but such is not its purpose. The analysis here is not placed at the
level of what in Chomskian terms would be called "surface
structures," or in Hjelmslevo-Greimassian terms stylistic "manifestation," but at the level of "immanent" temporal structures
that give the text its skeleton and its foundation—and without
which it would not exist [since in this case, without the system
of determinations and specifications we have reconstituted, the
text would necessarily, and flatly, be limited to its first sentence
alone]. And, as usual, the analysis of foundations discloses,
beneath the smooth horizontality of successive syntagms, the
uneven system of paradigmatic selections and relationships. If
the object of analysis is indeed to illuminate the conditions of

---

[53] A determination that is itself iterative, since it is repeated every year. The
opposition *spring/summer,* which at the level of a single year is pure determination, thus becomes, if one encompasses the totality of the Combray period, a
combination of determination and specification.

existence—of production—of the text, it is not done, as people
often say, by reducing the complex to the simple, but on the
contrary by revealing the hidden complexities that are the *secret
of the simplicity.*)

This "impressionist" theme of the variations, according to
time and season, in the illumination and thus in the very image
of the site[54]—the theme of what Proust calls the "varied landscape of the hours"—again governs the iterative descriptions of
the sea at Balbec, and particularly the one on pages 605–608 of
the *Jeunes Filles en fleurs:*

> Regularly, as the season advanced, the picture that I found there
> in my window changed. *At first* it was broad daylight. . . .
> *Presently* the days grew shorter. . . . *A few weeks later,* when I
> went upstairs, the sun had already set. Like the one that I used to
> see at Combray, behind the Calvary, when I was coming home
> from a walk and looking forward to going down to the kitchen
> before dinner, a band of red sky over the sea . . .

This first series, variations by determination, is followed by
another, variations by specification:

> I was on all sides surrounded by pictures of the sea.
> But *as often as not* they were, indeed, only pictures. . . . *At one
> time* it was an exhibition of Japanese colour-prints. . . . I had more
> pleasure *on evenings* when a ship . . . *Sometimes* the ocean . . .
> *Another day* the sea . . . *And sometimes* . . .

The same pattern occurs two pages later, apropos of the arrivals
at Rivebelle and even closer to the Combrayan version, although
that one is not recalled this time: "*At first,* when we arrived
there, the sun used just to have set, but it was light still. . . .
Presently night had always fallen when we left the carriage." In
Paris, in *La Prisonnière,* the mode of variation will be rather of an
auditory kind: it is the morning nuances of the sound of the bells
or the noises of the street that inform Marcel, still buried be-

---

[54] "Difference of lighting modifies no less the orientation of a place . . . than
would a distance in space actually traversed in the course of a long journey" (RH
I, 511/P I, 673).

neath his bedclothes, *what the weather is.*[55] Remaining constant
is the extraordinary sensitivity to variations of climate, the almost maniacal attention (which Marcel figuratively inherits from
his father) to the movements of the barometer within, and, with
respect to what concerns us here, the characteristic fertile bond
between the temporal and the meteorological, developing to its
furthest consequence the ambiguity of the *temps français*—I
mean the French word *temps*, expressing both time and weather:
an ambiguity already exploited by the magnificently premonitory title of one of the sections of *Les Plaisirs et les jours:*
"Rêveries couleur du Temps." The *return* of the hours, the days,
the seasons, the circularity of the cosmic movement, remains
both the most constant motif and the most exact symbol of what
I will readily call *Proustian iteratism.*

Such are the resources of strictly iterative diversification
(internal determination and internal specification). When these
are exhausted, two recourses still remain, whose common feature is that they put the singulative at the service of the iterative.
The first we already know: the convention of the pseudo-
iterative. The second is not a figure; it consists of invoking—in a
completely literal and avowed way—a singular event, either as
illustration and confirmation of an iterative series (*it is thus
that . . .*), or as exception to the rule that has just been established (*once, however . . .*). An example of the first function is this
passage from the *Jeunes Filles en fleurs:* "Now and then [this is the
iterative law] a pretty attention from one or another of them
would stir in me vibrations which dissipated for a time my desire for the rest. *Thus one day* Albertine [this is the singular
illustration] . . . "[56] An example of the second is the episode of
the steeples of Martinville, plainly presented as a deviation from
habit: ordinarily, once he was back from his outing, Marcel for-

[55] RH II, 383/P III, 9; RH II, 434/P III, 82, RI I II, 459/P III, 116.
[56] RH I, 682/P I, 911. I would hesitate, on the other hand, to say the same of the
three episodes that illustrate Marcel's "progress" with Gilberte ("One day," gift
of the agate marble; "Another time," gift of the pamphlet by Bergotte; "And . . .
another day": " 'you may call me "Gilberte," ' " RH I, 307–308/P I, 402–403), because these three "examples" perhaps exhaust the series, like the "three halting-
points" in the progress of forgetting after Albertine's death (RH II, 774–820/P III,
559–623). Which amounts to an anaphoric singulative.

got the impressions he had experienced and did not try to decipher their significance; "Once, however,"[57] he goes further
and writes down immediately the descriptive piece that is his
first work and the sign of his vocation. Even more explicit in its
role as exception is the incident of the syringas in *La Prisonnière*,
which begins in this way: "*I shall set apart* from the other days on
which I lingered at Mme. de Guermantes's, one that was distinguished by a trivial incident," after which the iterative narrative
picks up again in these terms: "*apart from this isolated incident*,
everything was quite normal when I returned from my visit to
the Duchess."[58] Thus, through the play of *once's, one day's*,
etc., the singulative itself is to some extent *integrated* into the
iterative, compelled to serve and illustrate it, positively or nega-
tively, either by respecting its code or by transgressing it, which
is another way of manifesting it.

Internal and External Diachrony

Up until now we have regarded the iterative unit as confined,
without any interference, within its own synthetic duration,
with real diachrony (singulative by definition) intervening only
to mark the limits of the constitutive series (determination) or to
diversify the contents of the constituted unit (internal determinations), but not really marking it with the passage of time, not
aging it; the *before* and the *after* have to some extent been for us
only two variants of the same theme. And in fact, an iterative
unit such as *sleepless night*, constituted from a series extending
over several years, can very well be narrated only in its own
successiveness, from evening to morning, without letting the
passage of "external" time—that is, the days and years separating the first sleepless night from the last—intervene in any way;
the typical night will remain similar to itself from the beginning
to the end of the series, *varying* without *evolving*. This is actually
what happens in the first pages of *Swann*, where the only temporal indications are either of the iterative-alternative type
(internal specifications) (*sometimes, or else, occasionally, often*,

[57] RH I, 138/P I, 179.
[58] RH II, 415–416/P III, 54–55.

now . . . now) or else are devoted to the internal duration of the synthetic night, whose unfolding governs the progression of the text *(when I had put out my candle . . . half an hour later . . . then . . . at the same time . . . gradually . . . then . . .*), without anything to indicate that the passage of years alters this unfolding in any way whatsoever.

But with the play of internal determinations, the iterative narrative can, as well, take real diachrony into account and integrate it into the iterative's own temporal progression—can recount, for example, the unit *Sunday in Combray*, or *walks about Combray*, noting the changes that the time elapsed (about ten years) in the course of the real series of weeks spent at Combray has brought to the unfolding of the unit. These changes can be looked at not as interchangeable variations, but as irreversible transformations: deaths (Léonie, Vinteuil), fallings-out (Adolphe), the hero's maturation and aging (new interests: Bergotte; new acquaintances: Bloch, Gilberte, the Duchesse de Guermantes; decisive experiences: discovery of sexuality; traumatizing scenes: "first concession," profanation at Montjouvain). Inevitably the question then arises of the relations between internal diachrony (that of the synthetic unit) and external diachrony (that of the real series), and of their possible interferences. That is what in fact takes place in *Combray II*, and J. P. Houston was able to maintain that there the narrative moved forward simultaneously along the three time periods of the day, the season, and the years.[59] Matters are not entirely so clear and systematic, but it is true that in the section devoted to Sundays, the morning comes at Easter and the afternoon and evening on Ascension Day, and that Marcel's pursuits in the morning seem to be those of a child and in the afternoon, those of an adolescent. Even more clearly, the two walks, and in particular the walk toward Méséglise, take account, in the succession of their singular or customary episodes, of the flow of the months of the year (lilacs and hawthorns in bloom at Tansonville, autumn rains at Roussainville) and the flow in the years of the hero's life (a very young child at Tansonville, an adolescent

[59] Houston, p. 38.

tormented by desire at Méséglise, with the final scene explicitly
later still).[60] And we have already noted the diachronic break
that the Duchess's appearance in church introduces into the
walks to Guermantes. In all these cases, therefore, Proust succeeds in treating the internal and external diachronies in an
approximately parallel way—thanks to a skillful arrangement of
episodes—without overtly departing from the frequentative
tense that he took as the base for his narrative. Likewise, the
love between Swann and Odette, between Marcel and Gilberte,
will develop to some extent by iterative plateaux, marked by a
very characteristic use of those *thenceforth*'s, *since*'s, *now*'s,[61]
which treat every story not as a train of events bound by a
causality but as a *succession of states* ceaselessly substituted for
each other, with no communication possible. More than usual,
the iterative here is the temporal mode (the aspect) of that sort of
perpetual forgetting, of innate incapacity on the part of the
Proustian hero (Swann always, Marcel before the revelation) to
perceive the continuity of his life, and thus the relation of one
"time" to another. When Gilberte, whose inseparable companion and "great favorite" he now is, points out to him the progress of their friendship since the time of the games of prisoner's
base on the Champs-Elysées, Marcel, for want of being able to
reconstitute in himself a situation now past and therefore destroyed, is as incapable of measuring that distance as he will be
later of conceiving how he could once have loved Gilberte, and
how he could have imagined the time when he would no longer
love her as so different from what in fact it becomes:

---

[60] "Some years later" (RH I, 122/P I, 159).

[61] "*Now* [translator: my translation], every evening . . . " (RH I, 180/P I, 234);
"there was one thing that was, *now*, invariable" (RH I, 180/P I, 235); "*Now* [his
jealousy] had food in store, and Swann could begin to grow uneasy afresh every
evening" (RH I, 217/P I, 283); "Gilberte's parents, who for so long had prevented
me from seeing her, *now* . . ." (RH I, 385/P I, 503); "*Now*, whenever I had to write
to Gilberte . . ." (RH I, 481/P I, 633). Let us leave to the computer the trouble
of making this list complete for the whole of the *Recherche*; here are three more
occurrences of it, very close together: "It was already night *now* when I exchanged
the warmth of the hotel . . . for the railway carriage into which I climbed with
Albertine" (RH II, 310/P II, 1036); "Included in the number of Mme. Verdurin's
regular frequenters . . . had been, for some months *now*, M. de Charlus" (RH II,
310/P II, 1037); "*Now* it was, quite unconsciously, because of that vice that they
found him more intelligent than the rest" (RH II, 313/P II, 1041).

She spoke of a change the occurrence of which I could verify only by observing it from without, finding no trace of it within myself, for it was composed of two separate states on both of which I could not, without their ceasing to be distinct from one another, succeed in keeping my thoughts fixed at one and the same time.[62]

To keep his thoughts fixed on two moments at the same time is almost always, for the Proustian creature, to consider them identical and to merge them: this strange equation is itself the law of the iterative.

Alternation, Transitions

It is as though Proustian narrative substituted for summary, which is the synthetic form of narration in the classical novel and which, as we saw, is absent from the *Recherche*, a different synthetic form, the iterative: a synthesis not by acceleration, but by assimilation and abstraction. Thus the rhythm of the narrative in the *Recherche* is essentially based not, like that of the classical novel, on the alternation of summary and scene, but on another alternation, that of iterative and singulative.

Generally that alternation overlays a system of functional subordinations that analysis can and should elucidate. We have already encountered the system's two basic types of relationship: the iterative section with a descriptive or explanatory function subordinated to (and generally inserted within) a singulative scene (example, the *wit of the Guermantes* in the dinner at Oriane's), and the singulative scene with an illustrative function subordinated to an iterative development (example, the *steeples of Martinville*, in the series of walks to Guermantes). But more complex structures exist: when, for example, a singular anecdote illustrates an iterative development that is itself subordinated to a singulative scene (for instance, Princesse Mathilde's reception,[63] illustrating the wit of the Guermantes), or inversely, when a singulative scene subordinated to an iterative section calls up in its turn an iterative parenthesis, which is what happens when the episode of the meeting with the Lady in pink—

---

[62] RH I, 410–411/P I, 538.
[63] RH I, 1052–1053/P II, 468–469.

told, as we have already seen, for its indirect effects on the hero's Sundays in Combray—opens with a development devoted to Marcel's youthful passion for the theatre and actresses, a development necessary to explain his unexpected visit to his Uncle Adolphe.[64]

But it sometimes happens that the relationship eludes all analysis, and even all definition, the narrative passing from one aspect to the other without worrying about their reciprocal functions, and even apparently without noticing them. Robert Vigneron came across such effects in the third part of *Swann*, and believed it possible to attribute what appeared to him "inextricable confusion" to the last-minute reshuffling imposed by the split edition of the first volume of the Grasset edition: in order to put the brilliant piece on the Bois de Boulogne "today" at the end of that volume (and thus at the end of *Du côté de chez Swann*) and connect it somehow or other to what precedes it, Proust supposedly had to change quite decidedly the order of the various episodes placed on pages 482–511 of the Grasset edition.[65] But these interpolations would have entailed various chronological difficulties that Proust would not have been able to mask except at the cost of a temporal "camouflage" whose crude and clumsy medium would be the (iterative) imperfect:

> To dissimulate this chronological and psychological confusion, the author tries to disguise single actions as repeated actions and slyly daubs his verbs with a whitewash of imperfects. Unfortunately, not only does the singularity of some actions make their habitual repetition unlikely, but, even worse, in places obstinate passés définis elude the whitewash and reveal the trick.[66]

Relying on this explanation, Vigneron went so far as to reconstitute by way of hypothesis the "original order" of the text that was so unseasonably disarranged. A most risky reconstitution, a

[64] RH I, 55–57/P I, 72–75.

[65] [Translator's note.] The pages Genette refers to from the Grasset edition appear in a slightly different version on RH I, 301–318/P I, 394–417.

[66] Robert Vigneron, "Structure de *Swann:* prétentions et défaillances," *MP,* 44 (November 1946), 127.

most fragile explanation: we have already met several examples of pseudo-iterative (for that is indeed what we are dealing with here) and of aberrant passés simples in the parts of the *Recherche* that did not suffer in any way from the forced truncation of 1913, and those that we can note at the end of *Swann* are not the most surprising ones.

Let us look a little more closely at one of the passages Vigneron incriminates: it is pages 486–489 of the Grasset edition.[67] Their subject is those winter days when the Champs-Elysées are covered with snow, but when a ray of unexpected sunlight in the afternoon sends Marcel and Françoise forth on an impromptu walk, with no hope of meeting Gilberte. As Vigneron says in different words, the first paragraph ("And on those days when") is iterative: its verbs are in the imperfect tense for repeated action. "In the next paragraph," writes Vigneron ("Françoise found it too cold"), "the imperfects and the passés simples follow each other with no apparent reason, as if the author, incapable of definitively adopting one point of view rather than the other, had left his temporal transpositions incomplete." To let the reader decide, I will quote that paragraph here as it appears in the edition of 1913:

Françoise *found* it too cold to stand about, so we *walked* to the Pont de la Concorde to see the Seine frozen over, on to which everyone, even children, *walked* fearlessly, as though upon an enormous whale, stranded, defenceless, and about to be cut up. We *returned* to the Champs-Elysées; I *was growing sick* with misery between the motionless wooden horses and the white lawn, caught in a net of black paths from which the snow *had been cleared*, while the statue that surmounted it *held* in its hand a long pendent icicle which *seemed* to explain its gesture. The old lady herself, having folded up her *Débats*, *asked* a passing nursemaid the time, thanking her with "How very good of you!" then begged the roadsweeper to tell her grandchildren to come, as she *felt* cold, adding "A thousand thanks. I am sorry to give you so much trouble!" Suddenly the sky was rent in two: between the punch-and-judy and the horses, against the opening horizon, I *had* just seen, like a

[67] RH I, 303–305/P I, 397–399.

miraculous sign, Mademoiselle's blue feather. And now Gilberte
was running at full speed towards me, sparkling and rosy beneath a
cap trimmed with fur, enlivened by the cold, by being late, by her
anxiety for a game; shortly before she reached me, she *slipped* on a
piece of ice and, either to regain her balance, or because it *appeared*
to her graceful, or else pretending that she was on skates, it was
with outstretched arms that she smilingly *advanced*, as though to
embrace me. "Bravo! bravo! that's splendid; 'topping,' I should
say, like you—'sporting,' I suppose I ought to say, only I'm a
hundred-and-one, a woman of the old school," *exclaimed* the lady,
uttering, on behalf of the voiceless Champs-Elysées, their thanks
to Gilberte for having come, without letting herself be frightened
away by the weather. "You are like me, faithful at all costs to our
old Champs-Elysées; we are two brave souls! You wouldn't believe me, I dare say, if I told you that I love them, even like this.
This snow (I know, you'll laugh at me), it makes me think of
ermine!" And the old lady *began* to laugh herself.

Françoise *avait* trop froid pour rester immobile, nous *allâmes* jus-
qu'au pont de la Concorde voir la Seine prise, dont chacun, et
même les enfants *s'approchaient* sans peur comme d'une immense
baleine échouée, sans défense, et qu'on *allait* dépecer. Nous *revenions* aux Champs-Elysées; je *languissais* de douleur entre les
chevaux de bois immobiles et la pelouse blanche prise dans le
réseau noir des allées dont on *avait* enlevé la neige et sur laquelle la
statue *avait* à la main un jet de glace ajouté qui *semblait* l'explica-
tion de son geste. La vieille dame elle-même ayant plié ses *Débats*
demanda l'heure à une bonne d'enfants qui *passait* et qu'elle *remercia* en lui disant: "Comme vous êtes aimable!" puis priant le can-
tonnier de dire à ses petits enfants de revenir, qu'elle *avait* froid,
ajouta: "Vous serez mille fois bon. Vous savez que je suis confuse!"
Tout à coup l'air se *déchirait:* entre le guignol et le cirque, à l'horizon embelli, sur le ciel entrouvert, je *venais* d'apercevoir, comme
un signe fabuleux, le plumet bleu de Mademoiselle. Et déjà Gilberte *courait* à toute vitesse dans ma direction, étincelante et rouge
sous un bonnet carré de fourrure, animée par le froid, le retard et
le désir du jeu; un peu avant d'arriver à moi, elle se *laissa* glisser
sur la glace et, soit pour mieux garder son équilibre, soit parce
qu'elle *trouvait* cela plus gracieux, ou par affectation du maintien
d'une patineuse, c'est les bras grands ouverts qu'elle *avançait* en
souriant, comme si elle avait voulu m'y recevoir. "Brava! Brava! ça
c'est très bien, je dirais comme vous que c'est chic, que c'est crâne,

si je n'étais pas d'un autre temps, du temps de l'ancien régime, *s'écria* la vieille dame prenant la parole au nom des Champs-Elysées silencieux pour remercier Gilberte d'être venue sans se laisser intimider par le temps. Vous êtes comme moi, fidèle quand même à nos vieux Champs-Elysées; nous sommes deux intrépides. Si je vous disais que je les aime même ainsi. Cette neige, vous allez rire de moi, ça me fait penser à de l'hermine!" Et la vieille dame se *mit* à rire.

Let us agree that in this "state" the text corresponds fairly well to Vigneron's harsh description of it: iterative and singulative forms are entangled in a way that leaves the verbal aspect in utter irresolution. But this ambiguity does not thereby justify the explanatory hypothesis of an "incomplete temporal transposition." I believe that I even glimpse a presumption, at least, to the contrary.

Indeed, if we examine more carefully the verbal forms italicized here, we notice that all the imperfects except one can be interpreted as imperfects of concomitance, which means that the whole of the piece may be defined as singulative, with all the verbs that strictly describe events, except one, being in the passé défini: we *walked* [*allâmes*], the old lady *asked* [*demanda; remercia, ajouta*], Gilberte *slipped* [se *laissa* glisser], the old lady *exclaimed, began* to laugh [*s'écria,* se *mit* à rire]. "Except one," I said, which is obviously, "Suddenly, the sky *was rent in two* [Tout à coup le ciel se *déchirait*]". The very presence of the adverb *suddenly* prevents this imperfect from being read as durative and requires it to be interpreted as iterative. It alone jars in an irreducible way in a context interpreted as singulative, and thus it alone introduces into the text that "inextricable confusion" Vigneron speaks of.[68] Now it happens that that form is corrected in the 1917 edition, which gives the expected form: "l'air se *déchira.*" That correction, it seems to me, is enough to pull this paragraph

---

[68] We can also, to tell the truth, hesitate at "We *returned* to the Champs-Elysées [nous *revenions* aux Champs-Elysées]," which does not easily reduce to an imperfect of concomitance, since the events that it would go with are a little subsequent to it ("The old lady... asked... the time [la vieille dame... demanda l'heure]"). But contamination by the context can sufficiently explain its presence.

from "confusion" and to push it entirely under the temporal aspect of the singulative. Vigneron's description does not apply, therefore, to the definitive text of *Swann*, the last to appear in the author's lifetime. And as to explaining the problem by calling it an "incomplete transposition" of the singulative into the iterative, we see that that one correction goes exactly in the opposite direction: far from "completing" in 1917 the "whitewashing with imperfects" of a text in which in 1913 he would carelessly have left too many passés simples, Proust[69] on the contrary brings over to the singulative the only undeniably iterative form on that page. Vigneron's interpretation, already fragile, thereupon becomes untenable.

We are talking only, I hasten to make clear, about the circumstantial explanation Vigneron quite uselessly sought for the confusions at the end of *Swann*, as if all the rest of the Proustian narrative were a model of coherence and clarity. The same critic, however, has rightly noticed elsewhere[70] the wholly retrospective unity imposed by Proust on "heteroclite" materials, and has described the entire *Recherche* as a "Harlequin's cloak whose multiple pieces, however rich the fabric may be, however industriously they may have been brought together, recut, adjusted and stitched, still betray, by differences in texture and color, their diverse origins."[71] That is undeniable, and the subsequent publication of the various "first versions" has done, and very probably will do, nothing but confirm that intuition. There is some "collage," or rather some "patchwork," in the *Recherche*, and its unity as narrative is indeed—like, according to Proust, the unity of the *Comédie humaine* or of the *Ring of the*

---

[69] Or perhaps somebody else: relying on a 1919 letter, Clarac and Ferré write, "It seems therefore that Proust may not have supervised the new edition of *Swann* which came out in 1917" (P I, xxi). But this uncertainty does not remove all authority from the correction, which, moreover, Clarac and Ferré themselves adopt. Besides, Proust cannot be totally unconnected with the variants of 1917: it certainly must have been he who requested the corrections shifting Combray, for the reasons we know, from Beauce to Champagne.

[70] Vigneron, "Structure de *Swann*: Combray ou le cercle parfait," *MP*, 45 (February 1948), 185–207.

[71] Vigneron, "Structure de *Swann*: Balzac, Wagner et Proust," *French Review*, 19 (May 1946), 384.

Nibelung—a unity *after the event*, claimed all the more keenly because it is constructed later and more laboriously with materials from every source and from every period. We know that Proust, far from considering this type of unity as "illusory" (Vigneron), judged it "not fictitious, perhaps indeed all the more real for being ulterior, for being born of a moment of enthusiasm when it is discovered to exist among fragments which need only to be joined together. A unity that has been unaware of itself, therefore vital and not logical, that has not banned variety, chilled execution."[72] We can only, it seems to me, grant his basic point, perhaps adding, however, that he underestimates here the fragments' resistance to being "joined together." It is no doubt this resistance that the chaotic (according to the norms of classical narration) episode of the Champs-Elysées (among others) bears the trace of, more than of a rushed publication. We can be convinced of this by comparing the passage in question here with two of its earlier versions: that in *Jean Santeuil*, which is purely singulative, and that in *Contre Sainte-Beuve*, which is completely iterative.[73] Proust, at the moment of connecting the pieces together for the last version, could have hesitated to choose, and could have finally decided, consciously or not, on the absence of choice.

Whatever the *cause*, the most relevant hypothesis as to how this should be read continues to be that this passage is composed of an iterative beginning (the first paragraph) and a singulative continuation (the second, which we have just examined, and the third, whose temporal aspect has no ambiguity): this would be banal if the temporal standing of this singulative in relation to the preceding iterative were indicated, if only by a

---

[72] RH II, 491/P III, 161. Cf. *Marcel Proust on Art*: "Some portions of [Balzac's] great sequences were not linked up . . . till afterwards. What does that matter? Wagner had composed *The Good Friday Music* before he thought of writing *Parsifal*, and put it into the opera later on. But the additions Balzac made, these lovely things that are brought in, the new relationships suddenly perceived by his genius between separate parts of his work, which rejoin each other, come to life, are henceforth inseparable, are they not his finest creative intuitions?" (p. 182).

[73] *Jean Santeuil*, trans. Hopkins, pp. 49–52; *Contre Sainte-Beuve*, ed. Fallois, p. 111 (*Marcel Proust on Art*, pp. 75–76).

"once" that would isolate it in the series to which it belongs.[74]
But nothing of the kind: the narrative passes without warning
from a habit to a singular event as if, instead of the event being
placed somewhere within or in connection to the habit, the habit
could become, indeed could *be at the same time*, a singular
event—which is, strictly speaking, inconceivable, and is thus, in
the Proustian text *as it is*, an occasion of irreducible unrealism.
There are others, of the same kind. For example, at the end of
Sodome et Gomorrhe, the account of M. de Charlus's trips in the
little train of La Raspelière and of his relations with the other
followers begins in a very precisely specified iterative ("Regularly, thrice weekly, . . . "), is then restricted by internal determination ("the very first times . . . "), and goes on for two pages
in an indeterminate singulative ("[Cottard] *said* [*dit*], either from
malice . . . ").[75] We see that here simply amending the iterative
plural ("the very first times") to a singular ("the very first time")
would be enough for everything to *become orderly again*. But
anyone who ventured to plunge into that course would have a
little more trouble with "Teaser Augustus," which is iterative on
pages 1049–1051 [RH I/P II, 464–466] but abruptly becomes singulative in the middle of page 1051 and continues so to the end
of the episode. And would have more trouble still, with the
narrative of the dinner at Rivebelle, in the *Jeunes Filles en fleurs*,
which is inextricably both a synthetic dinner, told in the imperfect ("At first, when we *arrived* there [Les premiers temps,
quand nous y *arrivions*]"), and a singular dinner, told in the
passé défini ("I *noticed* one of these servants. . . . A young, fair
[woman] . . . *gazed* at me [je *remarquai* un de ces servants. . . .
Une jeune fille blonde me *regarda*]"); and since it deals with the
evening of the first appearance of the young girls we can date it
accurately, but no temporal indication places it in relation to the

---

[74] The third paragraph does carry such an indication: "The first of these days
. . . " (called by Vigneron a "laboured connection" but habitual in Proust; for
example, at the inn in Doncières, RH I, 784/P II, 98, where "the first day"
associates a singulative illustration with a beginning of an iterative scene). But
this indication is not good retroactively for the second paragraph, whose inde-
terminateness it simply heightens through contrast.
[75] RH II, 310–312/P II, 1037–1040. [Translator's note: partly my translation.]

series it belongs to and in which it gives the impression—a rather disconcerting one—of *floating*.[76]

Most often, actually, these points of contact between iterative and singulative, with no assignable temporal relationship, are, deliberately or not, masked by the interposition of *neutral* sections whose aspect is indeterminate, whose function, as Houston observes, seems to be to prevent the reader from noticing the change of aspect.[77] These neutral sections can be of three kinds: they may be discursive excursuses in the present tense, such as a fairly long one in the transition between the iterative beginning and the singulative continuation of *La Prisonnière*;[78] but this kind obviously has extranarrative status. It is otherwise for the second type, accurately noted by Houston, which is *dialogue* (possibly restricted to a single rejoinder) *without a declarative verb*;[79] the example Houston cites is the conversation between Marcel and the Duchess about the dress she wore to the Sainte-Euverte dinner.[80] By definition, abruptive dialogue has no determination of aspect, since it is deprived of verbs. The third type is more subtle, for here the neutral section is in fact a mixed or, more exactly, an ambiguous section: it consists of interposing between iterative and singulative some imperfects whose aspectual value remains indeterminate. Here is an example taken from *Un amour de Swann*: we are first in the singulative; Odette one day asks Swann for money to go without him to Bayreuth with the Verdurins;

> Of him she *said* not a word; it *was* to be taken for granted that their presence at Bayreuth *would be a bar* to his [singulative descriptive imperfects].

---

[76] RH I, 609–619/P I, 808–822.
[77] Houston, pp. 35–36.
[78] RH II, 434–435/P III, 82–83.
[79] It is what Fontanier calls *abruption*: "The figure by which one removes the customary transitions between the parts of a dialogue, or before direct speech, in order to make its presentation more animated and more interesting" (*Les Figures du discours* [1821–1827; Paris: Flammarion, 1968], pp. 342–343).
[80] RH II, 403/P III, 37. The singulative section introduced here comes to an end further on (RH II, 408/P III, 43) with a new abruptive dialogue.

Then that annihilating answer, every word of which he *had* carefully *rehearsed* overnight, without venturing to hope that it could ever be used [ambiguous pluperfect], he *had* the satisfaction of having it conveyed to her [iterative imperfect].[81]

De lui, elle ne *disait* pas un mot, il *était* sous-entendu que leur présence *excluait* la sienne [singulative descriptive imperfects].
Alors cette terrible réponse dont il *avait arrêté* chaque mot la veille sans oser espérer qu'elle pourrait servir jamais [ambiguous pluperfect], il *avait* la joie de la lui faire porter [iterative imperfect].

A transformation even more effective in its abruptness is the return to the iterative that closes the singulative episode of the trees at Hudimesnil, in the *Jeunes Filles en fleurs:*

And when, the road having forked and the carriage with it, I turned my back on them and ceased to see them, while Mme. de Villeparisis *asked* me what I *was dreaming* about, I *was* as wretched as though I *had* just lost a friend, *had* died myself, *had* broken faith with the dead, or *had* denied my God [singulative imperfects].
It *was* time to be thinking of home [ambiguous imperfect]. Mme. de Villeparisis . . . *told* her coachman to take us back by the old Balbec road [iterative imperfect].[82]

Quand, la voiture ayant bifurqué, je leur tournai le dos et cessai de les voir, tandis que Mme. de Villeparisis me *demandait* pourquoi j'*avais* l'air rêveur, j'*étais* triste comme si je *venais* de perdre un ami, de mourir à moi-même, de renier un mort ou de méconnaître un dieu [singulative imperfects].
Il *fallait* songer au retour [ambiguous imperfect]. Mme. de Villeparisis . . . *disait* au cocher de prendre la vieille route de Balbec [iterative imperfect].

More drawn out, by contrast, but extraordinarily skillful in maintaining its irresoluteness for twenty or so lines, is this transition in *Un amour de Swann:*

[81] RH I, 231/P I, 301.
[82] RH I, 545/P I, 719.

But she *saw* that his eyes *remained* fixed upon the things that he *did* not *know*, and on that past era of their love, monotonous and soothing in his memory because it *was* vague, and now *rent*, as with a sword-wound, by the news of that minute on the Island in the Bois, by moonlight, while he was dining with the Princesse des Laumes. But he *had* so far *acquired* the habit of finding life interesting—of marvelling at the strange discoveries that there were to be made in it—that even while he was suffering so acutely that he did not believe it possible to endure such agony for any length of time, he *was saying* to himself: "Life is indeed astonishing, and holds some fine surprises; it appears that vice is far more common than one has been led to believe. Here is a woman in whom I had absolute confidence, who looks so simple, so honest, who, in any case, even allowing that her morals are not strict, seemed quite normal and healthy in her tastes and inclinations. I receive a most improbable accusation, I question her, and the little that she admits reveals far more than I could ever have suspected." But he *could* not confine himself to these detached observations. He *sought* to form an exact estimate of the importance of what she *had* just *told* him, so as to know whether he *might* conclude that she *had done* these things often, and *was likely* to do them again. He *repeated* her words to himself: "I knew quite well what she was after." "Two or three times." "I've heard that tale before." But they *did* not *reappear* in his memory unarmed; each of them *held* a knife with which it *stabbed* him afresh. *For a long time*, like a sick man who cannot restrain himself from attempting, every minute, to make the movement that, he knows, will hurt him, he *kept* on murmuring to himself.[83]

Mais elle *vit* que ses yeux *restaient* fixés sur les choses qu'il ne *savait* pas et que ce passé de leur amour, monotone et doux dans sa mémoire parce qu'il *était* vague, et que *déchirait* maintenant comme une blessure cette minute dans l'île du Bois, au clair de lune, après le dîner chez la princesse des Laumes. Mais il *avait* tellement *pris* l'habitude de trouver la vie intéressante—d'admirer les curieuses découvertes qu'on peut y faire—que tout en souffrant au point de croire qu'il ne pourrait pas supporter longtemps une pareille douleur, il se *disait*: "La vie est vraiment étonnante et réserve de belles surprises; en somme le vice est quelque chose de

[83] RH I, 281/P I, 366–367.

plus répandu qu'on ne le croit. Voilà une femme en qui j'avais confiance, qui a l'air si simple, si honnête, en tout cas, si même elle était légère, qui semblait bien normale et saine dans ses goûts: sur une dénonciation invraisemblable, je l'interroge, et le peu qu'elle m'avoue révèle bien plus que ce qu'on eût pu soupçonner." Mais il ne *pouvait* pas se borner à ces remarques désintéressées. Il *cherchait* à apprécier exactement la valeur de ce qu'elle lui *avait raconté*, afin de savoir s'il *devait* conclure que ces choses, elle les *avait faites* souvent, qu'elles se *renouvelleraient*. Il se *répétait* ces mots qu'elle *avait dits:* "Je voyais bien où elle voulait en venir," "Deux ou trois fois," "Cette blague!," mais ils ne *reparaissaient* pas désarmés dans la mémoire de Swann, chacun d'eux *tenait* son couteau et lui en *portait* un nouveau coup. *Pendant bien longtemps,* comme un malade ne peut s'empêcher d'essayer à toute minute de faire le mouvement qui lui est douloureux, il se *redisait* ces mots.

We see that the transformation is truly reached, unequivocally, only starting with "For a long time [Pendant bien longtemps]," which assigns a clearly iterative value to the imperfect "he kept on murmuring to himself [il se redisait ces mots]"—an iterative value that the whole of the following passage will keep. Apropos of a transition of this kind (but more elaborated—more than five pages—and, to tell the truth, less pure, since it also includes several paragraphs of reflections in the narrator's present and a brief interior monologue of the hero)—the transition in *La Prisonnière* separating and joining the narrative of an "ideal" Parisian day and the account of a certain real day in February[84]—J. P. Houston rightly evokes "those Wagnerian scores where the tonality shifts continuously without any change in the key signature."[85] Proust knew, indeed, how to exploit with great harmonic subtlety the capacities for *modulation* which the ambiguity of the French imperfect tense admits, as if he had wished, before mentioning it explicitly apropos of Vinteuil, to fashion almost a poetic equivalent of the chromaticism of *Tristan.*

All of that, we imagine, cannot be simply the result of material contingencies. Even if we must make (considerable) allowances

[84] RH II, 434–438/P III, 81–88.
[85] Houston, p. 37.

for external circumstances, there undoubtedly remains in Proust, at work in such pages just as we have already met it elsewhere, a sort of undertow of will—perhaps scarcely conscious— to liberate the forms of narrative temporality from their dramatic function, to let them play for their own sake, and (as he says apropos of Flaubert) to *treat them in terms of music*.[86]

The Game with Time

We still have a word to say on the category of narrative time as a whole, with respect to the general structure of the *Recherche* and with respect to the place that work has in the evolution of novelistic forms. More than once we were able to observe, indeed, the tight actual solidarity of various phenomena that we had to separate for purposes of exposition. For example, in traditional narrative, analepsis (an aspect of *sequence*) most often takes the form of summary (an aspect of *duration*, or of speed); summary frequently has recourse to the services of the iterative (an aspect of *frequency*); description is almost always at the same time pinpointed, durative, and iterative, without ever forbidding itself the beginnings of diachronic movement—and we have seen how in Proust this tendency goes so far as to reabsorb description into narrative; there exist frequentative forms of ellipsis (for example, all Marcel's Parisian winters during the period of Combray); the iterative syllepsis is not only an aspect of frequency: it also affects sequence (since by synthesizing "similar" events it abolishes their succession) and duration (since at the same time it eliminates their time intervals); and we could extend this list further. So we can characterize the temporal stance of a narrative only by considering at the same time all the relationships it establishes between its own temporality and that of the story it tells.

We observed in the chapter on sequence that the main anachronies of the *Recherche* all come at the beginning of the work,

---

[86] "With Balzac, the change of tempo has an active and documentary character. Flaubert was the first novelist to free this change from all parasitic growths of historical scavenging. He treated it in terms of music. Nobody before him had ever done that" (*Essais et articles*, Pléiade, p. 595; "About Flaubert's Style," in *Proust: A Selection*, p. 235).

chiefly in *Du côté de chez Swann*, where we saw the narrative
begin as if with difficulty, hesitatingly, interrupted by incessant
backs-and-forths between the remembering position of the "intermediary subject" and various diegetic positions, which were
sometimes redoubled (*Combray I* and *Combray II*), until, at *Balbec*, the narrative concluded a sort of general agreement with
chronological succession. We cannot miss connecting that aspect of sequence with an aspect of frequency just as unmistakable: the dominance of the iterative in this same section of text.
The initial narrative sections are mainly iterative plateaux
(childhood in Combray, Swann's love, Gilberte) that occur to
the mind of the intermediary subject—and, through him, to the
narrator—like so many almost motionless moments when the
passage of time is masked behind repetition. The anachronism
of the memories ("voluntary" or not) and their static nature are
obviously in league with each other in that they both arise from
the work of memory, which reduces (diachronic) periods to
(synchronic) epochs and events to pictures—epochs and pictures that memory arranges in an order not theirs, but its own.
The remembering activity of the intermediary subject is thus a
factor in (I should rather say a means of) the emancipation of the
narrative with respect to diegetic temporality on the two connected planes of simple anachronism and iteration, which is a
more complex anachronism. But starting with *Balbec*, and especially with *Guermantes*, the simultaneous restoration of
chronological order and the dominance of the singulative—
plainly associated with the gradual disappearance of the remembering instance and thus with the emancipation, this time,
of the story, which regains its hold over the narrative[87]—brings
us back to apparently more traditional paths, and one might
prefer the subtle temporal "confusion" of *Swann* to the sobered
arrangement of the *Balbec-Guermantes-Sodome* series. But with
that series the distortions of duration take over, subjecting a
temporality whose rights and norms have apparently been re-

---

[87] It is in fact as if the narrative, caught between what it tells (the story) and
what tells it (the narrating, led here by memory), had no choice except domination by the former (classical narrative) or domination by the latter (modern
narrative, inaugurated with Proust); but we will bring this point up again in the
chapter on *voice*.

established to a distorting operation (enormous ellipses, monstrous scenes) that no longer comes from the intermediary subject but directly from the narrator—who in his impatience and growing anguish is desirous both of *loading* his final scenes, like Noah his ark, to the bursting point, and of jumping to the denouement (for it is one) that will finally give him being and legitimate his discourse. This is to say that there we touch on another temporality, no longer the temporality of the narrative but in the final instance governing it: the temporality of the narrating itself. We will meet it again below.[88]

Interpolations, distortions, temporal condensations[89]— Proust, at least when he is aware of them (he seems never, for example, to have perceived the importance for him of the iterative narrative), justifies them constantly (according to an already old tradition that will not die with him) by a realistic motivation: he invokes in turn the concern to tell things as they were "lived" at the time and the concern to tell them as they were recalled after the event. Thus, the anachronism of the narrative is now that of existence itself,[90] now that of memory, which obeys other laws than those of time.[91] The variations in tempo, likewise, are

---

[88] Chapter 5. We may deplore this quartering of the problems of narrative temporality, but any other distribution would have the effect of underestimating the importance and the specificity of the narrating instance. In matters of "writing" our only choice is between drawbacks.

[89] Here these three terms obviously designate the three main kinds of temporal "distortion," according to whether they affect order, duration, or frequency. The iterative syllepsis condenses several events into a single narrative; the alternation scenes/ellipses distorts duration; finally, let us recall that Proust himself named "interpolations" the anachronies he admired in Balzac: "Make plain Balzac's ... interpolation of passages of time, like geological formations where lava from different epochs lies intermingled (*La Duchesse de Langeais, Sarrazine*)" (*Marcel Proust on Art*, p. 180).

[90] "For often we find a day, in [a season], that has strayed from another season, and makes us live in that other ... by inserting, out of its turn, too early or too late, this leaf, torn from another chapter, in the interpolated calendar of Happiness" (RH I, 295/P I, 386–387); "So it is that the different periods of our life overlap one another" (RH I, 476/P I, 626); " ... our life being so careless of chronology, interpolating so many anachronisms in the sequence of our days" (RH I, 488/P I, 642).

[91] "As our memory presents things to us, as a rule, not in their chronological sequence but as it were by a reflexion in which the order of the parts is reversed" (RH I, 440/P I, 578).

now the doing of "life,"[92] now the work of memory, or rather of forgetfulness.[93]

These contradictions and compliancies would dissuade us, if there were any need to, from granting too much credit to those retrospective rationalizations that great artists are never niggardly with, and this in direct proportion to their *genius*, in other words, to the lead their practice has over any theory—including their own. The role of the analyst is not to be satisfied with the rationalizations, nor to be ignorant of them, but rather, having "laid bare" the technique, to see how the motivation that has been invoked functions in the work as aesthetic medium. We would thus readily say, in the manner of the early Shklovsky, that in Proust, for example, "reminiscence" is at the service of metaphor and not the reverse; that the intermediary subject's selective amnesia is there so that the narrative of childhood may open with the "drama of going to bed"; that the "jog-trot" of Combray serves to trigger the horizontal escalator of iterative

[92] "In our life the days are not all equal. To reach the end of a day, natures that are slightly nervous, as mine was, make use, like motor-cars, of different 'speeds.' There are mountainous, uncomfortable days, up which one takes an infinite time to pass, and days downward sloping, through which one can go at full tilt, singing as one goes" (RH I, 298/P I, 390–391); "The time which we have at our disposal every day is elastic; the passions that we feel expand it, those that we inspire contract it; and habit fills up what remains" (RH I, 465/P I, 612).

[93] "Oblivion does not fail to alter profoundly our notion of time. There are optical errors in time as there are in space. . . . This oblivion of so many things . . . by its fragmentary, irregular interpolation in my memory . . . confused, destroyed my sense of distances in time, contracted in one place, extended in another, and made me suppose myself now farther away from things, now far closer to them than I really was" (RH II, 799–800/P III, 593–594). Throughout this we are dealing with time as it is lived or remembered "subjectively," with the "optical illusions of which our first sight . . . is composed," and of which Proust, like Elstir, wants to be the faithful interpreter. But we see him for that matter justify his ellipses, for example, by the concern to make perceptible to the reader a flight of time which "life," ordinarily, screens from us, and of which we have only a knowledge acquired from books: "In theory one is aware that the earth revolves, but in practice one does not perceive it, the ground upon which one treads seems not to move, and one can live undisturbed. So it is with Time in one's life. And to make its flight perceptible novelists are obliged, by wildly accelerating the beat of the pendulum, to transport the reader in a couple of minutes over ten, or twenty, or even thirty years" (RH I, 369/P I, 482). We see that realistic motivation adapts itself equally to subjectivism and scientific objectivity: sometimes I distort to show things as they are illusively experienced, sometimes I distort to show things as they really are, which experience conceals from us.

imperfects; that the hero makes two stays in a clinic to provide the narrator with two fine ellipses; that the little madeleine has broad shoulders. And Proust himself said it clearly at least once:

> Leaving aside, for the moment, all question of the value I attach to such unconscious memories, on which, in the final volume . . . I base my whole theory of art, let me concentrate attention on the purely compositional aspect of the matter, and point out that, in order to pass from one plane to another, I make use, not of "fact," but of something in which I find a greater degree of purity and significance, as a link—namely, a phenomenon of memory. Now, open the *Mémoires d'Outre-Tombe*, or Gérard de Nerval's *Filles du Feu*, and you will find that two great writers, whom it is the fashion to impoverish and devitalise by applying to them an over-formal interpretation, were perfectly familiar with this method of sudden transition.[94]

Involuntary memory, ecstasy of the intemporal, contemplation of eternity? Perhaps. But also, when we concentrate on the "purely compositional aspect of the matter," *significant link* and *method of transition*. And let us relish in passing, in this *craftsman's*[95] confession, that strange repentance about the writers "whom it is the fashion to impoverish and devitalise by applying to them an over-formal interpretation." That is one stone that falls back into its own garden, but it has not yet been shown how "over-formal" interpretation impoverishes and de-vitalizes. Or rather, Proust himself proved the contrary by point-ing out, for example about Flaubert, how a particular use "of the past definite, the past indefinite, the present participle, and of certain pronouns and prepositions, has renewed our vision of things almost to the same extent as Kant, with his Categories, renewed our theories of knowledge and of the reality of the external world."[96] To put it another way, and to parody Proust's own formula, *vision can also be a matter of style and of technique.*

[94] *Essais et articles*, Pléiade, p. 599; "About Flaubert's Style," in *Proust: A Selection*, p. 239.

[95] It is apropos of Wagner that Proust speaks of the "delight of the craftsman" (RH II, 491/P III, 161).

[96] *Essais et articles*, Pléiade, p. 586; "About Flaubert's Style," in *Proust: A Selection*, p. 224.

We know with what ambiguity—to all appearances unbearable—the Proustian hero devotes himself to the search for and the "adoration" of both the "extra-temporal" and "time in its pure state"; how he wants himself, and with him his future work, to be both together "outside time" and "in Time." Whatever the key to this ontological mystery may be, perhaps we see better now how this contradictory aim functions in and takes possession of Proust's work: interpolations, distortions, condensations—the Proustian novel is undoubtedly, as it proclaims, a novel of Time lost and found again, but it is also, more secretly perhaps, a novel of Time ruled, captured, bewitched, surreptitiously subverted, or better: *perverted*. Apropos of this novel, how could we not speak—as its author does about dreaming (and perhaps not without some ulterior motive of connection)—of the "formidable game it creates with Time"?[97]

[97] P III, 912. [Translator's note: my translation; the RH translation is on II, 1032.] In passing let us emphasize the verb used here: "*create* (and not: *play*) a game with Time" is not only to *play with Time*, it is also to *make a game of it*. But a "formidable" game. In other words, also a dangerous one.

4 Mood

Narrative Moods?

If the grammatical category of tense clearly applies to the stance of narrative discourse, that of mood might seem a priori to be irrelevant here. Since the function of narrative is not to give an order, express a wish, state a condition, etc., but simply to tell a story and therefore to "report" facts (real or fictive), its one mood, or at least its characteristic mood, strictly speaking can be only the indicative—and at that point we have said everything there is to say on this subject, unless we stretch the linguistic metaphor a little more than is fitting.

Without denying the metaphoric extension (and therefore the distortion), we can meet the objection by saying that there are not only differences between affirming, commanding, wishing, etc., but there are also differences between degrees of affirmation; and that these differences are ordinarily expressed by modal variations, be they the infinitive and subjunctive of indirect discourse in Latin, or, in French, the conditional that indicates information not confirmed. This obviously is the function the *Littré* dictionary is referring to when it defines the grammatical meaning of *mood:* "name given to the different forms of the verb that are used to affirm more or less the thing in question, and to express... the different points of view from which the life or the action is looked at," and this definition on good authority is very valuable to us here. Indeed, one can tell *more* or tell *less* what one tells, and can tell it *according to one point of view or another;* and this capacity, and the modalities of its use, are precisely what our category of <u>narrative mood</u> aims at. Narrative "representation," or, more exactly, narrative information, has its degrees: the narrative can furnish the reader with more or fewer details, and in a more or less direct way, and can thus seem (to adopt a common and convenient spatial metaphor, which is not to be taken literally) to keep at a greater or lesser *distance* from what it tells. The narrative can also choose to regulate the information it delivers, not with a sort of even screening, but according to the capacities of knowledge of one or another participant in the story (a character or group of characters), with the narrative adopting or seeming to adopt what we ordinarily call the participant's "vision" or "point of view"; the narrative seems in that case (continuing the spatial metaphor) to take on, with regard to the story, one or another *perspective.* "Distance" and "perspective," thus provisionally designated and defined, are the two chief modalities of that *regulation of narrative information* that is mood—as the view I have of a picture depends for precision on the distance separating me from it, and for breadth on my position with respect to whatever partial obstruction is more or less blocking it.

Distance

This problem was addressed for the first time, it seems, by Plato, in Book III of *The Republic.* [1] As we know, Plato contrasts two narrative modes, according to whether the poet "himself is the speaker and does not even attempt to suggest to us that anyone but himself is speaking" (this is what Plato calls *pure narrative*),[2] or whether, on the other hand, the poet "delivers a speech as if he were someone else" (as if he were such-and-such a character), if we are dealing with spoken words˙ (this is what Plato properly calls imitation, or *mimesis*). And to really exhibit

[1] Plato, *Republic,* 392 c to 395. [Translator's note: all quotations in this chapter from the *Republic* are from the translation of Paul Shorey, Cambridge, Mass.: Loeb Classical Library, 1937.] Cf. my *Figures II,* pp. 50–56.

[2] The common translation of *haplé diégésis* as "simple narrative" seems to me a little off the mark. *Haplé diégésis* is the narrative *not mixed* (in 397 b, Plato says: *akraton*) with mimetic elements: therefore, *pure*.

the difference, Plato goes so far as to rewrite as *diegesis* the end
of the scene between Chryses and the Achaeans, a scene which
Homer had treated as *mimesis*, that is, as direct speech in the
manner of drama. The scene in direct dialogue then becomes a
narrative mediated by the narrator, where the "replies" of the
characters are dissolved and condensed into indirect discourse.
Indirection and condensation—later we will again meet these
two distinctive features of "pure narrative," in contrast to
"mimetic" representation borrowed from the theatre. In these
terms, adopted provisionally, "pure narrative" will be taken to
be more *distant* than "imitation": it says less, and in a more
mediated way.

We know how this contrast—somewhat neutralized by Aristotle (who makes pure narrative and direct representation two
varieties of mimesis),[3] and (for that very reason?) neglected by
the classical tradition (which in any case paid little attention to
the problems of narrative discourse)—abruptly surged forth
again in novel theory in the United States and England at the
end of the nineteenth century and the beginning of the twentieth, with Henry James and his disciples, in the barely transposed terms of *showing* vs. *telling*, which speedily became the
Ormazd and the Ahriman[4] of novelistic aesthetics in the
Anglo-American normative vulgate.[5] From this normative point
of view, Wayne Booth, throughout his *Rhetoric of Fiction*, deci-
sively criticized that neo-Aristotelian valuing of the mimetic.[6]
From our own strictly analytic point of view it must be added (as
Booth's discussion, moreover, reveals in passing) that the very
idea of *showing*, like that of imitation or narrative representation
(and even more so, because of its naively visual character), is

<hr>

[3] Aristotle, *Poetics*, 1448 a.

[4] [Translator's note.] The Zoroastrian good and evil principles, respectively;
the first created and governs the world, while the second seeks to destroy the
other's beneficent work.

[5] See in particular Percy Lubbock, *The Craft of Fiction*. For Lubbock, "The art of
fiction does not begin until the novelist thinks of his story as a matter to be
shown, to be so exhibited that it will tell itself" (p. 62).

[6] Wayne C. Booth, *The Rhetoric of Fiction* (Chicago, 1961). Let us note that,
paradoxically, Booth belongs to the neo-Aristotelian school of the "Chicago
critics."

completely illusory: in contrast to dramatic representation, no narrative can "show" or "imitate" the story it tells. All it can do is tell it in a manner which is detailed, precise, "alive," and in that way give more or less the *illusion of mimesis*—which is the only narrative mimesis, for this single and sufficient reason: that narration, oral or written, is a fact of language, and language signifies without imitating.

Unless, of course, the object signified (narrated) be itself language. We observed just above, when we recalled the Platonic definition of mimesis (the poet can deliver a speech as someone else), that then we are dealing with spoken words. But what happens when we are dealing with something else: not words, but silent events and actions? How then does mimesis function, and how will the narrator "suggest to us that . . . he [is] someone else"? (I do not say the poet, or the author: whether the narrative be taken charge of by Homer or by Ulysses is simply to transfer the problem.) How can one handle the narrative object so that it literally "tells itself" (as Lubbock insists) without anyone having to speak for it? Plato knows better than to answer this question, and even than to ask it, as if his exercise in rewriting bore only on speech, and—for the opposition between diegesis and mimesis—contrasted only two kinds of dialogue, dialogue in indirect style and dialogue in direct style. The truth is that mimesis in words can only be mimesis of words. Other than that, all we have and can have is degrees of diegesis. So we must distinguish here between narrative of events and "narrative of words."

Narrative of Events

The Homeric "imitation" of which Plato offers a translation into "pure narrative" includes only a brief section that is not in dialogue. Here it is in its original version: "So said he, and the old man was afraid and obeyed his word, and fared silently along the shore of the loud-sounding sea. Then went that aged man apart and prayed aloud to king Apollo, whom Leto of the fair locks bare."[7] Here it is in its Platonic rewriting: "And the old

[7] *Iliad*, I, ll.33–36, trans. Lang, Leaf, and Myers.

man on hearing this was frightened and departed in silence, and having gone apart from the camp he prayed at length to Apollo."

The most evident difference is obviously in length (eighteen words to thirty in the Greek texts, twenty-six to forty-three in the English translations). Plato achieves this condensation by eliminating redundant information ("so said he," "obeyed," "whom Leto bare"), and also by eliminating circumstantial and "picturesque" indicators: "of the fair locks," and especially "along the shore of the loud-sounding sea." This *shore of the loud-sounding sea,* a detail functionally useless in the story, is—despite the stereotyped nature of the formula (which recurs several times in the *Iliad* and the *Odyssey*), and beyond the enormous differences in style between the Homeric epic and the realistic novel—fairly typical of what Barthes calls a *realistic effect.*[8] The loud-sounding shore serves no purpose other than to let us understand that the narrative mentions it only because *it is there,* and because the narrator, abdicating his function of choosing and directing the narrative, allows himself to be governed by "reality," by the presence of what is there and what demands to be "shown." A useless and contingent detail, it is the medium par excellence of the referential illusion, and therefore of the mimetic effect: it is a *connotator of mimesis.* So Plato, with a sure hand, suppresses it in his translation as a feature incompatible with pure narrative.

The narrative of events, however, whatever its mode, is always narrative, that is, a transcription of the (supposed) nonverbal into the verbal. Its mimesis will thus never be anything more than an illusion of mimesis, depending like every illusion on a highly variable relationship between the sender and the receiver. It goes without saying, for example, that the same text can be received by one reader as intensely mimetic and by another as an only slightly "expressive" account. Historical evolution plays a critical role here, and it is likely that the audience for the classics, which was so sensitive to Racinean "figuration," found more mimesis than we do in the narrative style of a

[8] Barthes, "L'Effet de réel," *Communications,* 11 (1968), 84–89.

d'Urfé or a Fénelon, but would undoubtedly have found the so richly and minutely described accounts in the naturalistic novel to be only chaotic proliferation and "murky mess," and would thus have missed the mimetic function of those accounts. We have to make allowance for this relationship, which varies according to individuals, groups, and periods, and does not, therefore, depend exclusively on the narrative text.

The strictly textual mimetic factors, it seems to me, come down to those two data already implicitly present in Plato's comments: the quantity of narrative information (a more developed or more *detailed* narrative) and the absence (or minimal presence) of the informer—in other words, of the narrator. "Showing" can be only a *way of telling*, and this way consists of both *saying about it* as much as one can, and *saying this "much"* as little as possible [*en dire* le plus possible, et ce plus, *le dire* le moins possible]: speaking, Plato says, "as if the poet were someone else"—in other words, making one forget that it is the narrator telling. Whence these two cardinal precepts of *showing*: the Jamesian dominance of *scene* (detailed narrative) and the (pseudo-)Flaubertian transparency of the narrator (canonic example: Hemingway's "The Killers," or "Hills Like White Elephants"). Cardinal precepts and, above all, *interrelated* precepts: pretending to show is pretending to be silent. Finally, therefore, we will have to mark the contrast between mimetic and diegetic by a formula such as: *information + informer = C*, which implies that the quantity of information and the presence of the informer are in inverse ratio, mimesis being defined by a maximum of information and a minimum of the informer, diegesis by the opposite relationship.

As we see immediately, this definition, on the one hand, sends us back to a temporal determination—narrative speed— since it goes without saying that the quantity of information is solidly in inverse ratio to the speed of the narrative; and on the other hand it sends us to a datum of voice—the degree to which the narrating instance is present. Mood here is simply a product of features that do not belong to it in its own right, and so we have no reason to linger over it—except to note this: that the *Recherche du temps perdu* in itself constitutes a paradox—or a contradiction—completely unassimilable by the mimetic "norm" whose implicit formula we have just elucidated. Indeed, as we saw in Chapter 2, Proustian narrative consists on the one hand almost exclusively of "scenes" (singulative or iterative), in other words, of a narrative form that is most rich in information, and thus most "mimetic"; but on the other hand, as we shall see more closely in the next chapter (and as the most unsophisticated reading readily testifies), the narrator's presence is constant, and so intense as to be completely contrary to the "Flaubertian" rule. The narrator is present as source, guarantor, and organizer of the narrative, as analyst and commentator, as stylist (as "writer," in Marcel Muller's vocabulary) and particularly—as we well know—as producer of "metaphors." Proust then would be—like Balzac, like Dickens, like Dostoevski, but in an even more pronounced and thus more paradoxical way—simultaneously at the extreme of *showing* and at the extreme of *telling* (and even a little further than that, in this discourse sometimes so liberated from any concern with a story to tell that it could perhaps more fittingly be called simply *talking*). All this is both well known and impossible to demonstrate without an exhaustive analysis of the text. As illustration, I will content myself here with invoking once again the scene of the bedtime in Combray, already quoted in Chapter 1.[9] Nothing is more intense than this vision of the father, "an immense figure in his white nightshirt, crowned with the pink and violet scarf of Indian cashmere in which . . . he used to tie up his head," candle in hand, with his fantastic reflection on the wall of the staircase, and the child's sobs, so long suppressed, bursting out when he is alone once more with his mother. But at the same time nothing is more explicitly mediated, avouched as *memory*, and as memory both very old and very recent, perceptible anew after years of oblivion, now that "life is more quiet" around a narrator on the threshold of death. It cannot be said that this narrator here lets the story tell itself, and it would be too little to say that he tells it without any care to efface himself before it: what we are dealing with is not the story, but the story's "image," its *trace* in a memory. But this trace, so delayed, so remote, so indirect, is also the presence itself. In this *mediated intensity* is a paradox which, quite obviously, is such only according to the norms of mimetic theory: a decisive transgression, a rejection pure and simple—as we watch—of the millennial opposition between *diegesis* and *mimesis*.

We know that for post-Jamesian partisans of the mimetic novel (and for James himself), the best narrative form is what Norman Friedman calls "the story told as if by a character in the story, but told in the third person" (a clumsy formula that evidently refers to the focalized narrative, told by a narrator who is not one of the characters but who adopts the point of view of one). Thus, continues Friedman summarizing Lubbock, "the reader perceives the action as it filters through the consciousness of one of the characters involved, yet perceives it *directly* as it impinges upon that consciousness, thus avoiding that removal to a distance necessitated by retrospective first-person narration."[10] The *Recherche du temps perdu*, a narration doubly, sometimes triply, retrospective, does not, as we know, avoid that distance; very much to the contrary, it maintains and cultivates it. But the marvel of Proustian narrative (like that of Rousseau's *Confessions*, which here again we must put side by side with it) is that this *temporal distance* between the story and the narrating instance involves no *modal distance* between the story and the narrative: no loss, no weakening of the mimetic illusion. Ex-

[10] Norman Friedman, "Point of View in Fiction," *PMLA*, 70 (1955); rpt. in Philip Stevick, ed., *The Theory of the Novel* (New York, 1967), p. 113. This alleged disability of the autobiographical novel is described more precisely by A. A. Mendilow: "Contrary to what might be expected, a novel in the first person rarely succeeds in conveying the illusion of presentness and immediacy. Far from facilitating the hero-reader identification, it tends to appear remote in time. The essence of such a novel is that it is retrospective, and that there is an avowed temporal distance between the fictional time—that of the events as they happened—and the narrator's actual time—his time of recording those events. There is a vital difference between writing a story forward from the past, as in the third person novel, and writing one backward from the present, as in the first person novel. Though both are equally written in the past, in the former the illusion is created that the action is taking place; in the latter, the action is felt as having taken place" (*Time and the Novel* [New York, 1952], pp. 106–107).

treme mediation, and at the same time utmost immediacy. That too is perhaps symbolized by the rapture of reminiscence.

Narrative of Words

If the verbal "imitation" of nonverbal events is simply a utopia of illusion, the "narrative of words" can, by contrast, seem condemned a priori to that absolute imitation which, as Socrates demonstrated to Cratylus, would, if it truly presided over the creation of words, make of language a reduplication of the world: "Everything would be duplicated, and no one could tell in any case which was the real thing and which the name."[11] When Marcel, on the last page of *Sodome et Gomorrhe*, declares to his mother, "It is absolutely necessary that I marry Albertine," there is no difference between the statement present in the text and the sentence purportedly spoken by the hero other than what derives from the transition from oral language to written. The narrator does not narrate the hero's sentence; one can scarcely say he imitates it: he *recopies* it, and in this sense one cannot speak here of narrative.

Yet that is indeed what Plato does when he imagines what the dialogue between Chryses and Agamemnon would become if Homer reported it "not as if made or being Chryses [and Agamemnon], but still as Homer," since he adds right here: "It would not be imitation but narration, pure and simple." It is worth the trouble to return again to that strange *rewriting*, even if the translation lets some nuances escape. Let us be satisfied with a single portion, composed of Agamemnon's answer to Chryses' supplications. Here is what this discourse was in the *Iliad*:

"Let me not find thee, old man, amid the hollow ships, whether tarrying now or returning again hereafter, lest the staff and fillet of the god avail thee naught. And her will I not set free; nay, ere that shall old age come on her in our house, in Argos, far from her native land, where she shall ply the loom and serve my couch. But

[11] Plato, *Cratylus*, 432 d, trans. H. N. Fowler (Cambridge, Mass.: Loeb Classical Library, 1926), p. 165.

depart, provoke me not, that thou mayest the rather go in peace."[12]

Here is what it becomes in Plato:

Agamemnon was angry and bade him depart and not come again lest the scepter and the fillets of the god should not avail him. And ere his daughter should be released, he said, she would grow old in Argos with himself, and he ordered him to be off and not vex him if he wished to get home safe.

Here we have side by side two possible states of the discourse of characters, which we shall provisionally describe in a rather rough way: in Homer, an "imitated" discourse—that is, discourse fictively *reported* as it supposedly was uttered by the character; in Plato, a *"narratized"* discourse—that is, discourse treated like one event among others and taken on as such by the narrator himself. In Plato's narratized discourse Agamemnon's speech becomes an action, and nothing external distinguishes between what comes from the answer Homer gives his hero (he "bade him depart") and what is taken from the narrative lines that precede (he "was angry")—in other words, nothing external distinguishes between what was words in the original and what was gesture, posture, state of mind. Without any doubt we could push further the reduction of speech to event, for example by writing once and for all: "Agamemnon refused and dismissed Chryses." There we would have the pure form of narratized speech. In Plato's text, the care to retain a few more details has disturbed that purity by introducing into it elements of a sort of intermediary degree, written in an indirect style, more or less closely subordinated ("his daughter should [not] be released, he said"; "lest the scepter ... should not avail him"). For this intermediary degree we will reserve the name of *transposed* speech. This tripartite division applies to "inner speech" as well as to words actually uttered, a distinction, moreover, that is not always relevant when we are dealing with a soliloquy. See,

[12] *Iliad*, I, ll.26–32, trans. Lang, Leaf, and Myers.

for example, that monologue—internal or external?—of Julien
Sorel receiving Mathilde's declaration of love, punctuated by
"Julien said to himself," "he cried," "he added": it would be
quite useless to wonder whether or not those expressions
should be taken literally.[13] The novelistic convention, perhaps
truthful in this case, is that thoughts and feelings are no different from speech, except when the narrator undertakes to
condense them into events and to relate them as such.

So we will distinguish these three states of characters' speech
(uttered or "inner"), connecting them to our present subject,
which is narrative "distance."

1. *Narratized,* or *narrated,* speech is obviously the most distant
and generally, as we have just seen, the most reduced. Let us
suppose that the hero of the *Recherche,* instead of reproducing
his dialogue with his mother, should simply write at the end of
Sodome: "I informed my mother of my decision to marry Albertine." If we were dealing not with his words but his "thoughts,"
the statement could be even briefer and closer to pure event: "I
decided to marry Albertine." On the other hand, the narrative of
the inner debate leading to that decision, conducted by the narrator in his own name, can be developed at greater length within
the form traditionally referred to by the term *analysis,* a form we
can consider to be like a narrative of thoughts, or narratized
inner speech.

2. *Transposed* speech, in indirect style: "I told my mother that I
absolutely had to marry Albertine" (uttered speech), "I thought
that I absolutely had to marry Albertine" (inner speech). Although a little more mimetic than narrated speech, and in principle capable of exhaustiveness, this form never gives the reader
any guarantee or above all any feeling—of literal fidelity to the
words "really" uttered: the narrator's presence is still too perceptible in the very syntax of the sentence for the speech to
impose itself with the documentary autonomy of a quotation. It

---

[13] Stendhal, *Le Rouge et le noir,* Book II, chap. 13 (Garnier, p. 301). Similarly,
Mathilde, busy sketching in her album, "*cried* with rapture" (II, chap. 19; Garnier,
p. 355). Julien goes so far as to "reflect" with a Gascon accent: " 'It's a question of
honnur,' he said to himself" (II, chap. 15; Garnier, p. 333).

is, so to speak, acknowledged in advance that the narrator is not satisfied with transposing the words into subordinate clauses, but that he condenses them, integrates them into his own speech, and thus *expresses* them in his own style, like Françoise representing the civilities of Mme. de Villeparisis.[14]

It is not entirely the same with the variant known by the name of "free indirect style," where economizing on subordination allows a greater extension of the speech, and thus a beginning of emancipation, despite the temporal transpositions. But the main difference is the absence of a declarative verb, an absence which can (unless the context provides indicators) involve a double confusion. First, between uttered speech and inner speech. In a statement such as, "I went to find my mother: it was absolutely necessary that I marry Albertine," the second clause can express equally well the thoughts Marcel has while seeking out his mother or the words he addresses to her. Next and especially, confusion between the speech (uttered or inner) of the character and that of the narrator. Marguerite Lips quotes some striking examples of this,[15] and we know the remarkable advantage Flaubert derived from this ambiguity, which permits him to make his own language speak this both loathsome and fascinating idiom of the "other" without being wholly compromised or wholly innocent.

⟶ 3. The most "mimetic" form is obviously that rejected by Plato, where the narrator pretends literally to give the floor to his character: "I said to my mother (or: I thought): it is absolutely necessary that I marry Albertine." This *reported* speech, dramatic in type, has been adopted since Homer as the basic form of dialogue (and of monologue) in the "mixed"[16] narrative first of the epic and then of the novel; and Plato's appeal for the

---

[14] " 'She said to me, "You'll be sure and bid them good day" ' " (RH I, 529/P I, 697). The paradox here is that the representation professes to be a literal quotation, emphasized by a vocal imitation. But if Françoise had been satisfied with a "She told me to bid you good day," she would be following the norm of indirect discourse.

[15] Marguerite Lips, *Le Style indirect libre* (Paris, 1926), pp. 57 ff.

[16] Mixing diegesis and mimesis in the Platonic sense.

purely narrative was all the less effective since Aristotle lost no time upholding, with the authority and success we know of, the superiority of the purely mimetic. We should not fail to appreciate the influence that this prerogative, massively granted to dramatic style, exerted for centuries on the evolution of narrative genres. It is expressed not only by the canonization of tragedy as the supreme genre in the entire classical tradition, but also, more subtly and well beyond classicism, in that sort of tutelage exercised over narrative by the dramatic model, expressed so well by the use of the word "scene" to designate the basic form of novelistic narration. Up to the end of the nineteenth century, the novelistic scene is conceived, fairly piteously, as a pale copy of the dramatic scene: mimesis at two degrees, imitation of imitation.

Curiously, one of the main paths of emancipation of the modern novel has consisted of pushing this mimesis of speech to its extreme, or rather to its limit, obliterating the last traces of the narrating instance and giving the floor to the character right away. Let us imagine a narrative beginning (but without quotation marks) with this sentence: "It is absolutely necessary that I marry Albertine," and continuing thus up to the last page, according to the order of the hero's thoughts, perceptions, and actions performed or undergone. "The reader [would be] installed in the thought of the main character from the first lines on, and it is the uninterrupted unfolding of that thought which, substituting completely for the customary form of narrative, [would] apprise us of what the character does and what happens to him." The reader has perhaps recognized this as Joyce's description of *Les Lauriers sont coupés* by Edouard Dujardin[17]—as, in other words, the most exact definition of what has been quite unfortunately christened "interior monologue," and which it would be better to call *immediate speech:* for the main point, which did not escape Joyce, is not that the speech should

[17] Reported by Valery Larbaud in his preface to the 10/18 edition of Dujardin's *Les Lauriers sont coupés*, p. 8. This conversation took place in 1920 or shortly thereafter. Let us recall that the novel dates from 1887.

be internal, but that it should be emancipated right away ("from the first lines") from all narrative patronage, that it should from the word go take the front of the "stage."[18]

We know, from Joyce to Beckett, to Nathalie Sarraute, to Roger Laporte, what that strange little book's posterity has been and what revolution in the history of the novel that new form effected in the twentieth century.[19] It is not part of our purpose to dwell on that here, but only to note the generally misunderstood relationship between immediate speech and "reported speech," which are formally distinguished from one another only by the presence or absence of a declarative introduction. As the example of Molly Bloom's monologue in *Ulysses* shows, or the first three sections of *The Sound and the Fury* (successive monologues of Benjy, Quentin, and Jason), the monologue does not have to be coextensive with the complete work to be accepted as "immediate"; it is sufficient, whatever the monologue's extent may be, for it to happen on its own, without the intermediary of a narrating instance which is reduced to silence and whose function the monologue takes on. We see here the essential difference between immediate monologue and free indirect style, which are sometimes erroneously confused or improperly put together: in free indirect speech, the narrator takes on the speech of the character, or, if one prefers, the character speaks through the voice of the narrator, and the two instances are then *merged*; in immediate speech, the narrator is obliterated and the character *substitutes* for him. In the case of an

[18] Dujardin himself insists more on a stylistic criterion, which is the necessarily formless—according to him—nature of interior monologue: "a discourse without an auditor and unspoken, by which a character expresses his most intimate thoughts, those closest to the unconscious, prior to all logical organization, or, simply, thought in its dawning state—expresses it by means of direct phrases reduced to their syntactical minimum, in such a way as to give the impression of a *hodgepodge*" (*Le Monologue intérieur* [Paris, 1931], p. 59). The bond here between intimacy of thought and the nonlogical and nonarticulated nature of it is, clearly, a prejudice of the age. Molly Bloom's monologue corresponds fairly well to that description, but those of Beckett's characters are, on the contrary, rather hyperlogical and ratiocinating.

[19] On this subject see L. E. Bowling, "What Is the Stream of Consciousness Technique?" *PMLA*, 65 (1950), 333–345; Robert Humphrey, *Stream of Consciousness in the Modern Novel* (Berkeley, 1954); Melvin Friedman, *Stream of Consciousness: A Study in Literary Method* (New Haven, 1955).

isolated monologue, one not taking up the whole of the narrative, as in Joyce or Faulkner, the narrating instance is maintained (but in the background) by the context: all the chapters before the last one in *Ulysses*, the fourth section in *The Sound and the Fury*. When the monologue blends with the whole of the narrative, as in the *Lauriers*, or *Martereau*, or *Fugue*, the higher (i.e., narrating) instance is annulled, and we are again in the presence of a narrative in the present tense and "in the first person." Here we verge on problems of *voice*. For the moment let us not go further, and let us return to Proust.

Needless to say, unless one is deliberately trying to prove a point (like the rejection, in Plato's rewriting of Homer, of all reported speech), the different forms we have just distinguished in theory will not be so clearly separated in the practice of texts. Thus, we have already been able to note in the text Plato proposed (or at any rate in its English translation) an almost imperceptible sliding from narrated speech to transposed speech, and from indirect style to free indirect style. The same chain is found, for example, in this passage of *Un amour de Swann*, where the narrator first describes in his own name the feelings of Swann admitted to Odette's and confronting the agonies customary to him in his present situation: "And then ... *all the terrible and disturbing ideas which he had formed of Odette melted away and vanished* in the charming creature who stood there before his eyes"; then, introduced by the phrase "He had the sudden suspicion," here is a whole series of the character's thoughts reported in indirect style:

> *that* this hour spent in Odette's house, in the lamp-light was, perhaps, after all, not an artificial hour ... , *that*, if he himself had not been there, she would have pulled forward the same armchair for Forcheville ... ; *that* the world inhabited by Odette was not that other world, fearful and supernatural, in which he spent his time in placing her—and which existed, perhaps, only in his imagination, but the real universe ... ;

then Marcel lends his voice, in free indirect style (and with the grammatical transpositions that implies) to Swann's own inner speech:

Ah! *had* fate but *allowed him* to share a single dwelling with Odette, so that in her house *he should be* in his own; if, when asking his servant what there would be for luncheon, it had been Odette's bill of fare that *he had learned* from the reply; if, when Odette wished to go for a walk, in the morning, along the Avenue du Bois-de-Boulogne, his duty as a good husband *had obliged him*, though *he had* no desire to go out, to accompany her... ; then how completely would all the trivial details of *Swann's* life, which *seemed to him* now so gloomy, simply because they would, at the same time, have formed part of the life of Odette, have taken on... a sort of superabundant sweetness and a mysterious solidity;

then, after that sort of mimetic atmosphere, the text returns to subordinated indirect style:

And yet *he was inclined to suspect that* the state for which he so much longed was a calm, a peace, which would not have created an atmosphere favourable to his love. . . . *He told himself that*, when he was cured of it, what Odette might or might not do would be indifferent to him,

to return finally to the opening mode of narratized speech (*"he feared* death itself no more than such a recovery"), a mode that allows the text imperceptibly to move on to the narrative of events: "After these quiet evenings, Swann's suspicions would be temporarily lulled; he would bless the name of Odette, and next day, in the morning, would order the most attractive jewels to be sent to her."[20]

These gradations or subtle blends of indirect style and narrated speech ought not to blind us to the Proustian narrative's characteristic use of reported inner speech. Whether Marcel is involved or Swann, the Proustian hero, especially in his moments of ardent emotion, readily articulates his thoughts as a genuine monologue, enlivened by a fully theatrical rhetoric. Here is Swann when angry:

"But I've been a fool, too," he would argue. "I'm paying for other men's pleasures with my money. All the same, she'd better take

[20] RH I, 229–230/P I, 298–300. (My emphasis.)

care, and not pull the string too often, for I might very well stop giving her anything at all. At any rate, we'd better knock off supplementary favours for the time being. To think that, only yesterday, when she said she would like to go to Bayreuth for the season, I was such an ass as to offer to take one of those jolly little places the King of Bavaria has there, for the two of us. However she didn't seem particularly keen; she hasn't said yes or no yet. Let's hope that she'll refuse. Good God! Think of listening to Wagner for a fortnight on end with her, who takes about as much interest in music as a fish does in little apples; it will be fun!"[21]

Or Marcel trying to reassure himself after Albertine's departure:

"All this means nothing," I told myself, "It is even better than I thought, for as she doesn't mean a word of what she says she has obviously written her letter only to give me a severe shock, so that I shall take fright, and not be horrid to her again. I must make some arrangement at once: Albertine must be brought back this evening. It is sad to think that the Bontemps are no better than blackmailers who make use of their niece to extort money from me. But what does that matter?"[22]

Moreover, sometimes it happens that Swann, at least, speaks "to himself, aloud," and, what is more, on the street, when he is returning home furious after having gotten himself excluded from the party at Chatou:

"What a fetid form of humour!" he exclaimed, *twisting his mouth into an expression of disgust so violent* that he could feel the muscles of his throat stiffen against his collar. . . . "I dwell so many miles above the puddles in which these filthy little vermin sprawl and crawl and bawl their cheap obscenities, that I cannot possibly be spattered by the witticisms of a Verdurin!" *he cried, tossing up his head* and arrogantly straightening his body. . . .

He had long since emerged from the paths and avenues of the Bois, he had almost reached his own house, and still, for he had not yet thrown off the intoxication of grief, or his whim of insincerity, but was ever more and more exhilarated by the *false intonation,*

---

[21] RH I, 231/P I, 300–301. This monologue is pseudo-iterative as well.
[22] RH II, 676–678/P III, 421–422.

the *artificial sonority of his own voice,* he continued to *perorate aloud* in the silence of the night.[23]

We see that here the sound of the voice and the factitious intonation form part of the thought, or rather reveal it beyond the emphatic disclaimers of bad faith:

> Doubtless Swann's voice shewed a finer perspicacity than his own when it refused to utter those words full of disgust at the Verdurins and their circle, and of joy at his having shaken himself free of it, save in an artificial and rhetorical tone, and as though his words had been chosen rather to appease his anger than to express his thoughts. The latter, in fact, while he abandoned himself to invective, were probably, though he did not know it, occupied with a wholly different matter.

This "matter," which is more than different from—which is diametrically opposed to—the scornful speech Swann addresses to himself, is obviously to reingratiate himself at any cost with the Verdurins and get himself invited to the dinner at Chatou. Such is often the duplicity of inner speech, and nothing can reveal it better than these insincere monologues uttered aloud, like a scene, a "comedy" that one is acting in for oneself. "Thought" is indeed speech, but at the same time this speech, "oblique" and deceitful like all the others, is generally unfaithful to the "felt truth"—the felt truth which no inner monologue can reveal and which the novelist must ultimately show glimpses of through the concealments of bad faith, which are "consciousness" itself. That is expressed fairly well in the passage of the *Temps retrouvé* which follows the famous assertion that "The function and task of a writer are those of a translator":

> And if in some cases—where we are dealing, for instance, with the inaccurate language of our own vanity—the rectification of an *oblique interior discourse* which deviates gradually more and more widely from the first and central impression, so that it is brought back into line and made to merge with the authentic words which the impression ought to have generated, is a laborious undertak-

[23] RH I, 219–222/P I, 286–289. (My emphasis.)

ing which our idleness would prefer to shirk, there are other circumstances—for example, where love is involved—in which this same process is actually painful. Here all our feigned indifferences, all our indignation at the lies of whomever it is we love (lies which are so natural and so like those that we perpetrate ourselves), in a word all that we have not ceased, whenever we are unhappy or betrayed, not only to say to the loved one but, while we are waiting for a meeting with her, to repeat endlessly to ourselves, *sometimes aloud in the silence of our room,* which we disturb with remarks like: "No, really, this sort of behavior is intolerable," and: "I have consented to see you once more, for the last time, and I don't deny that it hurts me," all this can only be brought back into conformity with the felt truth from which it has so widely diverged by the abolition of all that we have set most store by, all that in our solitude, in our feverish projects of letters and schemes, has been the substance of our *passionate dialogue with ourselves.* [24]

Although we would perhaps expect from Proust—chronologically situated as he is between Dujardin and Joyce—some movement in the direction of the "interior monologue" after the style of the *Lauriers* or *Ulysses,* [25] yet we know he presents almost nothing in his work which we can liken to that. It would be totally mistaken to describe as such the passage in the present tense ("I drink a second mouthful, in which I find nothing more than in the first . . . ") which is inserted in the episode of the madeleine[26] and whose stance much more recalls the narrative present of philosophical experience, as we find it for example in Descartes or Bergson; the hero's supposed soliloquy here is very firmly taken charge of by the narrator for obvious purposes of demonstration, and nothing is more remote than this from the spirit of the modern interior monologue, which encloses the character in the subjectivity of a "real experience"

---

[24] RH II, 1016/P III, 890–891. (My emphasis.)
[25] On this subject see Michel Raimond, *La Crise du roman* (Paris, 1966), pp. 277–282, who examines Robert Kemp's view, expressed in 1925, of a Proust employing the interior monologue, and decides, like Dujardin, in the negative: "These vistas seem to lead him sometimes to the frontiers of the interior monologue, but he never crosses them, and most of the time he stays clear of them."
[26] RH I, 34–35/P I, 45–46.

without transcendence or communication. The only case in which the form and spirit of immediate monologue appear in the *Recherche* is the one J. P. Houston notes—while describing it precisely as "quite a rarity in Proust"—on page 436 of *La Prisonnière*.[27] But Houston quotes only the opening lines of this passage, which despite all their animation perhaps come under free indirect style; and it is the subsequent lines which, abandoning all temporal transposition, constitute the genuine Joycean *hapax* of the *Recherche*. Here is the whole of this passage, in which I emphasize the several phrases where immediate monologue is incontestable:

> Those morning concerts at Balbec were not remote in time. And yet, at that comparatively recent moment, I had given but little thought to Albertine. Indeed, on the very first mornings after my arrival, I had not known that she was at Balbec. From whom then had I learned it? Oh, yes, from Aimé. It was a fine sunny day like this. He was glad to see me again. *But he does not like Albertine. Not everybody can be in love with her. Yes, it was he who told me that she was at Balbec.* But how did he know? Ah! he had met her, had thought that she had a bad style.[28]

When all is said and done, then, Proustian handling of inner speech is extremely traditional, although not completely for traditional reasons, showing a very marked—and to some people, paradoxical—aversion to what Dujardin calls the mental "hodgepodge," "thought in a dawning state," represented by an infraverbal flux reduced to the "syntactical minimum." Nothing is more foreign to Proustian psychology than the utopia of an authentic interior monologue whose inchoateness supposedly guarantees transparency and faithfulness to the deepest eddies of the "stream of consciousness"—or of unconsciousness.

The single apparent exception is the last sentence in Marcel's dream at Balbec:[29] "You know quite well I shall always stay

[27] Houston, p. 37.
[28] RH II, 436/P III, 84.
[29] RH II, 117–118/P II, 762.

beside her, dear, deer, deer, Francis Jammes, fork"—which contrasts with the perfectly articulate character of the words exchanged in this dream until then.[30] But if we look at it a little more closely, this contrast itself carries a very precise meaning: immediately after that sentence with the conspicuous incoherence, the narrator adds:

> But already I had retraced the dark meanderings of the stream, had ascended to the surface where the world of living people opens, so that if I still repeated: "Francis Jammes, deer, deer," the sequence of these words no longer offered me the limpid meaning and logic which they had expressed to me so naturally an instant earlier and which I could not now recall. I could not even understand why the word 'Aias' which my father had just said to me, had immediately signified: "Take care you don't catch cold," without any possible doubt.

This means that the infralinguistic sequence *deer, Francis Jammes, fork* is by no means given as an example of dream language, but as evidence of rupture and incomprehension, at waking, between that language and the alert consciousness. In the space of the dream, everything is clear and natural, expressed by speeches with perfect linguistic coherence. It is at waking—in other words, at the moment when this coherent universe gives up its place to another (whose logic is different)—that what was "limpid" and "logical" loses its transparency. Similarly, when the sleeper of the opening pages of *Swann* is emerging from his first sleep, the subject of his dream (his being a church, a quartet, the rivalry of François I and Charles V) "would *begin* to seem unintelligible, as the thoughts of a former existence must be to a reincarnate spirit."[31] The intralinguistic "hodgepodge" is thus in Proust never the speech of a supposedly alogical depth, even the depth of dream, but is only the means of representing, by a sort of transitory and borderline *misunderstanding*, the gulf between two logics, each as distinct as the other.

[30] As in Swann's, RH I, 290–292/P I, 378–381.
[31] RH I, 3/P I, 3. (My emphasis.)

As to "outer" speech—that is, the stance of what we traditionally call "dialogue," even if it involves more than two characters—we know that Proust here completely parts company with the Flaubertian practice of free indirect style. Marguerite Lips has noted two or three examples of it,[32] but they stand as exceptions. That ambiguous transfusion of speeches, that confusion of voices is deeply foreign to his style, which here is linked much more to the Balzacian model, marked by the predominance of reported speech and of what Proust himself calls "objectivized language"—that is, linguistic autonomy granted to the characters, or at any rate to some of them:

> Because in some respects Balzac is a slapdash writer, one might
> suppose that he did not trouble to make his characters talk like
> themselves, or that if he had tried to, he would not have been able
> to resist drawing attention to it at every turn. However, it is quite
> the opposite: the man who artlessly reels out his views on history,
> art, and so forth, keeps the most deep-laid schemes under cover,
> and leaves the truth of the dialogue to speak for itself, without
> attempting to underline what he does so artfully that it might go
> unnoticed. When he makes the lovely Mme. de Roguin, that born
> Parisian whom Tours knew as the country prefect's wife, talk

---

[32] The example of Françoise's menus, RH I, 54/P I, 71: "a brill, because the fish-woman had guaranteed its freshness; a turkey, because she had seen a beauty in the market at Roussainville-le-Pin, . . . " where the citational nature is not very marked, except in "a roast leg of mutton, because the fresh air made one hungry and there would be plenty of time for it to 'settle down' in the seven hours before dinner" (Lips, p. 46); and this other one, more obvious because of the interjection: "We would fly upstairs to my aunt Léonie's room to reassure her, to prove to her by our bodily presence that all her gloomy imaginings were false, that, on the contrary, nothing had happened to us, but that we had gone the 'Guermantes way,' and, good lord, when one took that walk, my aunt knew well enough that one could never say at what time one would be home" (RH I, 102–103/P I, 133–134; Lips, p. 99). Here is another, where the source of the discourse (again Françoise) increasingly stands out: "She was quite overcome because there had just been a terrible scene between the lovesick footman and the tale-bearing porter. It had required the Duchess herself, in her unfailing benevolence, to intervene, restore an apparent calm to the household and forgive the footman. For she was a good mistress, and that would have been the ideal 'place' if only she didn't listen to 'stories' " (RH I, 935/P II, 307). We see that Proust does not dare to take on the servant's lexicon without quotation marks: a sign of great timidity in the use of free indirect style.

about how the Rogrons have furnished their house, how infallibly all those sallies are *hers*, not Balzac's![33]

This autonomy is sometimes disputed, and Malraux, for example, deems it "altogether relative."[34] No doubt it is excessive to say, like Gaëtan Picon (whom Malraux is answering here), that Balzac "seeks to give each character a personal voice," if *personal voice* means own individual style. "Verbal features of character" emerge in Balzac (as in Molière) through meaning rather than through style, and the most conspicuous pronunciations (Nucingen's or Schmucke's German accent or the concierge parlance of La Cibot) are group languages rather than personal styles. Nonetheless, the attempt at characterization is obvious and, whether idiolect or sociolect, the characters' parlance is indeed "objectivized," with a marked differentiation between the narrator's speech and the characters' speech—and the mimetic effect is thus probably more intense than in the work of any previous novelist.

Proust, for his part, will push the effect much further, and the mere fact that he should have noted it and somewhat exaggerated its presence in Balzac shows well, as do all critical distortions of this type, what his own course was. Clearly no one else, either before him or after, and to my knowledge not in any language, has so nailed down the "objectivization"—and this time the individuation—of the characters' style. I have touched on this subject elsewhere;[35] an exhaustive study of it would require a comparative stylistic analysis of the speeches of Charlus, Norpois, Françoise, etc., not without unavoidable references to the "psychology" of these characters—and would require also a comparison between the technique of those imaginary (or partially imaginary) pastiches and the technique of the real pastiches of the *Affaire Lemoine* and elsewhere. To do that is not our purpose here. It is enough to recall the importance of the

---

[33] *Marcel Proust on Art*, p. 179.
[34] Gaëtan Picon, *Malraux par lui-même* (Paris, 1953), p. 40.
[35] *Figures II*, pp. 223–294. Cf. Tadié, *Proust et le roman*, chap. 6.

fact; but we must also mention the unevenness of its dispersion. Indeed, it would be excessive and hasty to say that all Proust's characters have an idiolect, and all with the same continuousness and intensity. The truth is that nearly all of them do present, at least at some time, some eccentric characteristic of language, an incorrect or dialectical or socially imprinted turn of phrase, a typical acquisition or borrowing, a blunder, howler, or tell-tale slip, etc.; we can say that none of them escapes that minimal state of connotative relationship with language, except perhaps the hero himself, who as such speaks very little, for that matter, and whose role here is rather as observer, apprentice, and decoder. At a second level are the characters marked by a recurrent linguistic characteristic, which belongs to them like a tic or a personal and/or class marker: Odette's Anglicisms, Basin's improprieties, Bloch's schoolboy pseudo-Homerisms, Saniette's archaisms, the blunders of Françoise or of the director at Balbec, Oriane's puns and provincialisms, Saint-Loup's social-club jargon, the Sévigné style of the hero's mother and grandmother, errors in pronunciation by the Princess Sherbatoff, Bréauté, Faffenheim, etc. This is where Proust is closest to the Balzacian model, and this is the practice which has been most often imitated since.[36] The highest level is that of personal style as such,[37] both specific and continuous, as we find it with Brichot (demagogic professor's pedantism and familiarism), with Norpois (officious truisms and diplomatic periphrases), with Jupien (classical purity), with Legrandin (decadent style), and especially with Charlus (furious rhetoric). "Stylized" speech is the extreme form of the mimesis of speech, where the author "imitates" his character not only in the tenor of his remarks but in the hyperbolic literalness of pastiche, which is always a little more idiolectical than the authentic text, as "imitation" is always a *caricature* through accumulation and accentuation of specific characteristics. And so Legrandin or Char-

---

[36] Even by Malraux, who did not fail to give tics of language to some of his heroes (Katow's elisions, Clappique's "my good man," Tchen's "Nong," Pradas's "concretely," Garcia's obsession with definitions, etc.).

[37] Which does not mean that here the idiolect is devoid of all representative value: Brichot speaks as a Sorbonne man, Norpois as a diplomat.

lus always gives the impression of imitating himself, and finally of caricaturing himself. Here the mimetic effect is thus at its height, or more exactly at its limit: at the point where the extreme of "realism" borders on pure unreality. The narrator's unerring grandmother says rightly that Legrandin talks "a little too much like a book."[38] In a larger sense, this risk lies heavy over any too-perfect mimesis of language, which finally annuls itself in the circularity—already noted by Plato—of the link to its shadow: Legrandin talks like Legrandin (in other words, like Proust imitating Legrandin), and speech, finally, sends one back to the text that "quotes" it (in other words, to the text that in fact constitutes it).

This circularity perhaps explains why a technique of "characterization" as effective as stylistic autonomy does not, in Proust, result in the composition of substantial and well-defined *characters* in the realistic sense of the term. We know that Proustian "characters" remain, or rather become, down through the pages more and more indefinable, ungraspable, "creatures in flight," and the incoherence of their behavior is obviously the main reason for this, and the reason most carefully arranged for by the author. But the hyperbolic coherence of their language, far from compensating for that psychological evanescence, quite often simply accentuates it and aggravates it. A Legrandin, a Norpois, even a Charlus does not completely escape the exemplary fate of lesser characters like the director at Balbec, Céleste Albaret, or the footman Périgot Joseph: blending with, to the point of amounting to, his language. Here the strongest verbal existence is the sign and the beginning of a disappearance. At the limit of stylistic "objectivization," the Proustian character finds this highly symbolic form of death: doing away with himself in his own speech.

Perspective

What we are calling, for the moment and through metaphor, narrative perspective—in other words, the second mode of regulating information, arising from the choice (or not) of a restric-

[38]RH I, 51/P I, 67–68.

tive "point of view"—is, of all the questions having to do with narrative technique, the one that has been most frequently studied since the end of the nineteenth century, with indisputable critical results, like Percy Lubbock's chapters on Balzac, Flaubert, Tolstoy, or James, or Georges Blin's chapter on "restrictions of field" in Stendhal.[39] However, to my mind most of the theoretical works on this subject (which are mainly classifications) suffer from a regrettable confusion between what I call here *mood* and *voice,* a confusion between the question *who is the character whose point of view orients the narrative perspective?* and the very different question *who is the narrator?*—or, more simply, the question *who sees?* and the question *who speaks?* We will return later to this apparently obvious but almost universally disregarded distinction. Thus Cleanth Brooks and Robert Penn Warren proposed in 1943, under the term *focus of narration*—which they explicitly (and very happily) proposed as an equivalent to "point of view"—a four-term typology, summed up in the table below.[40]

	Internal analysis of events	*Outside observation of events*
Narrator as a character in the story	1. Main character tells his story	2. Minor character tells main character's story
Narrator not a character in the story	4. Analytic or omniscient author tells story	3. Author tells story as observer

Now, it is obvious that only the vertical demarcation relates to "point of view" (inner or outer), while the horizontal bears on voice (the identity of the narrator), with no real difference in point of view between 1 and 4 (let us say *Adolphe* and *Armance*)

[39] Georges Blin, *Stendhal et les problèmes du roman* (Paris, 1954), Part II. For a "theoretical" bibliography on this subject, see Françoise van Rossum-Guyon, "Point de vue ou perspective narrative," *Poétique,* 4 (1970). From the historical angle, see Richard Stang, *The Theory of the Novel in England, 1850–1870* (New York, 1959), chap. 3; and Raimond, *La Crise du roman,* Part IV.

[40] Cleanth Brooks and Robert Penn Warren, *Understanding Fiction* (New York, 1943), p. 589.

and between 2 and 3 (Watson narrating Sherlock Holmes, and Agatha Christie narrating Hercule Poirot). In 1955, F. K. Stanzel distinguished three types of novelistic "narrative situations": the *auktoriale Erzählsituation*, which is that of the "omniscient" author (type: *Tom Jones*); the *Ich Erzählsituation*, where the narrator is one of the characters (type: *Moby Dick*); and the *personale Erzählsituation*, a narrative conducted "in the third person" according to the point of view of a character (type: *The Ambassadors*).[41] Here again, the difference between the second and third situations is not in "point of view" (whereas the first *is* defined according to that criterion), since Ishmael and Strether in fact occupy the same focal position in the two narratives: they differ only in that in one the focal character himself is the narrator, and in the other the narrator is an "author" absent from the story. In the same year Norman Friedman, on his part, presented a much more complex classification with eight terms: two types of "omniscient" narrating with or without "authorial intrusions" (Fielding or Thomas Hardy); two types of "first-person" narrating, I-witness (Conrad) or I-protagonist (Dickens, *Great Expectations*); two types of "selective-omniscient" narrating, that is, with restricted point of view, either "multiple" (Virginia Woolf, *To the Lighthouse*), or single (Joyce, *Portrait of the Artist*); finally, two types of purely objective narrating, the second of which is hypothetical and, moreover, not easily distinguishable from the first: the "dramatic mode" (Hemingway, "Hills Like White Elephants") and "the camera," a recording pure and simple, without selection or organization.[42] Clearly, the third and fourth types (Conrad and Dickens) are distinguished from the others only in being "first-person" narratives, and the difference between the first two (intrusions of the author or not: Fielding or Hardy) is likewise a fact of voice, relating to the narrator and not to the point of view. Let us recall that Friedman describes his sixth type (*Portrait of the Artist*) as "a story told as if by a character in the story, but told in the third

---

[41] F. K. Stanzel, *Narrative Situations in the Novel*, trans. J. P. Pusack (Bloomington, Ind., 1971).
[42] N. Friedman, "Point of View in Fiction."

person," a formulation that attests to obvious confusion between the focal character (what James called the "reflector") and
the narrator. The same assimilation, obviously intentional, occurs with Wayne Booth, who in 1961 gave the title "Distance
and Point of View" to an essay devoted in fact to problems of
voice (the distinction between *implied author* and *narrator*—a
narrator who is *dramatized* or *undramatized* and *reliable* or *unreliable*) as, for that matter, he explicitly stated in proposing "a
richer tabulation of the forms the author's voice can take."[43]
"Strether," continued Booth, "in large part 'narrates' his own
story, even though he is always referred to in the third person":
is his status, then, identical to Caesar's in the *Gallic War?* We see
what difficulties the confusion between mood and voice leads
to. In 1962, finally, Bertil Romberg took up Stanzel's typology
again, and completed it by adding a fourth type: objective narrative in the behaviorist style (Friedman's seventh type);[44] whence
this quadripartition: (1) narrative with omniscient author, (2)
narrative with point of view, (3) objective narrative, (4) narrative
in the first person—where the fourth type is clearly discordant
with respect to the principle of classification of the first three.
Here Borges would no doubt introduce a fifth class, typically
Chinese: that of narratives written with a very fine brush.

It is certainly legitimate to envisage a typology of "narrative
situations" that would take into account the data of both mood
and voice; what is not legitimate is to present such a classification under the single category of "point of view," or to draw up
a list where the two determinations compete with each other on
the basis of an obvious confusion. And so it is convenient here
to consider only the purely modal determinations, those that
concern what we ordinarily call "point of view" or, with Jean
Pouillon and Tzvetan Todorov, "vision" or "aspect."[45] Granting
this restriction, the consensus settles with no great difficulty on
a three-term typology. The first term corresponds to what

[43] Booth, "Distance and Point of View," *Essays in Criticism*, 11 (1961), 60–79.
[44] Bertil Romberg, *Studies in the Narrative Technique of the First-Person Novel*,
trans. Michael Taylor and Harold H. Borland (Stockholm, 1962).
[45] Jean Pouillon, *Temps et roman* (Paris, 1946); Todorov, "Les Catégories du
récit littéraire."

English-language criticism calls the narrative with omniscient narrator and Pouillon calls "vision from behind," and which Todorov symbolizes by the formula *Narrator > Character* (where the narrator knows more than the character, or more exactly *says* more than any of the characters knows). In the second term, *Narrator = Character* (the narrator says only what a given character knows); this is the narrative with "point of view" after Lubbock, or with "restricted field" after Blin; Pouillon calls it "vision with." In the third term, *Narrator < Character* (the narrator says less than the character knows); this is the "objective" or "behaviorist" narrative, what Pouillon calls "vision from without." To avoid the too specifically visual connotations of the terms *vision, field,* and *point of view,* I will take up here the slightly more abstract term *focalization*[46] which corresponds, besides, to Brooks and Warren's expression, "focus of narration."[47]

Focalizations

So we will rechristen the first type (in general represented by the classical narrative) as *nonfocalized narrative,* or narrative with *zero focalization*. The second type will be narrative with *internal focalization,* whether that be (a) *fixed*—canonical example: *The Ambassadors,* where everything passes through Strether; or, even better, *What Maisie Knew,* where we almost never leave the point of view of the little girl, whose "restriction of field" is particularly dramatic in this story of adults, a story whose significance escapes her; (b) *variable*—as in *Madame Bovary,* where the focal character is first Charles, then Emma, then again Charles;[48] or, in a much more rapid and elusive way, as with

[46] Already used in my *Figures II,* p. 191, apropos of Stendhalian narrative.
[47] We can draw a parallel between this tripartition and the four-term classification proposed by Boris Uspenski (*A Poetics of Composition,* trans. Valentina Zavarin and Susan Wittig [Berkeley, 1973]) for the "plane of psychology" of his general theory of point of view (see the "clarification" and documents presented by Todorov in *Poétique,* 9[February 1972]). Uspenski distinguishes two types in the point-of-view narrative, according to whether the point of view is constant (fixed on a single character) or not: this is what I propose to call *fixed* or *variable* internal focalization, but for me these are only subclasses.
[48] On this subject see Lubbock, *The Craft of Fiction,* chap. 6, and Jean Rousset, "Madame Bovary ou le Livre sur rien," *Forme et signification* (Paris, 1962).

Stendhal; or (c) multiple—as in epistolary novels, where the same event may be evoked several times according to the point of view of several letter-writing characters;[49] we know that Robert Browning's narrative poem *The Ring and the Book* (which relates a criminal case as perceived successively by the murderer, the victims, the defense, the prosecution, etc.) was for several years the canonical example of this type of narrative,[50] before being supplanted for us by the film *Rashomon*. Our third type will be the narrative with external focalization, popularized between the two world wars by Dashiell Hammett's novels, in which the hero performs in front of us without our ever being allowed to know his thoughts or feelings, and also by some of Hemingway's novellas, like "The Killers" or, even more, "Hills Like White Elephants," which carries circumspection so far as to become a riddle. But we should not limit this narrative type to a role only in works at the highest literary level. Michel Raimond remarks rightly that in the novel of intrigue or adventure, "where interest arises from the fact that there is a mystery," the author "does not tell us immediately all that he knows";[51] and in fact a large number of adventure novels, from Walter Scott to Jules Verne via Alexandre Dumas, handle their opening pages in external focalization. See how Phileas Fogg is looked at first from the outside, through the puzzled gaze of his contemporaries, and how his inhuman mysteriousness will be maintained until the episode that will reveal his generosity.[52] But many "serious" novels of the nineteenth century practice this type of enigmatic *introit:* examples, in Balzac, are *La Peau de chagrin* or *L'Envers de l'histoire contemporaine*, and even *Le Cousin Pons*, where the hero is described and followed for a long time as

---

[49] See Rousset, "Le Roman par lettres," *Forme et signification*, p. 86.
[50] See Raimond, pp. 313–314. Proust was interested in that book: see Tadié, p. 52.
[51] *La Crise du roman*, p. 300.
[52] It is the rescue of Aouda, in chapter 12. Nothing prevents a writer from indefinitely prolonging this external point of view with respect to a character who will remain mysterious up to the end: that is what Melville does in *The Confidence-Man*, or Conrad in *The Nigger of the "Narcissus."*

an unknown person whose identity is problematic.[53] And other motives can justify recourse to this narrative behavior, like the reason of propriety (or the roguish play with impropriety) for the scene of the carriage in *Bovary*, which is narrated entirely from the point of view of an external, innocent witness.[54]

As this last example certainly shows, the commitment as to focalization is not necessarily steady over the whole length of a narrative, and variable internal focalization, a formula already very flexible, does not apply to the whole of *Bovary*: not only is the scene of the carriage in external focalization, but we have already had occasion to say that the view of Yonville that begins the second part is not any more focalized than most Balzacian descriptions.[55] Any single formula of focalization does not, therefore, always bear on an entire work, but rather on a definite narrative section, which can be very short.[56] Furthermore, the distinction between different points of view is not always as clear as the consideration of pure types alone could lead one to believe. External focalization with respect to one character could sometimes just as well be defined as internal focalization through another: external focalization on Phileas Fogg is just as well internal focalization through Passepartout dumbfounded by his new master, and the only reason for being satisfied with

---

[53] This initial "ignorance" has become a topos of novelistic beginning, even when the mystery is to be immediately dispelled. For example, in the fourth paragraph of the *Education sentimentale:* "A young man eighteen years old with long hair and holding an album under his arm . . . " It is as if, to introduce him, the author had to pretend not to know him; once this ritual is over, he can go on without further affectations of mystery: "M. Frédéric Moreau, newly graduated . . . " The two periods may be very close together, but they must be distinct. This rule operates still, for example, in *Germinal*, where first the hero is "a man," until he introduces himself: "My name is Etienne Lantier," after which Zola will call him Etienne. On the other hand, the rule no longer operates in James, who from the very beginning establishes a familiar relationship with his heroes: "Strether's first question, when he reached the hotel . . . " (*The Ambassadors*); "She waited, Kate Croy, for her father to come in . . . " (*The Wings of the Dove*); "The Prince had always liked his London . . . " (*The Golden Bowl*). These variations would be worth an overall historical study.

[54] III, chap. 1. Cf. Sartre, *L'Idiot de la famille* (Paris, 1971), pp. 1277–1282.

[55] P. 101.

[56] See Raymonde Debray-Genette, "Du mode narratif dans les *Trois Contes*," *Littérature*, 2 (May 1971).

the first term is Phileas's status as hero, which restricts
Passepartout to the role of witness. And this ambivalence (or
reversibility) is equally noticeable when the witness is not per-
sonified but remains an impersonal, floating observer, as at the
beginning of *La Peau de chagrin*. Similarly, the division between
variable focalization and nonfocalization is sometimes very difficult to establish, for the nonfocalized narrative can most often
be analyzed as a narrative that is multifocalized *ad libitum*, in
accordance with the principle "he who can do most can do
least" (let us not forget that focalization is essentially, in Blin's
word, a *restriction*); and yet, on this point no one could confuse
Fielding's manner with Stendhal's or Flaubert's.[57]

We must also note that what we call internal focalization is
rarely applied in a totally rigorous way. Indeed, the very principle of this narrative mode implies in all strictness that the focal
character never be described or even referred to from the outside, and that his thoughts or perceptions never be analyzed
objectively by the narrator. We do not, therefore, have internal
focalization in the strict sense in a statement like this one, where
Stendhal tells us what Fabrice del Dongo does and thinks:

> Without hesitation, although ready to yield up his soul with dis-
> gust, Fabrizio flung himself from his horse and took the hand of the
> corpse which he shook vigorously; then he stood still as though
> paralysed. He felt that he had not the strength to mount again.
> What horrified him more than anything was that open eye.

On the other hand, the focalization is perfect in the following
statement, which is content to describe what its hero sees: "A
bullet, entering on one side of the nose, had gone out at the

---

[57] Balzac's position is more complex. One is often tempted to see Balzacian
narrative as the very type of narrative with an omniscient narrator, but to do that
is to neglect the part played by external focalization, which I have just referred to
as a technique of opening; and neglects also the part played by more subtle
situations, as in the first pages of *Une double famille*, where the narrative focalizes
sometimes on Camille and her mother, sometimes on M. de Granville—each of
these internal focalizations serving to isolate the other character (or group) in its
mysterious externality: a rearrangement of curiosities that can only quicken the
reader's own.

opposite temple, and disfigured the corpse in a hideous fashion. It lay with one eye still open."[58] Jean Pouillon very accurately notes the paradox when he writes that, in "vision with," the character is seen

> not in his innerness, for then we would have to emerge from the innerness whereas instead we are absorbed into it, but is seen in the image he develops of others, and to some extent through that image. In sum, we apprehend him as we apprehend ourselves in our immediate awareness of things, our attitudes with respect to what surrounds us—what surrounds us and is not within us. Consequently we can say in conclusion: vision as an image of others is not a result of vision "with" the main character, it is itself that vision "with."[59]

Internal focalization is fully realized only in the narrative of "interior monologue," or in that borderline work, Robbe-Grillet's *La Jalousie*,[60] where the central character is limited absolutely to—and strictly *inferred* from—his focal position alone. So we will take the term "internal focalization" in a necessarily less strict sense—that term whose minimal criterion has been pointed out by Roland Barthes in his definition of what he calls the *personal* mode of narrative.[61] According to Barthes, this criterion is the possibility of rewriting the narrative section under consideration into the first person (if it is not in that person already) without the need for "any alteration of the discourse other than the change of grammatical pronouns." Thus, a sentence such as "[James Bond] saw a man in his fifties, still young-looking . . . " can be translated into the first person ("I saw . . . ")—and so for us it belongs to internal focalization. On the other hand, Barthes continues, a sentence like "the tinkling of the ice cubes against the glass *seemed* to awaken in Bond a

[58] *Charterhouse of Parma*, chap. 3, trans. C. K. Scott Moncrieff (New York: Liveright, 1925), p. 48.

[59] *Temps et roman*, p. 79.

[60] Or, in the movies, Robert Montgomery's *The Lady in the Lake*, where the protagonist's part is played by the camera.

[61] Barthes, "An Introduction to the Structural Analysis of Narrative," p. 262.

sudden inspiration" cannot be translated into the first person without obvious semantic incongruity.[62] Here we are typically in external focalization, because of the narrator's marked ignorance with respect to the hero's real thoughts. But the convenience of this purely practical criterion should not tempt us to confuse the two instances of the focalizing and the narrating, which remain distinct even in "first-person" narrative, that is, even when the two instances are taken up by the same person (except when the first-person narrative is a present-tense interior monologue). When Marcel writes, "I saw a man of about forty, very tall and rather stout, with a very dark moustache, who, nervously slapping the leg of his trousers with a switch, kept fastened upon me a pair of eyes dilated with observation,"[63] the identity of "person" between the adolescent of Balbec (the hero) who notices a stranger and the mature man (the narrator) who tells this story several decades later and knows very well that that stranger was Charlus (and knows all that the stranger's behavior means) must not conceal the difference in function and, particularly, the difference in information. The narrator almost always "knows" more than the hero, even if he himself is the hero, and therefore for the narrator focalization through the hero is a restriction of field just as artificial in the first person as in the third. We will soon come again to this crucial question apropos of narrative perspective in Proust, but we must still define two ideas indispensable to that study.

Alterations

The variations in "point of view" that occur in the course of a narrative can be analyzed as changes in focalization, like those we have already met in *Madame Bovary:* in such a case we can speak of variable focalization, of omniscience with partial restrictions of field, etc. This is a perfectly defensible narrative course, and the norm of coherence raised to a point of honor by post-

[62] Proust notices in *Le Lys dans la vallée* this sentence that he rightly says *manages however it can:* "'... I walked down to the meadows to see once again the Indre and its islets, the valley and its hillsides, *of which I appeared a passionate admirer'"* (*Marcel Proust on Art*, p. 172).
[63] RH I, 568/P I, 751.

Jamesian criticism is obviously arbitrary. Lubbock requires the novelist to be "consistent on *some* plan, to follow the principle he has adopted,"[64] but why could this course not be absolute freedom and inconsistency? Forster[65] and Booth have well pointed out the futility of pseudo-Jamesian rules, and who today would take seriously Sartre's remonstrances against Mauriac?[66]

But a change in focalization, especially if it is isolated within a coherent context, can also be analyzed as a momentary infraction of the code which governs that context without thereby calling into question the existence of the code—the same way that in a classical musical composition a momentary change in tonality, or even a recurrent dissonance, may be defined as a modulation or alteration without contesting the tonality of the whole. Playing on the double meaning of the word *mode*, which refers us to both grammar and music,[67] I will thus give the general name *alterations* to these isolated infractions, when the coherence of the whole still remains strong enough for the notion of dominant mode/mood to continue relevant. The two conceivable types of alteration consist either of giving less information than is necessary in principle, or of giving more than is authorized in principle in the code of focalization governing the whole. The first type bears a name in rhetoric, and we have already met it apropos of completing anachronies:[68] we are dealing with lateral omission or *paralipsis*. The second does not yet bear a name; we will christen it *paralepsis*, since here we are no longer dealing with leaving aside (-lipsis, from *leipo*) information that should be taken up (and given), but on the contrary with taking up (-lepsis, from *lambano*) and giving information that should be left aside.

The classical type of paralipsis, we remember, in the code of

[64] *The Craft of Fiction*, p. 72.

[65] E. M. Forster, *Aspects of the Novel* (London, 1927).

[66] J. P. Sartre, "François Mauriac and Freedom," in *Literary and Philosophical Essays*, trans. Annette Michelson (New York, 1955), pp. 7–23.

[67] [Translator's note.] In French the word *mode* includes two meanings that in English require separate words: (grammatical) "mood" and (musical) "mode."

[68] P. 52.

internal focalization, is the omission of some important action or thought of the focal hero, which neither the hero nor the narrator can be ignorant of but which the narrator chooses to conceal from the reader. We know what use Stendhal made of this figure,[69] and Jean Pouillon evokes precisely this fact apropos of his "vision with," whose main disadvantage seems to him to be that the character is too well known in advance and holds no surprise in store—whence this defense, which Pouillon deems clumsy: deliberate omission. A solid example: Stendhal's dissimulation, in *Armance,* through so many of the hero's pseudo-monologues, of that hero's central thought, which obviously cannot leave him for a minute: his sexual impotence. That affectation of mystery, says Pouillon, would be normal if Octave were seen from without,

> but Stendhal does not remain outside; he makes psychological analyses, and in that case it becomes absurd to hide from us what Octave himself must certainly know; if he is sad, he knows the cause, and cannot experience that sadness without thinking of it: Stendhal therefore ought to inform us of it—which, unfortunately, he does not do; he obtains an effect of surprise when the reader has understood, but it is not the main purpose of a character in a novel to be an enigma.[70]

This analysis, we see, assumes the resolution of a question that has not been totally resolved, since Octave's impotence is not exactly a datum in the text, but never mind that here: let us take the example with its hypothesis. This analysis also includes some opinions that I will avoid adopting as my own. But it has the merit of describing well the phenomenon—which, of course, is not exclusive to Stendhal. Apropos of what he calls the "intermingling of the two systems," Barthes rightly mentions the "cheating" that, in Agatha Christie, consists of focalizing a narrative like *The Sittaford Mystery* or *The Murder of Roger Ackroyd* through the murderer while omitting from his "thoughts" simply the memory of the murder;[71] and we know that the most

---

[69] See my *Figures II,* pp. 183–185.
[70] *Temps et roman,* p. 90.
[71] Barthes, "An Introduction to the Structural Analysis of Narrative," p. 263.

classical detective story, although generally focalized through the investigating detective, most often hides from us a part of his discoveries and inductions until the final revelation.[72]

The inverse alteration, the excess of information or paralepsis, can consist of an inroad into the consciousness of a character in the course of a narrative generally conducted in external focalization. We can take to be such, at the beginning of the *Peau de chagrin*, statements like "the young man did not *understand* his ruin" or "he *feigned* the manner of an Englishman,"[73] which contrast with the very distinct course of external vision adopted until then, and which begin a gradual transition to internal focalization. Paralepsis can likewise consist, in internal focalization, of incidental information about the thoughts of a character other than the focal character, or about a scene that the latter is not able to see. We will describe as such the passage in *Maisie* devoted to Mrs. Farange's thoughts, which Maisie cannot know: "The day was at hand, and she saw it, when she should feel more delight in hurling Maisie at [her father] than in snatching her away."[74]

A final general comment before returning to Proustian narrative: we should not confuse the *information* given by a focalized narrative with the *interpretation* the reader is called on to give of it (or that he gives without being invited to). It has often been noted that Maisie sees or hears things that she does not understand but that the reader will decipher with no trouble. The eyes "opened wide with attention" of Charlus looking at Marcel at Balbec can, for the informed reader, be a sign, which completely escapes the hero, like the whole of the Baron's behavior with respect to him up to *Sodome I*. Bertil Romberg analyzes the case of a novel by J. P. Marquand, *H. M. Pulham, Esquire*, where the narrator, a trusting husband, is present at scenes between his wife and a male friend that he recounts without thinking anything amiss but whose meaning cannot escape the least subtle

---

[72] Another unmistakable paralipsis, in *Michel Strogoff*: starting with Part II, chapter 6, Jules Verne conceals from us what the hero knows very well, viz., that he was not blinded by Ogareff's incandescent sword.

[73] Garnier, p. 10.

[74] Henry James, *What Maisie Knew* (New York: Scribner's, 1908), p. 19.

reader.[75] This excess of implicit information over explicit information is the basis of the whole play of what Barthes calls *indices*,[76] which functions just as well in external focalization: in "Hills Like White Elephants," Hemingway reports the conversation between his two characters while fully abstaining from interpreting it; so here it is as if the narrator, like Marquand's hero, did not understand what he relates; this in no way prevents the reader from interpreting it in conformity with the author's intentions, as each time a novelist writes "he felt a cold sweat run down his back" we unhesitatingly construe "he was afraid." Narrative always says less than it knows, but it often makes known more than it says.

Polymodality

Let us repeat it again: use of the "first person," or better yet, oneness of person of the narrator and the hero,[77] does not at all imply that the narrative is focalized through the hero. Very much to the contrary, the "autobiographical" type of narrator, whether we are dealing with a real or a fictive autobiography, is—by the very fact of his oneness with the hero—more "naturally" authorized to speak in his own name than is the narrator of a "third-person" narrative. There is less indiscretion from Tristram Shandy in mixing the account of his present "opinions" (and thus of his knowledge) with the narrative of his past "life" than there is on Fielding's part in mixing the account of *his* with the narrative of the life of Tom Jones. The impersonal narrative therefore tends toward internal focalization by the simple trend (if it is one) toward discretion and respect for what Sartre would call the "freedom"—in other words, the ignorance—of its characters. The autobiographical narrator, having no obligation of discretion with respect to himself, does not have this kind of reason to impose silence on himself. The only focalization that he has to respect is defined in connection with his present in-

[75] Romberg, p. 119.
[76] Barthes, "An Introduction to the Structural Analysis of Narrative," p. 247.
[77] Or (as we will see in the following chapter) of the narrator and an observer of the Watson type.

formation as narrator and not in connection with his past information as hero.[78] He *can*, if he wants, choose this second form
of focalization (focalization through the hero), but he is not at all
required to; and we could just as well consider this choice, when
it is made, as a paralipsis, since the narrator, in order to limit
himself to the information held by the hero at the moment of the
action, has to suppress all the information he acquired later,
information which very often is vital.

It is obvious (and we have already seen one example) that
Proust to a great extent imposed that hyperbolic restriction on
himself, and that the narrative mood of the *Recherche* is very
often internal focalization through the hero.[79] In general it is the
"hero's point of view" that governs the narrative, with his restrictions of field, his momentary ignorances, and even what the
narrator inwardly looks on as his youthful errors, naivetés, "illusions to lose." In a famous letter to Jacques Rivière, Proust
insisted on his carefulness in dissimulating what was at the back
of his mind (identified here with the mind of Marcel-narrator)
up until the moment of the final revelation. The apparent meaning of the final pages of *Swann* (which, we must remember, tell
an experience in principle very recent) is, he says forcefully,

> the opposite of my conclusion. It is a stage, seemingly subjective
> and amateurish, on the way to the most objective and non-foolish
> conclusion. If one inferred from it that my meaning is a disil-
> lusioned skepticism, that would absolutely be as if a viewer, at the
> end of the first act of *Parsifal*, after seeing a character understand
> nothing of the ceremony and be chased off by Gurnemanz, as-
> sumed that Wagner meant that simplicity of heart leads to noth-
> ing.

[78] Of course, this distinction is relevant only for the classical form of autobiographical narrative, where the narrating is enough subsequent to the events for
the narrator's information to differ appreciably from the hero's. When the narrating is contemporaneous with the story (interior monologue, journal, correspondence), internal focalization on the narrator amounts to focalization on the
hero. J. Rousset shows this well for the epistolary novel (*Forme et signification*, p.
70). We will come back to this point in the following chapter.

[79] We know that he was interested in the Jamesian technique of point of view,
and especially the technique in *Maisie* (Walter Berry, *N.R.F.*, *hommage à Marcel
Proust* [Paris: Gallimard, 1927], p. 73).

Similarly, the experience of the madeleine (it too, however, is recent) is reported in *Swann*, but not explained, since the profound reason for the pleasure of the reminiscence is not disclosed: "I will not explain it until the end of the third volume." For the moment, one must respect the hero's ignorance, and deal carefully with the evolution of his thought and the slow work of vocation.

> But this evolution of a thought, I did not want to analyze it abstractly but to recreate it, make it live. So I am forced to paint the mistakes, without thinking I have to say that I take them for mistakes; too bad for me if the reader thinks I take them for the truth. The second volume will accentuate this misunderstanding. I hope that the last will dissipate it.[80]

We know that the last did not dissipate all of it. This is the obvious risk of focalization, a risk that Stendhal pretended to insure himself against by means of notes on the bottom of the page: "It is the opinion of the hero, who is mad and will reform."

It is obviously with respect to the main point—that is, with respect to the experience of involuntary memory, and the literary vocation connected to it—that Proust was most careful in handling the focalization, forbidding himself to give any premature sign, any indiscreet encouragement. The "proofs" of Marcel's inability to write, of his incurable dilettantism, of his growing distaste for literature, do not stop accumulating until the dramatic peripeteia in the courtyard of the Guermantes townhouse—all the more dramatic since the suspense has been built up for a long time by a focalization that on this point was very rigorous. But the principle of nonintervention bears on many other subjects—like homosexuality, for example, which, despite the premonitory scene of Montjouvain, will remain for the reader as for the hero, until the opening pages of *Sodome*, a continent one-hundred times met but never recognized.

The most massive investment in this narrative course (that is,

[80] *Choix de lettres*, ed. Philip Kolb (Paris, 1965), 7 February 1914, pp. 197–199.

focalization through the hero) is undoubtedly the handling of the amorous relationships of the hero, and also of that second-degree hero, Swann, in *Un amour de Swann*. Here internal focalization recovers the psychological function that the Abbé Prévost had given it in *Manon Lescaut:* systematically adopting the "point of view" of one of the protagonists permits an author to leave the feelings of the other one almost completely in shadow, and thus to construct for that other, at little cost, a mysterious and ambiguous personality, the very one for which Proust will coin the name "creature in flight" (fugitive). We do not know, at each state of their passion, any more than Swann or Marcel knows about the inner "truth" of an Odette, a Gilberte, an Albertine, and nothing could more effectively illustrate the essential subjectivity of love according to Proust than that constant evanescence of its object: the creature in flight is by definition the creature loved.[81] Let us not take up again here the list (already evoked apropos of analepses with a corrective function) of episodes (first meeting with Gilberte, false confession of Albertine, incident of the syringas, etc.) whose real significance will not be discovered by the hero—and with him by the reader—until long after.

To these temporary ignorances or misunderstandings we must add some points of definitive opaqueness, where the perspectives of hero and narrator coincide; for instance, we will never know what Odette's "true" feelings for Swann were, or Albertine's for Marcel. A passage in the *Jeunes Filles en fleurs* illustrates well this somewhat interrogative attitude of the narrative in the face of those impenetrable creatures, when Marcel, dismissed by Albertine, wonders for what reason the girl could possibly have refused him a kiss after a series of such clear advances:

> of her attitude during that scene I could not arrive at any satisfactory explanation. Taking first of all the supposition that she was absolutely chaste (a supposition with which I had originally accounted for the violence with which Albertine had refused to let

[81] On Marcel's ignorance with respect to Albertine, see Tadié, pp. 40–42.

herself be taken in my arms and kissed, though it was by no means essential to my conception of the goodness, the fundamentally honourable character of my friend), I could not accept it without a copious revision of its terms. It ran so entirely counter to the hypothesis which I had constructed that day when I saw Albertine for the first time. Then ever so many different acts, all acts of kindness towards myself (a kindness that was caressing, at times uneasy, alarmed, jealous of my predilection for Andrée) came up on all sides to challenge the brutal gesture with which, to escape from me, she had pulled the bell. Why then had she invited me to come and spend the evening by her bedside? Why had she spoken all the time in the language of affection? What object is there in your desire to see a friend, in your fear that he is fonder of another of your friends than of you; why seek to give him pleasure, why tell him, so romantically, that the others will never know that he has spent the evening in your room, if you refuse him so simple a pleasure and if to you it is no pleasure at all? I could not believe, all the same, that Albertine's chastity was carried to such a pitch as that, and I had begun to ask myself whether her violence might not have been due to some reason of coquetry, a disagreeable odour, for instance, which she suspected of lingering about her person, and by which she was afraid that I might be disgusted, or else of cowardice, if for instance she imagined, in her ignorance of the facts of love, that my state of nervous exhaustion was due to something contagious, communicable to her in a kiss.[82]

Again, we must interpret as indices of focalization those openings onto the psychology of characters other than the hero which the narrative takes care to make in a more or less hypothetical form, as when Marcel guesses or conjectures the thought of his interlocutor according to the expression on that person's face:

I could see in Cottard's eyes, as uneasy as though he were afraid of missing a train, that he was asking himself whether he had not allowed his natural good-humour to appear. He was trying to think whether he had remembered to put on his mask of coldness, as one looks for a mirror to see whether one has not forgotten to tie

[82] RH I, 703–704/P I, 940–941.

one's tie. In his uncertainty, and, so as, whatever he had done, to put things right, he replied brutally.[83]

Since Spitzer,[84] critics have often noted the frequency of those modalizing locutions (*perhaps, undoubtedly, as if, seem, appear*) that allow the narrator to say hypothetically what he could not assert without stepping outside internal focalization; and thus Marcel Muller is not wrong in looking on them as "the alibis of the novelist"[85] imposing his truth under a somewhat hypocritical cover, beyond all the uncertainties of the hero and perhaps also of the narrator. For here again the narrator to some extent shares the hero's ignorance; or, more exactly, the ambiguity of the text does not allow us to decide whether the *perhaps* is an effect of indirect style—and, thus, whether the hesitation it denotes is the hero's alone. Further, we must note that the often *multiple* nature of these hypotheses much weakens their function as unavowed paralepsis, while at the same time it accentuates their role as indicators of focalization. When the narrative offers us, introduced by three *perhaps*'s, three explanations to choose from for the brutality with which Charlus answers Mme. de Gallardon,[86] or when the silence of the elevator operator at Balbec is ascribed with no preference to eight possible causes,[87] we are not in fact any more "informed" than when Marcel questions himself before us on the reasons for Albertine's refusal. And here we can hardly go along with Muller, who reproaches Proust for replacing "the secret of each creature with a series of little secrets": Proust, in giving the idea that the real motive is necessarily found among those he enumerates, thus suggests,

---

[83] RH I, 381/P I, 498. Cf. an analogous scene with Norpois, RH I, 367/P I, 478–479.

[84] Leo Spitzer, "Zum Stil Marcel Prousts," in *Stilstudien* (Munich, 1928); trans. in *Etudes de style* (Paris, 1970), pp. 453–455.

[85] *Voix narratives*, p. 129.

[86] RH II, 41/P II, 653.

[87] "He vouchsafed no answer, whether from astonishment at my words, preoccupation with what he was doing, regard for convention, hardness of hearing, respect for holy ground, fear of danger, slowness of understanding, or by the manager's orders" (RH I, 505/P I, 665).

according to Muller, that "the behavior of a character is always amenable to a rational explanation."[88] The multiplicity of contradictory hypotheses suggests much more the insolubility of the problem, and at the very least the incapacity of the narrator to resolve it.

We have already noted the highly subjective nature of Proustian descriptions, always bound to a perceptual activity of the hero's.[89] Proustian descriptions are rigorously focalized: not only does their "duration" never exceed that of real contemplation, but their content never exceeds what is actually perceived by the contemplator. Let us not come back to this subject, which is well understood;[90] let us simply recall the symbolic importance in the *Recherche* of scenes to which the hero, through an often miraculous chance, comes unexpectedly, and of which he perceives only one part, and whose visual or auditory restriction the narrative scrupulously respects: Swann in front of the window which he takes for Odette's, able to see nothing between the "slanting bars of the shutters," but only to hear, "in the silence of the night, the murmur of conversation";[91] Marcel at Montjouvain, witness through the window of the scene between the two young women but unable to make out Mlle. Vinteuil's look or hear what her friend murmurs in her ear, and for whom the scene will stop when she comes, seeming "weary, awkward, preoccupied, sincere, and rather sad," to close the shutters and the window;[92] Marcel again, spying from the top of the staircase, then from the neighboring shop, on the "conjunction" of Charlus and Jupien, the second part of which will be reduced for him to a purely auditory perception;[93] Marcel still, coming unexpectedly on Charlus's flagellation in Jupien's male bordello via a "small oval window opening onto the corridor."[94] Critics

[88] *Voix narratives,* p. 128.
[89] Pp. 99–106.
[90] On the "perspectivism" of Proustian description, see Raimond, pp. 338–343.
[91] RH I, 209–211/P I, 272–275.
[92] RH I, 122–125/P I, 159–163.
[93] RH II, 8–9/P II, 609–610.
[94] RH II, 959/P III, 815.

generally insist, and rightly so, on the unlikelihood of these situations,[95] and on the hidden strain they inflict on the principle of point of view; but we should first recognize that here, as in any fraud, there is an implicit recognition and confirmation of the code: these acrobatic indiscretions, with their so marked restrictions of field, attest to the difficulty the hero experiences in satisfying his curiosity and in penetrating into the existence of another. Thus they are to be set down to internal focalization.

As we have already had occasion to note, the observance of this code goes sometimes so far as to become that form of hyperrestriction of field that we call paralipsis: the end of Marcel's passion for the Duchess, Swann's death, the episode of the little girl-cousin at Combray have provided us with some examples. It is true that the existence of these paralipses is known to us only by the disclosure made later by the narrator—is made known, thus, by an intervention that, for its part, would be due to paralepsis if we considered focalization through the hero to be what the autobiographical form requires. But we have already seen that this is not so, and that that very widespread idea follows simply from an equally widespread confusion between the two. The only focalization logically implied by the "first-person" narrative is focalization through the narrator, and we shall see that in the *Recherche* this second narrative mood coexists with the first.

One obvious manifestation of this new perspective is the *advance notices* we met in the chapter on order. When it is said, apropos of the scene at Montjouvain, that later this scene will exert a decisive influence on the hero's life, such notification cannot be the hero's doing, but must of course be the narrator's— like, more generally, all forms of prolepsis, which (except for an intervention of the supernatural, as in prophetic dreams) always exceed a hero's capacities for knowledge. Likewise, complemen-

---

[95] Beginning with Proust himself, clearly anxious to forestall criticism (and to divert suspicion): "Certainly, the affairs of this sort of which I have been a spectator have always been presented in a setting of the most imprudent and least probable character, as if such revelations were to be the reward of an action full of risk, though in part clandestine" (RH II, 8/P II, 608).

tary information introduced by locutions of the type *"I have learned since . . ."*[96]—which belongs to the subsequent experience of the hero, in other words, to the experience of the narrator— arises from anticipation. It is not correct to set such interventions down to the "omniscient narrator":[97] they represent simply the autobiographical narrator's share in the report of facts still unknown to the hero, but the narrator does not think himself obliged on that account to put off mentioning them until the hero should have acquired knowledge of them. Between the information of the hero and the omniscience of the novelist is the information of the narrator, who disposes of it according to his own lights and holds it back only when he sees a precise reason for doing so. The critic can contest the opportuneness of these complements of information, but not their legitimacy or their credibility in a narrative whose form is autobiographical.

Further, we must certainly recognize that this holds true not only for prolepses giving explicit and avowed information. Even Marcel Muller notes that a formula like "I was ignorant that . . ."[98]—a real defiance of focalization through the hero—"can mean *I have learned since*, and with these two *I*'s we would unquestionably be kept on the Protagonist's plane. The ambiguity is frequent," he adds, "and the choice between Novelist and Narrator for the attribution of a given item of information is often arbitrary."[99] It seems to me that methodological soundness here forces us, at least for a preliminary period, to attribute to the (omniscient) "Novelist" only what we really cannot attribute to the narrator. We see in this case that a certain amount of information which Muller attributes to the "novelist who can walk through walls"[100] can be ascribed without prejudice to the later

[96] RH I, 148/P I, 193; RH I, 1057/P II, 475; RH I, 1129/P II, 579; RH II, 290/P II, 1009; RH II, 506/P III, 182; RH II, 607/P III, 326; RH II, 995/P III, 864, etc. It is different for information of the type *I had been told that . . .* (as for *Un amour de Swann*), which is one of the hero's modes of knowledge (by hearsay).

[97] As Muller has correctly observed: "We are of course leaving aside the cases—fairly numerous—where the Narrator anticipates what is still the hero's future by drawing from what his own (the Narrator's) past is. In such cases there is no question of the Novelist's omniscience" (*Voix narratives*, p. 110).

[98] RH I, 1111/P II, 554; RH II, 288/P II, 1006.

[99] *Voix narratives*, pp. 140–141.

[100] *Voix narratives*, p. 110.

knowledge of the Protagonist: for instance, Charlus's visits to Brichot's class, or the scene that unfolds at Berma's while Marcel attends the Guermantes matinée, or even the dialogue between the relatives on the evening of Swann's visit, if indeed the hero really could not hear it at the time.[101] Similarly, many details about the relations between Charlus and Morel can in one way or another have come to the narrator's knowledge.[102] The same hypothesis holds for Basin's infidelities, his conversion to Dreyfusism, his late liaison with Odette, for M. Nissim Bernard's unhappy love affairs, etc.[103]—so many indiscretions and so much gossip, whether true or false, are not at all improbable in the Proustian universe. Let us remember finally that it is to a tale of this kind that the hero's knowledge of the past love between Swann and Odette is attributed, a knowledge so precise that the narrator thinks he has to make excuses for it in a way that may seem rather clumsy,[104] and that furthermore does not spare the only hypothesis capable of accounting for the focalization through Swann in this narrative within the narrative: namely, that whatever the eventual way stations, the first source can only have been Swann himself.

The real difficulty arises when the narrative reports to us, on the spot and with no perceptible detour, the thoughts of another character in the course of a scene where the hero himself is present: Mme. de Cambremer at the Opera, the usher at the Guermantes soirée, the historian of the Fronde or the librarian at the Villeparisis matinée, Basin or Bréauté in the course of the dinner at Oriane's.[105] In the same way we have access, without any apparent way station, to Swann's feelings about his wife or to Saint-Loup's about Rachel,[106] and even to the last thoughts of

[101] RH II, 583/P III, 291–292; RH II, 1098–1101/P III, 995–999; RH I, 26–27/P I, 35.

[102] Including the risqué scene of the Maineville bordello, the account of which is vouched for (RH II, 343/P II, 1082).

[103] RH II, 101/P II, 739; RH II, 1113–1115/P III, 1015–1018; RH II, 182/P II, 854–855.

[104] RH I, 143/P I, 186.

[105] RH I, 753–754/P II, 56–57; RH II, 29/P II, 636; RH I, 869/P II, 215; RH I, 893/P II, 248; RH I, 1090/P II, 524; RH I, 1025–1026/P II, 429–430.

[106] RH I, 398–401/P I, 522–525; RH I, 801/P II, 122; RH I, 826/P II, 156; RH I, 830–831/P II, 162–163.

Bergotte on his deathbed,[107] which, as has often been noted, cannot in point of fact have been reported to Marcel since no one—for a very good reason—could have knowledge of them. That is one paralepsis to end all paralepses; it is irreducible by any hypothesis to the narrator's information, and one we must indeed attribute to the "omniscient" novelist—and one that would be enough to prove Proust capable of transgressing the limits of his own narrative "system."

But evidently we cannot restrict the part played by paralepsis to this scene alone, on the pretext that this is the only one to present a physical impossibility. The decisive criterion is not so much material possibility or even psychological plausibility as it is textual coherence and narrative tonality. Thus, Michel Raimond attributes to the omniscient novelist the scene during which Charlus takes Cottard into a nearby room and talks to him without witnesses.[108] In principle nothing prohibits us from assuming that this dialogue, like others,[109] was reported to Marcel by Cottard himself, but nonetheless the reading of this passage gives the idea of an immediate narrating without way stations, and the same is true for all those that I mentioned in the preceding paragraph, and for some others as well. In all these Proust manifestly forgets or neglects the fiction of the autobiographical narrator and the focalization which that implies—and a fortiori the focalization through the hero that is its hyperbolic form—in order to handle his narrative in a third mood, which is obviously zero-focalization, in other words, the omniscience of the classical novelist. Which, let us note in passing, would be impossible if the *Recherche* were—as some people still want to see it—a true autobiography. Whence these scenes—scandalous, I would imagine, for the purists of "point of view"—where *I* and others are handled on the same footing, as if the narrator had exactly the same relationship to a Cambremer, a Basin, a Bréauté, and his own past "me": "Mme. de Cambremer remembered having heard Swann say . . . / For myself, the thought of the two

[107] RH II, 509/P III, 187.

[108] RH II, 335–336/P II, 1071–1072. Raimond, p. 337.

[109] For example, the conversation between the Verdurins about Saniette, RH II, 607/P III, 326.

cousins... / Mme. de Cambremer was trying to make out exactly how... / For my own part, I never doubted... "[110] Plainly such a text is constructed on the antithesis between Mme. de Cambremer's thoughts and Marcel's, as if somewhere there existed a point from which my thought and someone else's thought would seem symmetrical to me—the height of depersonalization, which unsettles a little the image of the famous Proustian subjectivism. Whence further that scene at Montjouvain, in which we have already noted the very rigorous focalization (through Marcel) with respect to visible and audible actions, but which for thoughts and feelings, on the other hand, is entirely focalized through Mlle. Vinteuil:[111] "she felt... she thought... she felt that she had been indiscreet, her sensitive heart took fright ... she pretended... she guessed... she realised... "—as if the witness could neither see all nor hear all, and nevertheless divined all the thoughts. But the truth quite obviously is that two concurrent codes are functioning here on two planes of reality which oppose each other without colliding.

This *double focalization*[112] certainly corresponds to the antithesis organizing the entire passage (like the entire character of Mlle. Vinteuil, "shy maiden" and "battered old campaigner"), an antithesis between the brutal immorality of the actions (perceived by the hero-witness) and the extreme delicacy of the feelings, which only an omniscient narrator, capable like God himself of seeing beyond actions and of sounding body and soul, can reveal.[113] But this scarcely conceivable coexistence can serve as an emblem of the whole of Proust's narrative practice,

[110] RH I, 754/P II, 57.

[111] With the exception of one sentence (RH I, 125/P I, 163) focalized through her friend, a "probably" (RH I, 123/P I, 161), and a "may well have" (RH I, 125/P I, 162). [Translator's note: partly my translation.]

[112] B. G. Rogers, *Proust's Narrative Techniques* (Geneva, 1965), p. 108, speaks of "double vision" apropos of the concurrence between the "subjective" hero and the "objective" narrator.

[113] On the technical and psychological aspects of this scene, see Muller's excellent commentary (pp. 148–153), which, in particular, points out well how the hero's mother and grandmother are indirectly but closely implicated in this act of filial "sadism," whose personal resonances in Proust are immense and which obviously recalls the "Confession d'une jeune fille" of *Les Plaisirs et les jours*, and the "Sentiments filiaux d'un parricide."

which plays without a qualm, and as if without being aware of it, in three modes of focalization at once, passing at will from the consciousness of his hero to that of his narrator, and inhabiting by turns that of his most diverse characters. This triple narrative position is not at all comparable to the simple omniscience of the classical novel, for it not only defies, as Sartre reproached Mauriac for defying, the conditions of the realistic illusion: it also transgresses a "law of the spirit" requiring that one cannot be inside and outside at the same time. To resume the musical metaphor used above, we could say that between a tonal (or modal) system with respect to which all infractions (paralipses and paralepses) can be defined as alterations, and an atonal (amodal?) system where no code prevails anymore and where the very notion of infraction becomes outworn, the *Recherche* illustrates quite well an intermediary state: a plural state, comparable to the polytonal (polymodal) system ushered in for a time, and in the very same year, 1913, by the *Rite of Spring*. One should not take this comparison too literally;[114] let it at least serve us to throw light on this typical and very troubling feature of Proustian narrative, which we would like to call its *polymodality*.

Let us recall to finish this chapter that this ambiguous—or rather, complex—and deliberately nonorganized position characterizes not only the system of focalization but the entire modal practice of the *Recherche:* at the level of the narrative of actions, the paradoxical coexistence of the greatest mimetic intensity and the presence of a narrator, which is in principle contrary to novelistic mimesis; the dominance of direct discourse, intensified by the stylistic autonomy of the characters

[114] We know (George Painter, *Proust: The Later Years* [New York: Atlantic-Little, Brown, 1965], pp. 340–342) what a fiasco the meeting arranged in May 1922 between Proust and Stravinsky (and Joyce) was. We could just as well draw a parallel between Proustian narrative practice and those multiple and superimposed visions so well expressed, still in the same period, by Cubism. Is it that kind of portrait that these lines from the preface to *Propos de peintre* refer to: "the admirable Picasso, who, in fact, has concentrated all Cocteau's features in a portrait of such noble rigidity . . ." (*Essais et articles*, Pléiade, p. 580; "Preface to Jacques Emile Blanche's Propos de Peintre: De David à Degas," in *Proust: A Selection*, p. 253)?

(the height of dialogic mimesis) but finally absorbing the characters in an immense verbal game (the height of literary gratuitousness, the antithesis of realism); and, finally, the concurrence of theoretically incompatible focalizations, which shakes the whole logic of narrative representation. Again and again we have seen this subversion of mood tied to the activity, or rather the presence, of the narrator himself, the disturbing intervention of the narrative source—of the narrating in the narrative. It is this last instance—that of *voice*—which we must now look at for its own sake, after having met it so often without wanting to.

5 Voice

The Narrating Instance

"For a long time I used to go to bed early": obviously, such a statement—unlike, let us say, "Water boils at one-hundred degrees Celsius" or "The sum of the angles of a triangle is equal to two right angles"—can be interpreted only with respect to the person who utters it and the situation in which he utters it. *I* is identifiable only with reference to that person, and the completed past of the "action" told is completed only in relation to the moment of utterance. To use Benveniste's well-known terms again, the *story* here is not without a share of *discourse*, and it is not too difficult to show that this is practically always the case.[1] Even historical narrative of the type "Napoleon died at Saint Helena" implies in its preterite that the story precedes the narrating, and I am not certain that the present tense in "Water boils at one-hundred degrees" (iterative narrative) is as atemporal as it seems. Nevertheless, the importance or the relevance of these implications is essentially variable, and this variability can justify or impose distinctions and contrasts that have at least an operative value. When I read *Gambara* or *Le Chef-d'oeuvre inconnu*, I am interested in a story, and care little to know who tells it, where, and when; if I read *Facino Cane*, at no time can I overlook the presence of the narrator in the story he tells; if it is

[1] On this subject see my *Figures II*, pp. 61–69.

La Maison Nucingen, the author makes it his business to draw my attention to the person of the talker Bixiou and the group of listeners he addresses; if it is *L'Auberge rouge,* I will undoubtedly give less attention to the foreseeable unfolding of the story Hermann tells than to the reactions of a listener named Taillefer, for the narrative is on two levels, and the second—*where someone narrates*—is where most of the drama's excitement is.

This kind of effect is what we are going to look at under the category of *voice:* "the mode of action," says Vendryès, "of the verb considered for its relations to the subject"—the subject here being not only the person who carries out or submits to the action, but also the person (the same one or another) who reports it, and, if need be, all those people who participate, even though passively, in this narrating activity. We know that linguistics has taken its time in addressing the task of accounting for what Benveniste has called *subjectivity in language,*[2] that is, in passing from analysis of statements to analysis of relations between these statements and their generating instance—what today we call their *enunciating.* It seems that poetics is experiencing a comparable difficulty in approaching the generating instance of narrative discourse, an instance for which we have reserved the parallel term *narrating.* This difficulty is shown especially by a sort of hesitation, no doubt an unconscious one, to recognize and respect the autonomy of that instance, or even simply its specificity. On the one hand, as we have already noted, critics restrict questions of narrative enunciating to questions of "point of view"; on the other hand they identify the narrating instance with the instance of "writing," the narrator with the author, and the recipient of the narrative with the reader of the work:[3] a confusion that is perhaps legitimate in the case of a historical narrative or a real autobiography, but not when we are dealing with a narrative of fiction, where the role of narrator is itself fictive, even if assumed directly by the author, and where the supposed narrating situation can be very different from the act of writing (or of dictating) which

[2] Benveniste, "Subjectivity in Language," *Problems,* pp. 223–230.
[3] For example Todorov, "Les Catégories du récit littéraire," pp. 146–147.

refers to it. It is not the Abbé Prévost who tells the love of Manon and Des Grieux, it is not even the Marquis de Renoncourt, supposed author of the *Mémoires d'un homme de qualité;* it is Des Grieux himself, in an oral narrative where "I" can designate only him, and where "here" and "now" refer to the spatiotemporal circumstances of that narrating and in no way to the circumstances of the writing of *Manon Lescaut* by its real author. And even the references in *Tristram Shandy* to the situation of writing speak to the (fictive) act of Tristram and not the (real) one of Sterne; but in a more subtle and also more radical way, the narrator of *Père Goriot* "is" not Balzac, even if here and there he expresses Balzac's opinions, for this author-narrator is someone who "knows" the Vauquer boardinghouse, its landlady and its lodgers, whereas all Balzac himself does is imagine them; and in this sense, of course, the narrating situation of a fictional account is *never* reduced to its situation of writing.

So it is this narrating instance that we have still to look at, according to the traces it has left—the traces it is considered to have left—in the narrative discourse it is considered to have produced. But it goes without saying that the instance does not necessarily remain identical and invariable in the course of a single narrative work. Most of *Manon Lescaut* is told by Des Grieux, but some pages revert to M. de Renoncourt; inversely, most of the *Odyssey* is told by "Homer," but Books IX–XII revert to Ulysses; and the baroque novel, *The Thousand and One Nights,* and *Lord Jim* have accustomed us to much more complex situations.[4] Narrative analysis must obviously take charge of the

---

[4] On the *Thousand and One Nights,* see Todorov, "Narrative-Men," in *Poetics of Prose:* "The record [for embedding] seems to be held by the narrative which offers us the story of the bloody chest. Here
    Scheherazade tells that
      Jaafer tells that
        the tailor tells that
          the barber tells that
            his brother (and he has six brothers) tells that . . .
The last story is a story to the fifth degree" (p. 71). But the term "embedding" does not do justice to the fact precisely that each of these stories is at a higher "degree" than the preceding one, since its narrator is a character in the preceding one; for stories can also be "embedded" at the same level, simply by digression, without any shift in the narrating instance: see Jacques's parentheses in the *Fataliste.*

study of these modifications—or of these permanences: for if it is remarkable that Ulysses' adventures are told by two different narrators, it is proper to find it just as noteworthy that the loves of Swann and of Marcel are told by the same narrator.

A narrating situation is, like any other, a complex whole within which analysis, or simply description, cannot *differentiate* except by ripping apart a tight web of connections among the narrating act, its protagonists, its spatio-temporal determinations, its relationship to the other narrating situations involved in the same narrative, etc. The demands of exposition constrain us to this unavoidable violence simply by the fact that critical discourse, like any other discourse, cannot say everything at once. Here again, therefore, we will look successively at elements of definition whose actual functioning is simultaneous: we will attach these elements, for the most part, to the categories of *time of the narrating, narrative level,* and *"person"* (that is, relations between the narrator—plus, should the occasion arise, his or their narratee[s][5]—and the story he tells).

Time of the Narrating

By a dissymmetry whose underlying reasons escape us but which is inscribed in the very structures of language (or at the very least of the main "languages of civilization" of Western culture), I can very well tell a story without specifying the place where it happens, and whether this place is more or less distant from the place where I am telling it; nevertheless, it is almost impossible for me not to locate the story in time with respect to my narrating act, since I must necessarily tell the story in a present, past, or future tense.[6] This is perhaps why the temporal determinations of the narrating instance are manifestly more important than its spatial determinations. With the exception of

[5] This is what I will call the receiver of the narrative, patterned after the contrast between *sender* and *receiver* proposed by A. J. Greimas (*Sémantique structurale* [Paris, 1966], p. 177).

[6] Certain uses of the present tense do indeed connote temporal indefiniteness (and not simultaneousness between story and narrating), but curiously they seem reserved for very particular forms of narrative (joke, riddle, scientific problem or experiment, plot summary) and literature does not have much investment in them. The case of the "narrative present" with preterite value is also different.

second-degree narratings, whose setting is generally indicated by the diegetic context (Ulysses with the Phaeacians, the landlady of *Jacques le fataliste* in her inn), the narrating place is very rarely specified, and is almost never relevant:[7] we know more or less where Proust wrote the *Recherche du temps perdu*, but we are ignorant of where Marcel is considered to have produced the narrative of his life, and we scarcely think of worrying about it. On the other hand, it is very important to us to know, for example, how much time elapses between the first scene of the *Recherche* (the "drama of going to bed") and the moment when it is evoked in these terms: "Many years have passed since that night. The wall of the staircase, up which I had watched the light of his candle gradually climb, was long ago demolished"; for this temporal interval, and what fills it up and gives it life, is an essential element in the narrative's significance.

The chief temporal determination of the narrating instance is obviously its position relative to the story. It seems evident that the narrating can only be subsequent to what it tells, but this obviousness has been belied for many centuries by the existence of "predictive" narrative[8] in its various forms (prophetic, apocalyptic, oracular, astrological, chiromantic, cartomantic, oneiromantic, etc.), whose origin is lost in the darkness of time—and has been belied also, at least since *Les Lauriers sont coupés*, by the use of narrative in the present tense. We must consider, further, that a past-tense narrating can to some extent be split up and inserted between the various moments of the story, much like a "live" running commentary[9]—a common

---

[7] It could be, but for reasons which are not exactly spatial in kind: for a "first-person" narrative to be produced in prison, on a hospital bed, in a psychiatric institution, can constitute a decisive element of advance notice about the denouement.

[8] I borrow the term "predictive" from Todorov, *Grammaire du Décaméron* (The Hague, 1969), p. 48, to designate any kind of narrative where the narrating precedes the story.

[9] Radio or television reporting is obviously the most perfectly live form of this kind of narrative, where the narrating follows so closely on the action that it can be considered practically simultaneous, whence the use of the present tense. We find a curious literary use of simultaneous narrative in chapter 29 of *Ivanhoe*, where Rebecca is telling the wounded Ivanhoe all about the battle taking place at the foot of the castle, a battle she is following from the window.

practice with correspondence and private diary, and therefore
with the "novel by letters" or the narrative in the form of a
journal (*Wuthering Heights, Journal d'un curé de campagne*). It is
therefore necessary, merely from the point of view of temporal
position, to differentiate four types of narrating: *subsequent* (the
classical position of the past-tense narrative, undoubtedly far
and away the most frequent); *prior* (predictive narrative, generally in the future tense, but not prohibited from being conju-
gated in the present, like Jocabel's dream in *Moyse sauvé*); *simultaneous* (narrative in the present contemporaneous with the action); and *interpolated* (between the moments of the action).

The last type is a priori the most complex, since it involves a
narrating with several instances, and since the story and the
narrating can become entangled in such a way that the latter has
an effect on the former. This is what happens particularly in the
epistolary novel with several correspondents,[10] where, as we
know, the letter is at the same time both a medium of the narrative and an element in the plot.[11] This type of narrating can
also be the most delicate, indeed, the one most refractory to
analysis, as for example when the journal form loosens up to
result in a sort of monologue after the event, with an indefinite, even incoherent, temporal position: attentive readers of
L'Etranger have not missed these uncertainties, which are one of
the audacities—perhaps unintentional—of that narrative.[12] Finally, the extreme closeness of story to narrating produces here,
most often,[13] a very subtle effect of friction (if I may call it that) between the slight temporal displacement of the narrative of
events ("Here is what happened to me today") and the complete
simultaneousness in the report of thoughts and feelings ("Here

[10] On the typology of epistolary novels according to the number of correspondents, see Rousset, "Une forme littéraire: le roman par lettres," *Forme et
signification*, and Romberg, *Studies*, pp. 51 ff.

[11] An example is when, in *Les Liaisons dangereuses*, Mme. de Volanges discovers Danceny's letters in her daughter's writing desk—a discovery whose consequences Danceny is notified of in letter 62, typically "performative." Cf. Todorov, *Littérature et signification* (Paris, 1967), pp. 44–46.

[12] See B. T. Fitch, *Narrateur et narration dans "l'Etranger" d'Albert Camus*, 2d rev.
ed. (Paris, 1968) pp. 12–26.

[13] But there also exist *delayed* forms of journal narrating: for example, the "first
notebook" of the *Symphonie pastorale*, or the complex counterpoint of *L'Emploi du
temps*.

is what I think about it this evening"). The journal and the epistolary confidence constantly combine what in broadcasting language is called the live and the prerecorded account, the quasi-interior monologue and the account after the event. Here, the narrator is at one and the same time still the hero and already someone else: the events of the day are already in the past, and the "point of view" may have been modified since then; the feelings of the evening or the next day are fully of the present, and here focalization through the narrator is at the same time focalization through the hero. Cécile Volanges writes to Mme. de Merteuil to tell her how she was seduced, last night, by Valmont, and to confide to her her remorse; the seduction scene is past, and with it the confusion that Cécile no longer feels, and can no longer even imagine; what remains is the shame, and a sort of stupor which is both incomprehension and discovery of oneself: "What I reproach myself for most, and what, however, I must talk to you about, is that I am afraid I didn't defend myself as much as I could have. I don't know how that happened: surely I don't love M. de Valmont, very much the opposite; and there were moments when I acted as if I did love him. . . ."[14] The Cécile of yesterday, very near and already far off, is seen and spoken of by the Cécile of today. We have here two successive heroines, (only) the second of whom is (also) the narrator and gives her point of view, the point of view—displaced just enough to create dissonance—of the immediate *post-event* future.[15] We know how the eighteenth-century novel, from *Pamela* to *Obermann*, exploited that narrative situation propitious to the most subtle and the most "irritating" counterpoints: the situation of the tiniest temporal interval.

The third type (simultaneous narrating), by contrast, is in principle the simplest, since the rigorous simultaneousness of story and narrating eliminates any sort of interference or temporal game. We must observe, however, that the blending of the instances can function here in two opposite directions, according to whether the emphasis is put on the story or on the narra-

<hr>

[14] Letter 97.

[15] Compare letter 48, from Valmont to Tourvel, written in Emilie's bed, "live" and, if I may say so, *at the event*.

tive discourse. A present-tense narrative which is "behaviorist" in type and strictly of the moment can seem like the height of objectivity, since the last trace of enunciating that still subsisted in the Hemingway-style narrative (the mark of temporal interval between story and narrating, which the use of the preterite unavoidably comprises) now disappears in a total transparency of the narrative, which finally fades away in favor of the story. That is how the works that come under the heading of the French "new novel," and especially Robbe-Grillet's early novels,[16] have generally been received: "objective literature," "school of the look"—these designations express well the sense of the narrating's absolute transitivity which a generalized use of the present tense promotes. But inversely, if the emphasis rests on the narrating itself, as in narratives of "interior monologue," the simultaneousness operates in favor of the discourse; and then it is the action that seems reduced to the condition of simple pretext, and ultimately abolished. This effect was already noticeable in Dujardin, and became more marked in a Beckett, a Claude Simon, a Roger Laporte. So it is as if use of the present tense, bringing the instances together, had the effect of unbalancing their equilibrium and allowing the whole of the narrative to tip, according to the slightest shifting of emphasis, either onto the side of the story or onto the side of the narrating, that is, the discourse. And the facility with which the French novel in recent years has passed from one extreme to the other perhaps illustrates this ambivalence and reversibility.[17]

The second type (prior narrating) has until now enjoyed a much smaller literary investment than the others, and certainly even novels of anticipation, from Wells to Bradbury—which nevertheless belong fully to the prophetic genre—almost always postdate their narrating instances, making them implicitly subsequent to their stories (which indeed illustrates the autonomy of this fictive instance with respect to the moment of actual

[16] All written in the present tense except *Le Voyeur*, whose temporal system, as we know, is more complex.

[17] An even more striking illustration is *La Jalousie*, which can be read *ad libitum* in the objectivist mode with no jealous person in the narrating, or purely as the interior monologue of a husband spying on his wife and imagining her adventures. Indeed, when this work was published in 1959 it played a pivotal role.

writing). Predictive narrative hardly appears at all in the literary corpus except on the second level: examples, in Saint-Amant's *Moyse sauvé*, are Aaron's prophetic narrative (sixth part) and Jocabel's long premonitory dream (fourth, fifth, and sixth parts), both of which are connected with Moses' future.[18] The common characteristic of these second narratives is obviously that they are predictive in relation to the immediate narrating instance (Aaron, Jocabel's dream) but not in relation to the final instance (the implied author of *Moyse sauvé*, who explicitly identifies himself with Saint-Amant): clear examples of prediction after the event.

Subsequent narrating (the first type) is what presides over the immense majority of the narratives produced to this day. The use of a past tense is enough to make a narrative subsequent, although without indicating the temporal interval which separates the moment of the narrating from the moment of the story.[19] In classical "third-person" narrative, this interval appears generally indeterminate, and the question irrelevant, the preterite marking a sort of ageless past:[20] the story can be dated, as it often is in Balzac, without the narrating being so.[21] It sometimes happens, however, that a relative contemporaneity of story time and narrating time is disclosed by the use of the present tense, either at the beginning, as in *Tom Jones*[22] or *Le*

[18] See my *Figures II*, pp. 210–211.
[19] With the exception of the passé composé, which in French connotes relative closeness: "The perfect creates a living connection between the past event and the present in which its evocation takes place. It is the tense for the one who relates the facts as a witness, as a participant; it is thus also the tense that will be chosen by whoever wishes to make the reported event ring vividly in our ears and to link it to the present" (Benveniste, "The Correlations of Tense in the French Verb," *Problems*, p. 210). *L'Etranger*, of course, owes a great deal to the use of this tense.
[20] Käte Hamburger (*The Logic of Literature*, trans. Marilynn J. Rose, 2d ed. [Bloomington, Ind., 1973]) has gone so far as to deny any temporal value to the "epic preterite." In this extreme and strongly contested position there is a certain hyperbolic truth.
[21] On the other hand, Stendhal does like to date, and more precisely to ante-date, for reasons of political prudence, the narrating instance of his novels: *Le Rouge* (written in 1829–1830) at 1827, *La Chartreuse* (written in 1839) at 1830.
[22] "In that Part of the western Division of this Kingdom, which is commonly called *Somersetshire, there lately lived (and perhaps lives still)* a Gentleman whose Name was *Allworthy*" (*Tom Jones*, Book I, chap. 2 [Norton, p. 27]).

Père Goriot,[23] or at the end, as in *Eugénie Grandet*[24] or *Madame Bovary.*[25] These effects of final convergence (the more striking of the two types) play on the fact that the very length of the story gradually lessens the interval separating it from the moment of the narrating. But the power of these final convergences results from their unexpected disclosure of a temporal isotopy (which, being temporal, is also to a certain extent diegetic) between the story and its narrator, an isotopy which until then was hidden (or, in the case of *Bovary,* long forgotten). In "first-person" narrative, on the other hand, this isotopy is evident from the beginning, where the narrator is presented right away as a character in the story, and where the final convergence is the rule,[26] in accordance with a mode that the last paragraph of *Robinson Crusoe* can furnish us with a paradigm of: "And here, resolving to harrass my self no more, I am preparing for a longer Journey than all these, having liv'd 72 Years, a Life of infinite Variety, and learn'd sufficiently to know the Value of Retirement, and the Blessing of ending our Days in Peace."[27] No dramatic effect here, unless the final situation should itself be a violent denouement, as in *Double Indemnity,* in which the hero writes the last line of his confession-narrative before slipping with his

[23] "Madame Vauquer, whose maiden name was De Conflans, is an elderly woman who for forty years has kept, in Paris, a family boardinghouse" (*Père Goriot,* trans. J. M. Sedgwick [New York: Rinehart, 1950], p. 1).

[24] "Her face is very pale and quiet now, and there is a tinge of sadness in the low tones of her voice. She has simple manners" (*Eugénie Grandet,* trans. E. Marriage [Philadelphia: Gebbie, 1899], p. 223).

[25] "The devil himself doesn't have a greater following than [M. Homais]: the authorities treat him considerately, and public opinion is on his side. He has just been awarded the cross of the Legion of Honor" (*Madame Bovary,* trans. F. Steegmuller [New York: Random House, 1957], p. 396). Let us remember that the opening pages ("*We were* in study-hall . . ." [Steegmuller, p. 3]) already indicate that the narrator is contemporary with the hero, and is even one of his fellow students.

[26] The Spanish picaresque seems to form a notable exception to this "rule," at any rate *Lazarillo,* which ends in suspense ("It was the time of my prosperity, and I was at the height of all good fortune"). *Guzman* and *Buscon* also, but while promising a continuation and end, which will not come.

[27] *Robinson Crusoe* (Oxford: Blackwell, 1928), III, 220. Or, in a more ironic mode, *Gil Blas:* "It is three years since then, my friend the reader, that I have been leading a delightful life with such dear people. As a crowning satisfaction, heaven was pleased to bestow on me two children, whose upbringing will become the pastime of my old age, and whose father I dutifully think I am."

accomplice into the ocean where a shark awaits them: "I didn't hear the stateroom door open, but she's beside me now while I'm writing. I can feel her. / The moon."[28]

In order for the story to overtake the narrating in this way, the duration of the latter must of course not exceed the duration of the former. Take Tristram's comic aporia: in one year of writing having succeeded in telling only the first day of his life, he observes that he has gotten 364 days behind, that he has therefore moved backward rather than forward, and that, living 364 times faster than he writes, it follows that the more he writes the more there remains for him to write; that, in short, his undertaking is hopeless.[29] Faultless reasoning, whose premises are not at all absurd. Telling takes time (Scheherazade's life hangs by that one thread), and when a novelist puts on his stage an oral narrating in the second degree, he rarely fails to take that into account: many things happen at the inn while the landlady of *Jacques* tells the story of the Marquis des Arcis, and the first part of *Manon Lescaut* ends with the remark that since the Chevalier spent more than an hour on his tale, he certainly needs supper in order to "get a little rest." We have a few reasons to think that Prévost, for his part, spent much more than an hour writing those some one-hundred pages, and we know, for example, that Flaubert needed almost five years to write *Madame Bovary*. Nevertheless—and this is finally very odd—the fictive narrating of that narrative, as with almost all the novels in the world except *Tristram Shandy,* is considered to have no duration; or, more exactly, everything takes place as if the question of its duration had no relevance. One of the fictions of literary narrating—perhaps the most powerful one, because it passes unnoticed, so to speak—is that the narrating involves an instantaneous action, without a temporal dimension. Sometimes it is dated, but it is never measured: we know that M. Homais has just received the cross of the Legion of Honor at the moment when the narrator writes that last sentence, but we do not know

[28] James M. Cain, *Double Indemnity,* in *Cain X3* (New York: Knopf, 1969), p. 465.

[29] Sterne, *Tristram Shandy,* Book IV, chap. 13.

what was happening while the narrator was writing his first one. Indeed, we even know that this question is absurd: nothing is held to separate those two moments of the narrating instance except the atemporal space of the narrative as text. Contrary to simultaneous or interpolated narrating, which exist through their duration and the relations between that duration and the story's, subsequent narrating exists through this paradox: it possesses at the same time a temporal situation (with respect to the past story) and an atemporal essence (since it has no duration proper).[30] Like Proustian reminiscence, it is rapture, "a moment brief as a flash of lightning," a miraculous syncope, "a minute freed from the order of [T]ime."[31]

The narrating instance of the *Recherche* obviously corresponds to this last type. We know that Proust spent more than ten years writing his novel, but Marcel's act of narrating bears no mark of duration, or of division: it is instantaneous. The narrator's present, which on almost every page we find mingled with the hero's various pasts, is a single moment without progression. Marcel Muller thought he found in Germaine Brée the hypothesis of a double narrating instance—before and after the final revelation—but this hypothesis has no basis, and in fact all I see in Germaine Brée is an improper (although common) use of "narrator" for *hero*, which perhaps led Muller into error on that point.[32] As for the feelings expressed on the final pages of *Swann*, which we know do not correspond to the narrator's final conviction, Muller himself shows very well that they do not at all prove the existence of a narrating instance prior to the revelation;[33] on the contrary, the letter to Jacques Rivière quoted above[34] shows that Proust was anxious to tune the narrator's

[30] Temporal indications of the kind "we have *already* said" and "we will see *later*," etc., do not in fact refer to the temporality of the narrating, but to the space of the text (= *we have said above, we will see further on . . .*) and to the temporality of reading.

[31] RH II, 1001 and 1002/P III, 872 and 873.

[32] Muller, p. 45; Germaine Brée, *Marcel Proust and Deliverance from Time*, trans. C. J. Richards and A. D. Truitt, 2d ed. (New Brunswick, N.J., 1969), pp. 19–20.

[33] Muller, p. 46.

[34] Pp. 199–200.

discourse to the hero's "errors," and thus to impute to the narrator a belief not his own, in order to avoid disclosing his own
mind too early. Even the narrative Marcel produces after the
Guermantes soirée, the narrative of his beginnings as a writer
(seclusion, rough drafts, first reactions of readers), which necessarily takes into account the length of writing ("like him
too, . . . I had something to write. But my task was longer than
his, my words had to reach more than a single person. My task
was long. By day, the most I could hope for was to try to sleep.
If I worked, it would be only at night. But I should need many
nights, a hundred perhaps, or even a thousand")[35] and the interrupting fear of death—even this narrative does not gainsay
the fictive instantaneousness of its narrating: for the book Marcel
then begins to write *in the story* cannot legitimately be identified
with the one Marcel has then almost finished writing *as narrative*—and which is the *Recherche* itself. Writing the fictive book,
which is the subject of the narrative, is, like writing every book, a
"task [that] was long." But the actual book, the narrative-book,
does not have knowledge of its own "length": it does away with
its own duration.

The present of Proustian narrating—from 1909 to 1922—
corresponds to many of the "presents" of the writing, and we
know that almost a third of the book—including, as it happens,
the final pages—was written by 1913. The fictive moment of
narrating has thus *in fact* shifted in the course of the real writing;
today it is no longer what it was in 1913, at the moment when
Proust thought his work concluded for the Grasset edition.
Therefore, the temporal intervals he had in mind—and wanted
to signify— when he wrote, for example apropos of the bedtime
scene, "Many years have passed since that night," or apropos of
the resurrection of Combray by the madeleine, "I can measure
the resistance, I can hear the echo of great spaces traversed"—
these spaces have increased by more than ten years simply because the story's time has lengthened: the signified of these
sentences is no longer the same. Whence certain irreducible contradictions like this one: the narrator's *today* is obviously, for us,

35 RH II, 1136/P III, 1043.

later than the war, but the "Paris today" of the last pages of *Swann* remains in its historical determinations (its referential content) a prewar Paris, as it was seen and described in its better days. The novelistic *signified* (the moment of the narrating) has become something like 1925, but the historical *referent*, which corresponds to the moment of the writing, did not keep pace and continues to say: 1913. Narrative analysis must register these shifts—and the resulting discordances—as effects of the actual genesis of the work; but in the end analysis can look at the narrating instance only as it is given in the final state of the text, as a single moment without duration, necessarily placed several years after the last "scene," therefore after the war, and even, as we have seen,[36] after the death of Marcel Proust. This paradox, let us remember, is not one: Marcel is not Proust, and nothing requires him to die with Proust. What is required, on the other hand, is that Marcel spend "many years" after 1916 in a clinic, which necessarily puts his return to Paris and the Guermantes matinée in 1921 at the earliest, and the meeting with an Odette "showing signs of senility" in 1923.[37] That consequence is a must.

Between this single narrating instant and the different moments of the story, the interval is necessarily variable. If "many years" have elapsed since the bedtime scene in Combray, it is only "of late" that the narrator has again begun to hear his childhood sobs, and the interval separating the narrating instant from the Guermantes matinee is obviously smaller than the interval separating narrating instant and the hero's first arrival in Balbec. The system of language, the uniform use of the past tense, does not allow this gradual shrinking to be imprinted in the very texture of the narrative discourse, but we have seen that to a certain extent Proust had succeeded in making it felt, by modifications in the temporal pacing of the narrative: gradual disappearance of the iterative, lengthening of the singulative scenes, increasing discontinuity, accentuation of the rhythm—

---

[36] P. 91.
[37] This episode takes place (RH II, 1063/P III, 951) "Less than three years"— thus more than two years—after the Guermantes matinée.

as if the story time were tending to dilate and make itself more and more conspicuous while drawing near its end, *which is also its origin.*

According to what we have already seen to be the common practice of "autobiographical" narrating, we could expect to see the narrative bring its hero to the point where the narrator awaits him, in order that these two hypostases might meet and finally merge. People have sometimes, a little quickly, claimed that this is what happens.[38] In fact, as Marcel Muller well notes, "between the day of the reception at the Princess's and the day when the Narrator recounts that reception there extends a whole era which maintains a gap between the Hero and the Narrator, a gap that cannot be bridged: the verbal forms in the conclusion of the *Temps retrouvé* are all in the past tense."[39] The narrator brings his hero's story—his own story—precisely to the point when, as Jean Rousset says, "the hero is about to become the narrator";[40] I would say rather, *is beginning to become* the narrator, since he actually starts in on his writing. Muller writes that "if the Hero overtakes the Narrator, it is like an asymptote: the interval separating them approaches zero, but will never reach it," but his image connotes a Sterneian play on the two durations that does not in fact exist in Proust. There is simply the narrative's halt at the point when the hero has discovered the truth and the meaning of his life: at the point, therefore, when this "story of a vocation"—which, let us remember, is the avowed subject of Proustian narrative—comes to an end. The rest, whose outcome is already known to us by the very novel that concludes here, no longer belongs to the "vocation" but to the effort that follows it up, and must therefore be only sketched

---

[38] In particular Louis Martin-Chauffier: "As in memoirs, the man who writes and the man whose life we see are distinct in time, but tend to catch up with each other in the long run; they are moving towards the day when the progress of the hero through his life stops at the table, where the narrator, no longer separated from him in time nor tied to him by memory, invites him to sit down beside him so that both together may write: the End" ("Proust and the Double I," *Partisan Review*, 16 [October 1949], 1012).

[39] Muller, pp. 49–50. Let us remember, however, that certain anticipations (like the last meeting with Odette) cover a part of that "era."

[40] Rousset, p. 144.

in. The subject of the *Recherche* is indeed "Marcel becomes a writer," not "Marcel the writer": the *Recherche* remains a novel of development, and to see it as a "novel about the novelist," like the *Faux Monnayeurs* [*The Counterfeiters*], would be to distort its intentions and above all to violate its meaning; it is a novel about the future novelist. "The continuation," Hegel said, precisely apropos of the Bildungsroman, "no longer has anything novelistic about it." Proust probably would have been glad to apply that formulation to his own narrative: what is novelistic is the quest, the *search* [*recherche*], which ends at the discovery (the revelation), not at the use to which that discovery will afterward be put. The final discovery of the truth, the late encounter with the vocation, like the happiness of lovers reunited, can be only a denouement, not an interim stopping place; and in this sense, the subject of the *Recherche* is indeed a traditional subject. So it is necessary that the narrative be interrupted before the hero overtakes the narrator; it is inconceivable for them both together to write: The End. The narrator's last sentence is when—is *that*—the hero finally reaches his first. The interval between the end of the story and the moment of the narrating is therefore the time it takes the hero to write this book, which is and is not the book the narrator, in his turn, reveals to us in a moment brief as a flash of lightning.

Narrative Levels

When Des Grieux, having reached the end of his narrative, states that he has just sailed from New Orleans to Havre-de-Grâce, then from Havre to Calais to meet his brother who is waiting for him several miles away, the temporal (and spatial) interval that until then separated the reported action from the narrating act becomes gradually smaller until it is finally reduced to zero: the narrative has reached the *here* and the *now*, the story has overtaken the narrating. Yet a distance still exists between the final episodes of the Chevalier's loves and the room in the "Lion d'or" with its occupants, including the Chevalier himself and his host, where after supper he recounts these episodes to the Marquis de Renoncourt: the distance between episodes and inn lies neither in time nor in space, but in the difference between the relations which both the episodes and the inn maintain at that point with Des Grieux's narrative. We will distinguish those relations in a rough and necessarily inadequate way by saying that the episodes of the Chevalier's loves are inside (meaning inside the narrative) and the inn with its occupants is outside. What separates them is less a distance than a sort of threshold represented by the narrating itself, a difference of *level*. The "Lion d'or," the Marquis, the Chevalier in his function as narrator are for us inside a particular narrative, not Des Grieux's but the Marquis's, the *Mémoires d'un homme de qualité;* the return from Louisiana, the trip from Havre to Calais, the Chevalier in his function as hero are inside another narrative, this one Des Grieux's, which is *contained* within the first one, not only in the sense that the first frames it with a preamble and a conclusion (although the latter is missing here), but also in the sense that the narrator of the second narrative is already a character in the first one, and that the act of narrating which produces the second narrative is an event recounted in the first one.

We will define this difference in level by saying that *any event a narrative recounts is at a diegetic level immediately higher than the level at which the narrating act producing this narrative is placed.* M. de Renoncourt's writing of his fictive *Mémoires* is a (literary) act carried out at a first level, which we will call extradiegetic; the events told in those *Mémoires* (including Des Grieux's narrating act) are inside this first narrative, so we will describe them as diegetic, or intradiegetic; the events told in Des Grieux's narrative, a narrative in the second degree, we will call *metadiegetic.*[41] In

---

[41] These terms have already been put forth in my *Figures II*, p. 202. The prefix *meta-* obviously connotes here, as in "metalanguage," the transition to the second degree: the *metanarrative* is a narrative within the narrative, the *metadiegesis* is the universe of this second narrative, as the *diegesis* (according to a now widespread usage) designates the universe of the first narrative. We must admit, however, that this term functions in a way opposite to that of its model in logic and linguistics: metalanguage is a language in which one speaks of another language, so metanarrative should be the first narrative, within which one would tell a second narrative. But it seemed to me that it was better to keep the simplest and most common designation for the first degree, and thus to reverse the direction of interlocking. Naturally, the eventual third degree will be a meta-metanarrative, with its meta-metadiegesis, etc.

the same way, M. de Renoncourt as "author" of the *Mémoires* is extradiegetic: although fictive, he addresses the actual public, just like Rousseau or Michelet; the same Marquis as hero of the same *Mémoires* is diegetic, or intradiegetic, and so also is Des Grieux the narrator at the "Lion d'or," as well as the Manon noticed by the Marquis at the first meeting in Pacy; but Des Grieux the hero of his own narrative, and Manon the heroine, and his brother, and the minor characters, are metadiegetic. These terms (metadiegetic, etc.) designate, not individuals, but relative situations and functions.[42]

The narrating instance of a first narrative is therefore extradiegetic by definition, as the narrating instance of a second (metadiegetic) narrative is diegetic by definition, etc. Let us emphasize the fact that the possibly fictive nature of the first instance does not modify this state of affairs any more than the possibly "real" nature of the subsequent instances does: M. de Renoncourt is not a "character" in a narrative taken charge of by the Abbé Prévost; he is the *fictive author* of *Mémoires*, whose real author, of course, is Prévost, just as Robinson Crusoe is the fictive author of the novel by Defoe that bears his name; subsequently, each of them (the Marquis and Crusoe) becomes a character in his own narrative. Neither Prévost nor Defoe enters the space of our inquiry, which, let us recall, bears on the narrating instance, not on the literary instance. M. de Renoncourt and Crusoe are author-narrators, and as such they are at the same narrative level as their public—that is, as you and me. This is not the case with Des Grieux, who never addresses himself to us, but only to the patient Marquis; and inversely, even if this fictive Marquis had met a real person at Calais (say, Sterne on a journey), this person would nonetheless be diegetic, even though real—just like Richelieu in Dumas, Napoleon in Balzac, or the

---

[42] The same character can, moreover, assume two identical (parallel) narrative functions at different levels: for example, in *Sarrasine*, the extradiegetic narrator himself becomes intradiegetic narrator when he tells his companion the story of Zambinella. Thus he tells us that he tells this story—a story of which he is not the hero: this situation is the exact opposite of the (much more common) one of *Manon*, where the first narrator becomes on the second level the listener of another character who tells his own story. The situation of a *double narrator* occurs only, to my knowledge, in *Sarrasine*.

Princesse Mathilde in Proust. In short, we shall not confound extradiegetic with real historical existence, nor diegetic (or even metadiegetic) status with fiction: Paris and Balbec are at the same level, although one is real and the other fictive, and every day we are subjects of a narrative, if not heroes of a novel.

But not every extradiegetic narrating is necessarily taken up as a literary work with its protagonist an author-narrator in a position to address himself, like the Marquis de Renoncourt, to a public termed such.[43] A novel in the form of a diary (like the *Journal d'un curé de campagne* or the *Symphonie pastorale*) does not in principle aim at any public or any reader, and it is the same with an epistolary novel, whether it include a single letter writer (like *Pamela, Werther*, or *Obermann*, often described as journals disguised as correspondence)[44] or several (like *La Nouvelle Héloïse* or *Les Liaisons dangereuses*). Bernanos, Gide, Richardson, Goethe, Senancour, Rousseau, and Laclos present themselves here simply as "editors," but the fictive authors of these diaries or "letters collected and published by... "—as distinct from Renoncourt, or Crusoe, or Gil Blas—obviously did not look on themselves as "authors." What is more, extradiegetic narrating is not even necessarily handled as written narrating: nothing claims that Meursault or The Unnamable wrote the texts we read as their interior monologues, and it goes without saying that the text of the *Lauriers sont coupés* cannot be anything but a "stream of consciousness"—not written, or even spoken—mysteriously caught and transcribed by Dujardin. It is the nature of immediate speech to preclude any formal determination of the narrating instance which it constitutes.

Inversely, every intradiegetic narrating does not necessarily produce, like Des Grieux's, an oral narrative. It can consist of a written text, like the memoir with no recipient written by Adolphe, or even a fictive literary text, a work within a work, like the "story" of the Curious Impertinent discovered in a cloak bag by the curate in *Don Quixote*, or the novella "L'Ambitieux

---

[43] See the "Notes by the Author" published at the head of *Manon Lescaut*.
[44] There remains, however, an appreciable difference between these "epistolary monodies," as Rousset calls them, and a diary: the difference is the existence of a receiver (even a mute one), and his traces in the text.

par amour" published in a fictive magazine by the hero of *Albert Savarus*, the intradiegetic author of a metadiegetic work. But the second narrative can also be neither oral nor written, and can present itself, openly or not, as an inward narrative (for instance, Jocabel's dream in *Moyse sauvé*) or (more frequently and less supernaturally) as any kind of recollection that a character has (in a dream or not). Thus (and this detail made a strong impression on Proust) the second chapter of *Sylvie* is interrupted by the episode ("memory half dreamed") of Adrienne's song: "I went back to bed and could find no rest there. As I lay between sleeping and waking, my whole youth passed through my memory. . . . I visualized a château from the time of Henry IV."[45] Finally, the second narrative can be handled as a nonverbal representation (most often visual), a sort of iconographic document, which the narrator converts into a narrative by describing it himself (the print representing the desertion of Ariadne, in *The Nuptial Song of Peleus and Thetis*, or the tapestry of the flood in *Moyse sauvé*), or, more rarely, by having another character describe it (like the tableaux of Joseph's life commented on by Amram, also in *Moyse sauvé*).

Metadiegetic Narrative

Second-degree narrative is a form that goes back to the very origins of epic narrating, since Books IX–XII of the *Odyssey*, as we know, are devoted to the narrative Ulysses makes to the assembled Phaeacians. Via Virgil, Ariosto, and Tasso, this technique (which the *Thousand and One Nights* has an enormous investment in, as we know in another connection) enters the novelistic tradition in the baroque period, and a work like *Astrée*, for example, is in large part composed of narratives obtained by one or another character. The practice continues in the

---

[45] So we have there an analepsis which is metadiegetic—obviously not the case of every analepsis. For example, in that same *Sylvie*, the retrospection of chapters 4, 5, and 6 is taken on by the narrator himself and not obtained through the hero's memory: "While the carriage is climbing the slopes, let us recollect the time when I came here so often." Here the analepsis is purely diegetic—or, if we wish to mark more clearly the equality of narrative level, it is *isodiegetic*. (Proust's comments are in *Marcel Proust on Art*, p. 147, and the *Recherche*, RH II, 1038/P III, 919.)

eighteenth century, despite the competition of new forms like the epistolary novel; we certainly see it in *Manon Lescaut*, or *Tristram Shandy*, or *Jacques le fataliste*. And even the advent of realism does not prevent it from surviving in Balzac (*La Maison Nucingen, Autre étude de femme, L'Auberge rouge, Sarrasine, La Peau de chagrin*) and Fromentin (*Dominique*); we can even observe a certain exacerbation of the topos with Barbey, or in *Wuthering Heights* (Isabella's narrative to Nelly, reported by Nelly to Lockwood, noted by Lockwood in his journal), and especially in *Lord Jim*, where the entanglement reaches the bounds of general intelligibility. The formal and historical study of this technique would go well beyond our intention, but for the sake of what follows it is necessary here at least to differentiate the main types of relationships that can connect the metadiegetic narrative to the first narrative, into which it is inserted.

The first type of relationship is direct causality between the events of the metadiegesis and those of the diegesis, conferring on the second narrative an *explanatory* function. It is the Balzacian "this is why," but taken on here by a character, whether the story he tells is someone else's (*Sarrasine*) or, more often, his own (Ulysses, Des Grieux, Dominique). All these narratives answer, explicitly or not, a question of the type "What events have led to the present situation?" Most often, the curiosity of the intradiegetic listener is only a pretext for replying to the curiosity of the reader (as in the expository scenes of classical drama), and the metadiegetic narrative only a variant of the explanatory analepsis. Whence certain discordances between the alleged function and the real function—generally resolved in favor of the latter. For instance, in Book XII of the *Odyssey*, Ulysses interrupts his narrative at the arrival on Calypso's island, although most of his audience does not know what follows; the pretext is that he told it briefly the day before to Alcinous and Arete (Book VII); the real reason is obviously that the reader knows it in detail by the direct narrative in Book V. "It liketh me not twice," says Ulysses, "to tell a plain-told tale":[46] this reluctance is, to begin with, the poet's own.

[46] *Odyssey*, Book XII, ll.452–453, trans. S. H. Butcher and A. Lang (New York: Modern Library, 1950), p. 194.

The second type consists of a purely *thematic* relationship, therefore implying no spatio-temporal continuity between metadiegesis and diegesis: a relationship of contrast (the deserted Ariadne's unhappiness, in the midst of Thetis' joyous wedding) or of analogy (as when Jocabel, in *Moyse sauvé*, hesitates to execute the divine command and Amram tells her the story of Abraham's sacrifice). The famous *structure en abyme*, not long ago so prized by the "new novel" of the 1960's, is obviously an extreme form of this relationship of analogy, pushed to the limits of identity. Thematic relationship can, moreover, when it is perceived by the audience, exert an influence on the diegetic situation: Amram's narrative has as its immediate effect (and, moreover, as its aim) to convince Jocabel; it is an *exemplum* with a function of persuading. We know that regular genres, like the parable or the apologue (the fable), are based on that monitory effect of analogy: before the rebelling populace, Menenius Agrippa tells the story of the *Members* [of the body] *and the Belly;* then, adds Titus Livius, "Drawing a parallel from this to show how *like* was the internal dissension of the bodily members to the anger of the plebs against the Fathers, he prevailed upon the minds of his hearers."[47] In Proust we will find a less curative illustration of this *force of example*.

The third type involves no explicit relationship between the two story levels· it is the act of narrating itself that fulfills a function in the diegesis, independently of the metadiegetic content—a function of distraction, for example, and/or of obstruction. Surely the most illustrious example is found in the *Thousand and One Nights,* where Scheherazade holds off death with renewed narratives, whatever they might be (provided they interest the sultan). We notice that, from the first type to the third, the importance of the narrating instance only grows. In the first type, the relationship (of linking) is direct; it is not via the narrative, which could very well be dispensed with: whether Ulysses tells about it or not, the storm is what cast him up on the shore of Phaeacia, and the only transformation his narrative introduces is of a purely cognitive order. In the second type, the

---

[47] Livy, *From the Founding of the City,* Book II, chap. 32, trans. B. O. Foster (London: Loeb Classical Library, 1925), p. 325.

relationship is indirect, rigorously mediated by the narrative, which is indispensable to the linking: the adventure of the members and the belly calms the populace *on condition* that Menenius tell it to the plebs. In the third type, the relationship is only between the narrating act and the present situation, with the metadiegetic content (almost) not mattering any more than a Biblical message does during a filibuster at the rostrum of the United States Senate. This relationship indeed confirms, if there were a need to, that narrating is an *act* like any other.

Metalepses

The transition from one narrative level to another can in principle be achieved only by the narrating, the act that consists precisely of introducing into one situation, by means of a discourse, the knowledge of another situation. Any other form of transit is, if not always impossible, at any rate always transgressive. Cortazar tells the story of a man assassinated by one of the characters in the novel he is reading;[48] this is an inverse (and extreme) form of the narrative figure the classics called *author's metalepsis*, which consists of pretending that the poet "himself brings about the effects he celebrates,"[49] as when we say that Virgil "has Dido die" in Book IV of the *Aeneid*, or when Diderot, more equivocally, writes in *Jacques le fataliste:* "What would prevent me from *getting the Master married* and *making him a cuckold?*" or even, addressing the reader, "If it gives you pleasure, *let us set* the peasant girl back in the saddle behind her escort, *let us let* them go and *let us come back* to our two travelers."[50] Sterne pushed the thing so far as to entreat the intervention of the reader, whom he beseeched to close the door or help Mr. Shandy get back to his bed, but the principle is the same: any intrusion by the extradiegetic narrator or narratee into the dieget-

---

[48] Cortazar, "Continuidad de los Parques," in *Final del Juego.*

[49] Pierre Fontanier, *Commentaire raisonné sur "Les Tropes" de Dumarsais,* vol. 2 of Dumarsais' *Les Tropes* (1818; repr. Geneva: Slatkine Reprints, 1967), p. 116. *Moyse sauvé* inspires Boileau (*Art poétique,* I, 25–26) with this unsparing metalepsis: "And [Saint Amant], following Moses o'er the sandy plain, / Perished with Pharaoh in the Arabian main" (*The Art of Poetry: The Poetical Treatises of Horace, Vida, and Boileau,* trans. Soame, ed. Albert S. Cook [Boston: Ginn and Co., 1892], p. 160).

[50] Garnier, pp. 495 and 497.

ic universe (or by diegetic characters into a metadiegetic universe, etc.), or the inverse (as in Cortazar), produces an effect of
strangeness that is either comical (when, as in Sterne or Diderot,
it is presented in a joking tone) or fantastic.

We will extend the term *narrative metalepsis*[51] to all these
transgressions. Some of them, as ordinary and innocent as those
of classical rhetoric, play on the double temporality of the story
and the narrating. Here, for example, is Balzac, in a passage
already quoted from *Illusions perdues:* "While the venerable
churchman climbs the ramps of Angoulême, it is not useless to
explain . . . ," as if the narrating were contemporaneous with the
story and had to fill up the latter's dead spaces. This is the very
prevalent model Proust follows when he writes, for example,
"but I have no time left now, *before my departure for Balbec* . . . , to
start upon a series of pictures of society," or "I confine myself at
present, *as the train halts and the porter calls out 'Doncières,'*
'Grattevast,' 'Maineville,' etc., to noting down the particular
memory that the watering-place or garrison town recalls to me,"
or again: *"But it is time to rejoin* the Baron as he advances . . ."[52] Sterne's temporal games, of course, are a bit
bolder, a bit more *literal,* in other words, as when the digressions of Tristram the (extradiegetic) narrator require his father
(in the diegesis) to prolong his nap by more than an hour,[53] but
here, too, the principle is the same.[54] In a certain way, the
Pirandello manner of *Six Characters in Search of an Author* or *Tonight We Improvise,* where the same actors are in turn characters
and players, is nothing but a vast expansion of metalepsis; so is
everything deriving from that manner in the plays of Genet, for
example, and so are the changes of level in the Robbe-Grillet
type of narrative (characters escaped from a painting, a book,
a press clipping, a photograph, a dream, a memory, a fantasy,

[51] *Metalepsis* here forms a system with *prolepsis, analepsis, syllepsis,* and *paralep sis,* with this specific sense: "taking hold of (telling) by changing level."
[52] RH II, 102–103/P II, 742; RH II, 339/P II, 1076; RH II, 530/P III, 216. Or again, RH II, 292/P II, 1011: "Let us for the moment say simply this, *while Albertine waits for me* . . . "
[53] Sterne, *Tristram Shandy,* III, chap. 38, and IV, chap. 2.
[54] I owe the distant revelation of the metaleptic game to this lapse, perhaps a deliberate one, by a history teacher: "We are going to study the Second Empire now from the coup d'état to the Easter vacation."

etc.). All these games, by the intensity of their effects, demonstrate the importance of the boundary they tax their ingenuity to
overstep, in defiance of verisimilitude—a boundary *that is precisely the narrating (or the performance) itself:* a shifting but sacred
frontier between two worlds, the world in which one tells, the
world of which one tells. Whence the uneasiness Borges so well
put his finger on: "Such inversions suggest that if the characters
in a story can be readers or spectators, then we, their readers or
spectators, can be fictitious."[55] The most troubling thing about
metalepsis indeed lies in this unacceptable and insistent
hypothesis, that the extradiegetic is perhaps always diegetic,
and that the narrator and his narratees—you and I—perhaps
belong to some narrative.

A less audacious figure, but one we can connect to metalepsis,
consists of telling as if it were diegetic (as if it were at the same
narrative level as its context) something that has nevertheless
been presented as (or can easily be guessed to be) metadiegetic
in its principle or, if one prefers, in its origin: as if the Marquis de
Renoncourt, after having acknowledged that he has gotten the
story of Des Grieux's loves from Des Grieux himself (or even
after having let Des Grieux speak for several pages), subsequently took back the floor to tell that story himself, no longer
"speaking," Plato would say, "as if he had become Des Grieux."
The prototype of this technique is undoubtedly the *Theaetetus*,
which, as we know, consists of a conversation among Socrates,
Theodorus, and Theaetetus, which Socrates himself told to Eucleides, who tells it to Terpsion. But, says Eucleides, "to avoid in
the written account the tiresome effect of bits of narrative interrupting the dialogue, such as 'and I said' or 'and I remarked'
wherever Socrates was speaking of himself, and 'he asserted' or
'he did not agree,' where he reported the answer," the conversation has been reworded into the form of "a direct conversation
between the actual speakers."[56] These forms of narrating where

[55] Borges, *Other Inquisitions, 1937–1952*, trans. R. Simms (Austin, 1964), p. 46.
[56] Plato, *Theaetetus*, 143 c, in *Plato's Theory of Knowledge: The "Theaetetus" and
the "Sophist" of Plato*, trans. Francis M. Cornford (London: Routledge and Kegan
Paul, 1935), p. 17.

the metadiegetic way station, mentioned or not, is immediately ousted in favor of the first narrator, which to some extent economizes on one (or sometimes several) narrative level(s)— these forms we will call *reduced metadiegetic* (implying: reduced to the diegetic), or *pseudo-diegetic*.

In fact, the reduction is not always obvious; more precisely, the difference between metadiegetic and pseudo-diegetic is not always perceptible in the literary narrative text, which (unlike the cinematographic text) does not have at hand features capable of indicating the metadiegetic nature of a section,[57] except by a shift in person: if M. de Renoncourt took Des Grieux's place to tell the latter's adventures, the substitution would be indicated immediately in the transition from *I* to *he*; but when the hero of *Sylvie* relives in a dream a moment from his youth, nothing allows us to decide whether the narrative is then a narrative of that dream or a direct narrative, beyond the dream instance, of the earlier moment.

From *Jean Santeuil* to the *Recherche*, or The Triumph of the Pseudo-diegetic

After that additional detour, it will be easier for us to characterize the narrative choice Proust made, deliberately or not, in the *Recherche du temps perdu*. But before we can do that we must remember what the choice was in his first large narrative work, or, more precisely, in the first version of the *Recherche*, that is, in *Jean Santeuil*. In that book the narrating instance is split in two: the extradiegetic narrator, who does not have a name (but he is a first hypostasis of the hero, and we see him in situations later assigned to Marcel), is on vacation with a friend at the Bay of Concarneau, the two young men strike up a friendship with a writer named C. (the second hypostasis of the hero), who at their request undertakes each evening to read them the pages he wrote, during the day, of a novel in progress. These fragmentary readings are not transcribed, but some years later, after C.'s

---

[57] Such as the blur, slow motion, voice-off, transition from color to black and white or the reverse, etc. Conventions of this kind, moreover, could have been established in literature (italics, bold-faced type, etc.).

death, the narrator, who has somehow gotten hold of a copy of the novel, decides to publish it: it is *Jean Santeuil,* whose hero is obviously a third outline of Marcel. This domino structure is fairly archaic, differing only in two minor ways from the tradition represented by *Manon Lescaut:* the intradiegetic narrator here does not tell his own story, and his narrative is not oral but written, and even literary, since it involves a novel. We will return later to the first difference, which touches on the problem of "person," but here we must emphasize the second, which, at a period when those techniques were no longer much used, attests to a certain timidity at novelistic writing and an obvious need for "distancing" with respect to this biography of Jean— much closer to autobiography than the *Recherche* is. The narrative splitting in two is further heightened by the literary—and, what is more, fictive (because novelistic)—nature of the metadiegetic narrative.

From this first attempt we should retain the fact that Proust was familiar with the use of "Chinese-box" narrative, and that he had submitted to its temptation. Moreover, he alludes to this technique at one point in *La Fugitive:*

> Novelists sometimes pretend in an introduction that while travelling in a foreign country they have met somebody who has told them the story of a person's life. They then withdraw in favour of this casual acquaintance, and the story that he tells them is nothing more or less than their novel. Thus the life of Fabrice del Dongo was related to Stendhal by a Canon of Padua. How gladly would we, when we are in love, that is to say when another person's existence seems to us mysterious, find some such well-informed narrator! And undoubtedly he exists. Do we not ourselves frequently relate, without any trace of passion, the story of some woman or other, to one of our friends, or to a stranger, who has known nothing of her love-affairs and listens to us with keen interest?[58]

We see that the comment does not concern only literary creation, but extends to the most common narrative activity, such as

[58] RH II, 768/P III, 551.

can be pursued, for example, in Marcel's existence: these narratives told by X to Y apropos of Z are the very fabric of our "experience," a large part of which is narrative in kind.

Those antecedents and that allusion only throw into greater relief the dominant feature of the narrating in the *Recherche,* which is *the almost systematic elimination of metadiegetic narrative.* In the first place, the fiction of the discovered manuscript disappears in favor of a direct narrating in which the narrator-hero openly presents his narrative as a literary work, and thus takes up the role of (fictive) author, like Gil Blas or Crusoe, in immediate contact with the public. Whence the use of the phrase "these volumes" or "this work"[59] to refer to his narrative; whence the editorial "we,"[60] those addresses to the reader,[61] and even this humorous pseudo-dialogue in Sterne's or Diderot's manner: " 'All this,' the reader will remark, 'tells us nothing as to . . . ' It is indeed a pity, gentle reader. And sadder than you think. . . . 'In a word, did Mme. d'Arpajon introduce you to the Prince?' No, but be quiet and let me go on with my story."[62] The fictive novelist of *Jean Santeuil* did not permit himself that much, and this difference measures the progress achieved in emancipating the narrator. Second, metadiegetic insertions are almost completely missing from the *Recherche:* under this heading we can hardly point to anything except Swann's narrative to Marcel about his conversation with the Prince de Guermantes who has converted to Dreyfusism,[63] Aimé's reports about Albertine's past behavior,[64] and above all the narrative assigned to the Goncourts about a dinner at the Verdurins'.[65] We will notice, moreover, that in these three cases the narrating instance is

---

[59] "That invisible vocation of which *these volumes* are the history" (RH I, 1002/P II, 397); "The proportions of *this work* . . . " (RH II, 33/P II, 642); "*this book* in which there is not a single incident which is not fictitious . . . " (RH II, 981/P III, 846).

[60] "*We suppose* M. de Charlus . . . " (RH II, 291/P II, 1010).

[61] "We must warn *the reader* . . . " (RH II, 406/P III, 40); "Before we come back to Jupien's shop, the author would like to say how deeply he would regret it should *any reader* be offended . . . " (RH II, 410/P III, 46).

[62] RH II, 39–40/P II, 651–652.

[63] RH II, 77–82/P II, 705–712.

[64] RH II, 744–745/P III, 515–516; RH II, 750–751/P III, 524–525.

[65] RH II, 880–885/P III, 709–717.

highlighted and competes in importance with the event being related: Swann's naive partiality interests Marcel much more than the Prince's conversion does; Aimé's writing style, with its parentheses and quotation marks, is an imaginary pastiche; and the pseudo-Goncourt, a real pastiche, serves here as a page from literature and a testimony to the vanity of Letters much more than as evidence about the Verdurin salon. For these various reasons it was not possible to *reduce* those metadiegetic narratives, that is, to have the narrator take control of them.

Everywhere else, on the other hand, the narrative in the *Recherche* constantly practices what we have christened the pseudo-diegetic: that is, a narrative second in its origin is immediately brought to the first level and taken charge of, whatever its source might be, by the narrator-hero. Most of the analepses noted in Chapter 1 originate either in memories the hero recalls (and thus in a sort of *inward narrative* in the manner of Nerval) or else in reports made to the hero by a third person. Coming under the first type, for example, are the last pages of the *Jeunes Filles en fleurs,* evoking the sun-bathed mornings of Balbec—but doing so through the memory of them that the hero, back in Paris, has preserved: "What my mind's eye did almost invariably see when I thought of Balbec were the hours which every morning during the fine weather... ";[66] after this the evocation forgets its memory-elicited pretext and to the last line unfolds on its own account as direct narrative, so that many readers do not notice the spatio-temporal detour that gave rise to it and think it a simple isodiegetic "return backward" without a change in narrative level. Also coming under the first type is the return to 1914, during the stay in Paris in 1916, introduced with this sentence: "*I reflected that* it was a long time since I had seen any of the personages who have been mentioned in this work. In 1914, it was true... ";[67] then comes a direct narrative about that first return, as if it were not a memory evoked during the second return, or as if the memory were in this case only a narrative pretext, what Proust precisely calls a "method of tran-

[66] RH I, 712–713/P I, 953.
[67] RH II, 900/P III, 737.

sition." Another example of the first type comes some pages later, where the passage devoted to Saint-Loup's visit,[68] which begins as an isodiegetic analepsis, ends with a sentence which reveals, after the event, its source as memory: "*As I turned over in my mind* this recent meeting with Saint-Loup. . . ." But above all we should remember that *Combray I* is an insomniac's reverie, that *Combray II* is an "involuntary memory" called forth by the taste of the madeleine, and that everything after that, starting with *Un amour de Swann,* is again an evocation of the insomniac. The whole *Recherche* is in fact a huge pseudo-diegetic analepsis in the name of the memories of the "intermediary subject"— memories which the final narrator immediately claims and takes control of.

To the second type (reports made to the hero by a third person) belong all those episodes, evoked in the preceding chapter apropos of the problems of focalization, that took place out of the hero's presence and that the narrator could therefore not be informed of except by an *intermediary narrative.* Examples are the circumstances of Swann's marriage, the negotiations between Norpois and Faffenheim, Bergotte's death, Gilberte's conduct after Swann's death, the missed reception at Berma's.[69] As we have seen, the source of all this information is sometimes stated, sometimes implicit, but in every case Marcel jealously incorporates into his own narrative what he has gotten from Cottard, from Norpois, from the Duchess, or from God knows whom, as if he could not bear to give up to anyone else the slightest part of his narrative privilege.

The most typical and naturally the most important case is *Un amour de Swann.* With respect to its source this episode is doubly metadiegetic, first since the details were reported to Marcel by an undetermined narrator at an undetermined time, and then because Marcel is remembering these details in the course of certain sleepless nights. These are memories of earlier narratives, therefore, from which the extradiegetic narrator once

[68] RH II, 914–919/P III, 756–762.
[69] RH I, 358–361/P I, 467–471; RH I, 899–904/P II, 257–263; RH II, 506–510/P III, 182–188; RH II, 786–792/P III, 574–582; RH II, 1098–1101/P III, 995–998.

again gathers up the whole kitty and in his own name tells this whole story that took place before he was born—not without introducing into it subtle marks of his subsequent existence,[70] which are there like a signature and prevent the reader from forgetting him for too long: a fine example of narrative egocentrism. In *Jean Santeuil* Proust had savored the antiquated pleasures of the metadiegetic, and it is as if he had vowed not to come back to them any more, and to reserve for himself (or for his spokesman) the whole of the narrating function. An *Amour de Swann* told by Swann himself would have compromised this unity of instance and this monopoly by the hero. In the definitive economy of the *Recherche*, Swann, the ex-hypostasis of Marcel,[71] must be no more than an unhappy and imperfect precursor. He therefore has no right to the "floor," that is, to the narrative—and even less (we will come back to this) to the discourse that transmits it, accompanies it, and gives it its meaning. This is why it is Marcel, and only Marcel, who in the final instance, and scorning all the others, must recount that love affair which is not his own.

But which prefigures his (as everyone knows) and to a certain extent brings it to pass. Here again we meet the indirect influence, analyzed above, of certain metadiegetic narratives: Swann's love for Odette in principle has no direct impact on Marcel's fate,[72] and on that ground the classical norm would undoubtedly deem Swann's love purely *episodic;* but on the other hand its indirect impact—that is, the influence of the knowledge Marcel has of that love, gained through a narrative—is considerable, as he himself testifies in this passage from *Sodome:*

[70] "*I* used often to recall to myself when, many years later, *I* began to take an interest in his character because of the similarities which, in wholly different respects, it offered to *my own . . .*" (RH I, 148/P I, 193); "And he did not have (as *I* had, afterwards, at Combray in *my* childhood) . . ." (RH I, 227/P I, 295); "as *I* myself was to go . . .*" (RH I, 228/P I, 297); "*my* grandfather" (RH I, 149, 238/P I, 194, 310); "*my* uncle" (RH I, 239–240/P I, 311–312), etc.

[71] In *Jean Santeuil,* the two characters appear merged; and again in certain sketches of the *Cahiers.* See for example André Maurois, *Proust: Portrait of a Genius,* trans. Gerard Hopkins (New York, 1950), p. 152.

[72] Unless we count as such the very existence of Gilberte, the "fruit" of that love.

I thought then of all that I had been told about Swann's love for Odette, of the way in which Swann had been tricked all his life. Indeed, when I come to think of it, the hypothesis that made me gradually build up the whole of Albertine's character and give a painful interpretation to every moment of a life that I could not control in its entirety, was the memory, the rooted idea of Mme. Swann's character, as it had been *described* to me. These *accounts* helped my imagination, in after years, to take the line of supposing that Albertine might, instead of being a good girl, have had the same immorality, the same faculty of deception as a reformed prostitute, and I thought of all the sufferings that would in that case have been in store for me had I ever really been her lover. [73]

"*These accounts helped* . . . ": it is *because* of the narrative of Swann in love that Marcel will one day be able actually to imagine an Albertine like Odette—unfaithful, given to vice, unattainable—and *consequently* to fall in love with her. We know what happens then. The power of narrative . . .

Let us not forget, after all, that if Oedipus can do what every man, so they say, goes only so far as wishing to do, it is because an oracle *told* in advance that one day he would kill his father and marry his mother: without the oracle, no exile, thus no incognito, thus no parricide and no incest. The oracle in *Oedipus the King* is a metadiegetic narrative in the future tense, the mere uttering of which will throw into gear the "infernal machine" capable of carrying it out. This is not a prophecy that comes true; it is a trap in the form of a narrative, a trap that "takes." Yes, the power (and cunning) of narrative. Some give life (Scheherazade), some take life. And we do not properly understand *Un amour de Swann* unless we realize that this love *told* is an instrument of Destiny.

Person

Readers may have noticed that until now we have used the terms "first-person—or third-person—narrative" only when paired with quotation marks of protest. Indeed, these common locutions seem to me inadequate, in that they stress variation in the element of the narrative situation that is in fact invariant—to

[73] RH II, 147/P II, 804.

wit, the presence (explicit or implicit) of the "person" of the narrator. This presence is invariant because the narrator can be in his narrative (like every subject of an enunciating in his enunciated statement) *only* in the "first person"—except for an enallage of convention as in Caesar's *Commentaries*; and stressing "person" leads one to think that the choice the narrator has to make—a purely grammatical and rhetorical choice—is always of the same order as Caesar's in deciding to write his Memoirs "in" one or another person. In fact, of course, this is not the issue. The novelist's choice, unlike the narrator's, is not between two grammatical forms, but between two narrative postures (whose grammatical forms are simply an automatic consequence): to have the story told by one of its "characters,"[74] or to have it told by a narrator outside of the story. The presence of first-person verbs in a narrative text can therefore refer to two very different situations which grammar renders identical but which narrative analysis must distinguish: the narrator's own designation of himself as such, as when Virgil writes "*I* sing of arms and the man... ," or else the identity of person between the narrator and one of the characters in the story, as when Crusoe writes "*I* was born in the year 1632, in the city of York.... " The term "first-person narrative" refers, quite obviously, only to the second of these situations, and this dissymmetry confirms its unfitness. Insofar as the narrator can at any instant intervene *as such* in the narrative, every narrating is, by definition, to all intents and purposes presented in the first person (even if in the editorial plural, as when Stendhal writes, "*We* will confess that... *we* have begun the story of *our* hero... "). The real question is whether or not the narrator can use the first person to designate *one of his characters*. We will therefore distinguish here two types of narrative: one with the narrator absent from the story he tells (example: Homer in the *Iliad*, or Flaubert in *L'Education sentimen-*

[74] This term [*personnages*]is used here for lack of a more neutral or more extensive term which would not unduly connote, as this one does, the "humanness" of the narrative agent, even though in fiction nothing prevents us from entrusting that role to an animal (*Mémoires d'un âne* [*Memoirs of a Donkey*]) or indeed to an "inanimate" object (I don't know whether we should put into this category the successive narrators of the *Bijoux indiscrets* [*Indiscreet Jewels*]).

tale), the other with the narrator present as a character in the
story he tells (example: *Gil Blas,* or *Wuthering Heights*). I call the
first type, for obvious reasons, *heterodiegetic,* and the second
type *homodiegetic.*

But from the examples selected no doubt a dissymmetry in the
status of these two types already emerges. Homer and Flaubert
are both totally, and therefore *equally,* absent from the two narratives in question; on the other hand, we cannot say that Gil
Blas and Lockwood are equally present in their respective narratives: Gil Blas is incontestably the hero of the story he tells,
Lockwood is incontestably not (and we could easily find examples of even weaker "presence"; I will come back to this
momentarily). Absence is absolute, but presence has degrees.
So will have to differentiate within the homodiegetic type at
least two varieties: one where the narrator is the hero of his
narrative (*Gil Blas*) and one where he plays only a secondary
role, which almost always turns out to be a role as observer and
witness: Lockwood, the anonymous narrator of *Louis Lambert,*
Ishmael in *Moby Dick,* Marlow in *Lord Jim,* Carraway in *The
Great Gatsby,* Zeitblom in *Doctor Faustus*—not to mention the
most illustrious and most representative one of all, the transparent (but inquisitive) Dr. Watson of Conan Doyle.[75] It is as if the
narrator cannot be an ordinary walk-on in his narrative: he can
be only the star, or else a mere bystander. For the first variety
(which to some extent represents the strong degree of the
homodiegetic) we will reserve the unavoidable term *autodiegetic.*

Defined this way, the narrator's relationship to the story is in
principle invariable: even when Gil Blas and Watson
momentarily disappear as characters, we know that they belong
to the diegetic universe of their narrative and that they will
reappear sooner or later. So the reader unfailingly takes the
transition from one status to the other—when he perceives
it—as an infraction of an implicit norm: for instance the (discreet) disappearance of the initial witness-narrator of the *Rouge*

[75] A variant of this type is the narrative with a collective witness as narrator:
the crew of *The Nigger of the "Narcissus,"* the inhabitants of the small town in "A
Rose for Emily." We remember that the opening pages of *Bovary* are written in
this mode.

or *Bovary*, or the (noisier) one of the narrator of *Lamiel*, who openly leaves the diegesis "in order to become a man of letters. Thus, O benevolent reader, farewell; you will hear nothing more of me."[76] An even more glaring violation is the shift in grammatical person to designate the same character: for instance, in *Autre étude de femme*, Bianchon moves all of a sudden from "I" to "he,"[77] as if he were unexpectedly abandoning the role of narrator; for instance, in *Jean Santeuil*, the hero moves inversely from "he" to "I."[78] In the field of the classical novel, and still in Proust, such effects obviously result from a sort of narrative pathology, explicable by last-minute reshufflings and states of textual incompleteness. But we know that the contemporary novel has passed that limit, as it has so many others, and does not hesitate to establish between narrator and character(s) a variable or floating relationship, a pronominal vertigo in tune with a freer logic and a more complex conception of "personality." The most advanced forms of this emancipation[79] are perhaps not the most perceptible ones, because the classical attributes of "character"—proper name, physical and moral "nature"—have disappeared and along with them the signs that direct grammatical (pronominal) traffic. It is undoubtedly Borges who offers us the most spectacular example of this violation— spectacular precisely because it is put down in a completely traditional narrative system, which accentuates the contrast—in the story entitled "The Form of the Sword":[80] the hero begins to tell his vile adventure while identifying himself with his victim, before confessing that he is in fact *the other*, the dastardly informer who until then was dealt with, with all due contempt, in the "third person." Moon himself supplies the "ideological" comment on this narrative technique: "What one man does is

---

[76] Stendhal, *Lamiel* (Paris: Divan, 1948), p. 43. The inverse case, the sudden appearance of an autodiegetic "I" in a heterodiegetic narrative, seems more rare. The Stendhalian "I believe" (*Leuwen*, p. 117, *Chartreuse*, p. 76) can belong to the narrator as such.
[77] Balzac, *Autre étude de femme* (Geneva: Skira), pp. 75–77.
[78] *Jean Santeuil*, Pléiade, p. 319; trans. Hopkins, pp. 118–119.
[79] See for example J. L. Baudry, *Personnes* (Paris: Seuil, 1967).
[80] In *Ficciones*, ed. Anthony Kerrigan (New York: Grove Press, 1962), pp. 117–122.

something done, in some measure, by all men. . . . I am all others, any man is all men." The Borgesian fantastic, in this respect
emblematic of a whole modern literature, does *not accept person.*

I do not intend to stretch Proustian narrating in this direction,
although in Proust the process of the disintegration of "character" is amply (and notoriously) begun. The *Recherche* is fundamentally an autodiegetic narrative, where, as we have seen, the
narrator-hero never, as it were, yields the privilege of the narrative function to anyone. Here what is most important is not the
presence of this completely traditional form, but first the conversion it results from, and next the difficulties it encounters in a
novel like this one.

Since it is a "disguised autobiography," it seems on the whole
quite natural and a matter of course that the *Recherche* should be
a narrative in autobiographical form written "in the first person." This naturalness is obviously deceptive, for Proust's initial
plan, as Germaine Brée suspected in 1948 and as the publication
of *Jean Santeuil* has since confirmed, made no place (except a
preliminary one) for that narrative course. *Jean Santeuil,* let us
remember, is deliberately heterodiegetic in form. Such a detour
prohibits us, then, from looking on the narrative form of the
Recherche as the direct extension of an authentically personal
discourse, whose discordances with respect to the real life of
Marcel Proust would constitute only secondary deviations. "His
use of the first person then," Germaine Brée accurately observes, "was the result of a conscious esthetic choice and not
proof that he considered his work as a confession or an autobiography."[81] To have "Marcel's" life be told by "Marcel"
himself, after having had "Jean's" be told by the writer "C.,"
arises indeed from a narrative choice as distinct, and thus as
significant, as Defoe's choice for *Robinson Crusoe* or Lesage's for
Gil Blas—and even more significant, because of the detour. But
we cannot fail to notice also that that conversion from the heterodiegetic to the autodiegetic accompanies and completes the other
conversion, already mentioned, of the metadiegetic to the diege-

[81] Brée, p. 8.

tic (or pseudo-diegetic). From *Santeuil* to the *Recherche*, the hero could move from "he" to "I" without the stratification of the narrating instances necessarily disappearing: it would be enough for C.'s "novel" to be autobiographical, or even simply auto-diegetic in form. Inversely, the double instance could be reduced without modifying the relationship between hero and narrator: it would be enough to suppress the preamble and begin with something like, "For a long time Marcel had gone to bed early...." We must therefore look at the full significance of the dual conversion enacted by the transition from the narrative system of *Jean Santeuil* to the narrative system of the *Recherche*.

If in every narrative we define the narrator's status both by its narrative level (extra- or intradiegetic) and by its relationship to the story (hetero- or homodiegetic), we can represent the four basic types of narrator's status as follows: (1) *extradiegetic-heterodiegetic*—paradigm: Homer, a narrator in the first degree who tells a story he is absent from; (2) *extradiegetic-homodiegetic*—paradigm: Gil Blas, a narrator in the first degree who tells his own story; (3) *intradiegetic-heterodiegetic*—paradigm: Scheherazade, a narrator in the second degree who tells stories she is on the whole absent from; (4) *intradiegetic-homodiegetic*—paradigm: Ulysses in Books IX-XII, a narrator in the second degree who tells his own story. In this system the (second) narrator of the quasi-totality of the narrative in *Santeuil*, the fictive novelist C., falls into the same category that Scheherazade does as intra-heterodiegetic, and the (single) narrator of the *Recherche* into the diametrically (diagonally) opposite category (whatever arrangement the entries are given) that Gil Blas does, as extra-homodiegetic:

LEVEL: RELATIONSHIP:	*Extradiegetic*	*Intradiegetic*
Heterodiegetic	Homer	Scheherazade C.
Homodiegetic	Gil Blas *Marcel*	Ulysses

We are dealing here with an absolute reversal, since we move from a situation characterized by the complete dissociation of the instances (first and extradiegetic author-narrator: "I"; second narrator, intradiegetic novelist: "C."; metadiegetic hero: "Jean") to the inverse situation, characterized by the merging of all three instances in one single "person": the author-narrator-hero Marcel. Most obviously significant in this turn-around is the late, and deliberate, assumption of the *form* of direct autobiography, which we must immediately connect to the apparently contradictory fact that the narrative content of the *Recherche* is less directly autobiographical than the narrative content of *Santeuil*[82]—as if Proust first had had to conquer a certain adhesion to himself, had to detach himself from himself, in order to win the right to say "I," or more precisely the right to have this hero who is neither completely himself nor completely someone else say "I." So the conquest of the *I* here is not a return to and attendance on himself, not a settling into the comfort of "subjectivity,"[83] but perhaps exactly the opposite: the difficult experience of relating to oneself with (slight) distance and off-centering—a relationship wonderfully symbolized by that barely suggested, seemingly accidental semihomonymy of the narrator-hero and the signatory.[84]

But this explanation clearly pays particular attention to the

---

[82] See Tadić, pp. 20-23.

[83] The famous Proustian "subjectivism" is nothing less than a proof of subjectivity. And Proust himself did not fail to get angry at the too-facile conclusions people drew from his narrative choice: "As I had the misfortune to begin my book with *I* and could not change it anymore, I am 'subjective' in aeternum. If I had begun instead, 'Roger Mauclair was occupying a summer house,' I would be classified 'objective'" (to J. Boulanger, 30 November 1921, *Correspondance générale* [Paris, 1932], III, 278)

[84] On this controversial question, see M. Suzuki, "Le 'je' proustien," *Bulletin de la Société des amis de Marcel Proust*, 9 (1959); Harold Waters, "The Narrator, not Marcel," *French Review*, 33 (February 1960), 389–392; and Muller, pp. 12 and 164–165. We know that the only two occurrences of this first name in the *Recherche* are late (RH II, 429 and 488/P III, 75 and 157), and that the first is not without a reservation. But it seems to me that this is not enough for us to reject it. If we were to contest everything that is said only once . . . On the other hand, naming the hero Marcel is obviously not identifying him with Proust; but this partial and fragile coincidence is highly symbolic.

transition from heterodiegetic to autodiegetic and leaves somewhat in the background the suppression of the metadiegetic
level. The ruthless condensing of instances was perhaps already
underway in those pages of *Jean Santeuil* where the "I" of the
narrator (but which one?) supplanted as if inadvertently the
"he" of the hero: a result of impatience, undoubtedly, but not
necessarily impatience to "express himself" or to "narrate himself" by removing the mask of the novelistic fiction; irritation,
rather, at the obstructions or hindrances that the dissociation of
instances puts in the way of the stance of the discourse—which,
even in *Santeuil*, is not just a narrative discourse. Undoubtedly,
to a narrator so eager to accompany his "story" with that sort of
running commentary that is its underlying justification, nothing
is more annoying than to have to shift "voice" incessantly, narrating the hero's experiences "in the third person" and then
commenting on them in his own name, with a continually repeated and always discordant intrusion. Whence the temptation
to leap over the obstruction, and lay claim to and finally annex
the experience itself, as in the passage where the narrator, after
having told the "feelings recaptured" by Jean when the countryside of Lake Geneva reminds him of the sea at Beg Meil,
continues with his own reminiscences, and his resolution to
write "only of what the past brings suddenly to life in a smell, in
a sight, in what has, as it were, exploded within *me* and set the
imagination quivering, so that the accompanying joy stirs *me* to
inspiration."[85] We see that here we are no longer dealing with
inadvertence: it is the narrative course as a whole chosen for
Santeuil which is revealed as inadequate, and which finally gives
way before the deepest needs and *instances* of the discourse. Such
"accidents" prefigure both the failure (or rather the approaching
abandonment) of *Santeuil* and its later resumption in the right
voice of the *Recherche*, the voice of direct autodiegetic narrating.

But, as we saw in the chapter on mood, this new course itself
is not without problems, since now into a narrative in autobiographical form there has to be integrated a whole social chronicle
that often goes beyond the field of the hero's direct knowledge

[85] *Jean Santeuil*, Pléiade, p. 401; trans. Hopkins, p. 410.

and sometimes, as is the case with *Un amour de Swann*, does not easily enter even the narrator's knowledge. In fact, as B. G. Rogers has shown, the Proustian novel manages only with much difficulty to reconcile two contradictory courses.[86] The first is that of an omnipresent speculative discourse, which barely accommodates itself to classical "objective" narrating and which requires the experience of the hero to merge with the past of the narrator, who will thus be able to comment on it without seeming to intrude (whence the ultimate adoption of a direct autodiegetic narrating where the voices—of hero, narrator, and an author turned toward a public to instruct and persuade—may mingle and blend). The second is that of a comprehensive narrative content that widely overflows the hero's inner experience and at times requires a quasi-"omniscient" narrator (whence the embarrassments and pluralities of focalization we have already met).

The narrative course in *Jean Santeuil* was doubtless untenable, and its abandonment seems to us retrospectively "justified"; the course in the *Recherche* is better suited to the needs of Proustian discourse, but it is not by any means perfectly coherent. In fact, the Proustian plan could be fully satisfied by neither the one nor the other: neither the too-remote "objectivity" of heterodiegetic narrative, which kept the narrator's discourse set apart from the "action" (and thus from the hero's experience), nor the "subjectivity" of autodiegetic narrative, too personal and seemingly too confined to encompass without improbability a narrative content widely overflowing that experience. We are dealing here, let us make clear, with the fictive experience *of the hero*, which Proust, for well-known reasons, wished more limited than his own personal experience. In a sense, nothing in the *Recherche* exceeds Proust's experience, but everything he thought it necessary to assign to Swann, Saint-Loup, Bergotte, Charlus, Mlle. Vinteuil, Legrandin, and many others obviously exceeds Marcel's experience: a deliberate dispersion of the autobiographical "material," which is responsible for certain narrative problems. So—to cite only the two most flagrant paralepses—we can find it strange that Marcel should have had access to Bergotte's final

[86] Rogers, pp. 120–141.

thoughts, but not that Proust should have, since he had "lived" them himself at the Jeu de Paume on a certain day in May 1921; similarly, we can wonder that Marcel should so well read Mlle. Vinteuil's ambiguous feelings at Montjouvain, but much less, I think, that Proust should have been able to ascribe them to her. All this, and a lot more, comes from Proust, and we will not go so far in disdaining the "referent" as to pretend to be unaware of it; but we also know that he wanted to get it off his hands by getting it off his hero's hands. So he needs both an "omniscient" narrator capable of dominating a moral experience which is now *objectivized* and an autodiegetic narrator capable of personally taking up, authenticating, and illuminating by his own commentary the spiritual experience which gives all the rest its ultimate meaning and which, for its part, remains the hero's privilege. Whence that paradoxical—and to some people shameful—situation of a "first-person" narrating that is nevertheless occasionally omniscient. Here again—without wanting to, perhaps unknowingly, and for reasons that result from the profound (and profoundly contradictory) nature of its purpose—the *Recherche* attacks the best-established convention of novelistic narrating by cracking not only its traditional "forms," but also—a more hidden and thus more decisive loosening—the very logic of its discourse.

Hero/Narrator

As in any narrative in autobiographical form,[87] the two *actants* that Spitzer called *erzählendes Ich* (the narrating I) and *erzähltes Ich* (the narrated I) are separated in the *Recherche* by a difference in age and experience that authorizes the former to treat the latter with a sort of condescending or ironic superiority, very noticeable for example in the scene of Marcel's missed introduction to Albertine, or that of the kiss denied.[88] But peculiar to the *Recherche*, distinguishing it from almost all other autobiographies real or fictive, is that added to this essentially variable

---

[87] In question here is classical autobiography, with subsequent narrating, and not interior monologue in the present tense.
[88] RH I, 642–643/P I, 855–856 and RH I, 698–699/P I, 933–934.

difference, inevitably decreasing in proportion as the hero pro-
gresses in "apprenticeship" to life, is a more radical and
seemingly absolute difference that is not reducible simply to
"development": the difference caused by the final revelation,
the decisive experience of involuntary memory and aesthetic
vocation. Here the *Recherche* parts company with the Bildungsroman tradition and approaches certain forms of religious
literature, like Saint Augustine's *Confessions:* the narrator does
not simply know *more*, empirically, than the hero; he *knows* in
the absolute sense, he understands the Truth—a truth which the
hero does not approach with a gradual and continuous movement, but which, quite to the contrary, despite the omens and
notices that have here and there preceded it, rushes in on him at
the very moment when in a certain way he feels himself more
distant than ever from it: "one knocks at all the doors which lead
nowhere, and then one stumbles without knowing it on the only
door through which one can enter—which one might have
sought in vain for a hundred years—and it opens of its own
accord."[89]

This particular characteristic of the *Recherche* involves a crucial
consequence with respect to relations between the hero's discourse and the narrator's. Up until that moment, indeed, these
two discourses had been juxtaposed, interwoven, but, except
for two or three exceptions,[90] never completely merged: the
voice of error and tribulation could not be identified with the
voice of understanding and wisdom—Parsifal's voice with Gur-
nemanz's. On the contrary, starting with the *final revelation* (to
turn inside out the term Proust applied to *Sodome I*), the two
voices can blend and merge, or spell each other in a single

---

[89] RH II, 997/P III, 866.
[90] Usually during moments of aesthetic meditation, apropos of Elstir (RH I,
1017–1020/P II, 419–422), Wagner (RH II, 489–492/P III, 158–162), or Vinteuil (RH
II, 555–559/P III, 252–258), when the hero has a presentiment which will be
confirmed by the final revelation. *Sodome I*, which in one sense is a first revelation scene, also presents features of coincidence between the two discourses, but
there the narrator takes care, at least once, to correct an error of the hero's (RH II,
24–25/P II, 630–631). An inverse exception is the final group of pages in *Swann*,
where it is the narrator who makes a pretense of sharing the point of view of
the character.

speech, since henceforth the hero's *I thought* can be written "I understood," "I observed," "I began to divine," "I was aware," "I knew," "I saw clearly," "the thought came to me," "I had arrived then at the conclusion," "I understood," etc.[91]—that is, can coincide with the narrator's *I know*. Whence that sudden proliferation of indirect discourse, and its alternation with the narrator's present discourse, without opposition or contrast. As we have already noticed, the hero of the matinée is not yet identified with the final narrator *in act,* since the work written by the latter is yet to come for the former; but the two instances have already met in "thought," that is, in speech, since they share the same truth, which now can slip without clashing and the need for correction from one discourse to the other, from one tense (the hero's imperfect) to the other (the narrator's present)—as is made very clear by this final sentence, so supple, so free (so *omnitemporal,* Auerbach would say), a perfect illustration of its own subject:

> But at least, if strength *were granted* me for long enough to accomplish my work, I *should not fail,* even if the result *were* to make them resemble monsters, to describe men first and foremost as occupying a place, a very considerable place compared with the restricted one which *is* allotted to them in space, a place on the contrary immoderately prolonged—for simultaneously, like giants plunged into the years, they *touch* epochs that are immensely far apart, separated by the slow accretion of many, many days—in the dimension of Time.

> Du moins, si elle m'*était laissée* assez longtemps pour accomplir mon oeuvre, ne *manquerais*-je pas d'abord d'y décrire les hommes (cela *dût*-il les faire ressembler à des êtres monstrueux) comme occupant une place si considérable, à côté de celle si restreinte qui leur *est* réservée dans l'espace, une place au contraire prolongée sans mesure—puisqu'ils *touchent* simultanément, comme des géants plongés dans les années, à des époques si distantes, entre lesquelles tant de jours *sont venus* se placer—dans le Temps.

[91] RH II, 999–1023/P III, 869–899.

Functions of the Narrator

That final modification, therefore, involves in a very perceptible way one of the main functions of the Proustian narrator. It
can seem strange, at first sight, to attribute to any narrator a role
other than the actual narrating, the act of telling the story, but in
fact we know well that the narrator's discourse, novelistic or
not, can take on other functions. Perhaps it is worth the trouble
to make a quick survey of them in order to appreciate better the
distinctiveness, in this respect, of Proustian narrating. It seems
to me that we can distribute these functions (rather as Jakobson
distributes the functions of language)[92] in accordance with the
several aspects of narrative (in the broad sense) to which they
are connected.

The first of these aspects is obviously the *story*, and the function connected to it is the properly *narrative function*, which no
narrator can turn away from without at the same time losing his
status as narrator, and to which he can quite well try—as some
American novelists have—to reduce his role. The second aspect
is the narrative *text*, which the narrator can refer to in a discourse that is to some extent metalinguistic (metanarrative, in
this case) to mark its articulations, connections, interrelation-
ships, in short, its internal organization: these "stage directions"
of the discourse,[93] which Georges Blin called "directing indications,"[94] belong to a second function that we can call *directing function*.

The third aspect is the *narrating situation* itself, whose two
protagonists are the narratee—present, absent, or implied—and
the narrator. The function that concerns the narrator's orientation toward the narratee—his care in establishing or maintaining
with the narratee a contact, indeed, a dialogue (actual, as in *La
Maison Nucingen*, or fictive, as in *Tristram Shandy*)—recalls both

---

[92] Roman Jakobson, "Closing Statement: Linguistics and Poetics," in Thomas
A. Sebeok, ed., *Style in Language* (Cambridge, Mass.: M.I.T. Press, 1960), pp.
350–377.
[93] Barthes, "Le Discours de l'histoire," p. 66.
[94] *Regiebemerkungen* (*Stendhal et les problèmes du roman*, p. 222).

Jakobson's "phatic" (verifying the contact) and his "conative" (acting on the receiver) functions. Rogers calls narrators of the Shandian type, always turned toward their public and often more interested in the relationship they maintain with that public than in their narrative itself, "raconteurs."[95] At one time they would have been called "talkers," and perhaps we should name the function they tend to privilege the *function of communication*. We know what importance it acquires in the epistolary novel, and perhaps particularly in those forms that Jean Rousset calls "epistolary monodies," such as, obviously, the *Lettres portuguaises*, where the absent presence of the receiver becomes the dominant (obsessive) element of the discourse.

The narrator's orientation toward himself, finally, brings about a function very homologous with the one Jakobson names, a little unfortunately, the "emotive" function: this is the one accounting for the part the narrator as such takes in the story he tells, the relationship he maintains with it—an affective relationship, of course, but equally a moral or intellectual one. It may take the form simply of an attestation, as when the narrator indicates the source of his information, or the degree of precision of his own memories, or the feelings which one or another episode awakens in him.[96] We have here something which could be called *testimonial function*, or function of *attestation*. But the narrator's interventions, direct or indirect, with regard to the story can also take the more didactic form of an authorized commentary on the action. This is an assertion of what could be called the narrator's *ideological function;*[97] and we know that Balzac, for example, greatly developed this form of explanatory and

---

[95] Rogers, p. 55.

[96] "In writing this I feel my pulse quicken yet; those moments will always be with me, were I to live a hundred thousand years" (Rousseau, *Confessions*, already quoted on pp. 67–68). But the narrator's attestation may also bear on events contemporary with the act of narrating and unconnected to the story he is telling: for example, the pages in *Doctor Faustus* on the war that rages while Zeitblom is writing his memories of Leverkühn.

[97] Which is not necessarily the author's: the judgments of Des Grieux do not a priori commit the Abbé Prévost, and those of the fictive author-narrator of *Leuwen* or the *Chartreuse* by no means commit Henry Beyle.

justificatory discourse—for him, as for so many others, a vehicle of realistic motivation.

These five functions are certainly not to be put into watertight compartments; none of the categories is completely unadulterated and free of complicity with others, none except the first is completely indispensable, and at the same time none, however carefully an author tries, can be completely avoided. It is rather a question of emphasis and relative weight: everyone knows that Balzac "intervenes" in his narrative more than Flaubert, that Fielding addresses the reader more often than Mme. de La Fayette does, that the "directing indications" are more indiscreet in James Fenimore Cooper[98] or Thomas Mann[99] than in Hemingway, etc., but we will not claim to derive some cumbersome typology from that.

Nor will we go back to the various manifestations, already encountered elsewhere, of the Proustian narrator's extranarrative functions: addresses to the reader, organization of the narrative by means of advance notices and recalls, indications of source, memory-elicited attestations. What remains for us to emphasize, here, is the situation of the narrator's quasi-monopoly with regard to what we have christened the ideological function, and the deliberate (nonobligatory) nature of this monopoly. In fact, of all the extranarrative functions, this is the only one that does not of necessity revert to the narrator. We know how careful great ideological novelists like Dostoevski,

---

[98] "It is necessary, in order that the thread of the narrative should not be spun to a length which might fatigue the reader, that he should imagine a week to have intervened between the scene with which the preceding chapter closed and the events with which it is our intention to resume its relation in this"; "It is proper that the course of the narrative should be stayed, while we revert to those causes which have brought in their train of consequences, the singular contest just related. The interruption must necessarily . . ." etc. (James Fenimore Cooper, *The Prairie*, chaps. 8, 15 [New York: Holt, Rinehart and Winston, 1950], pp. 92, 178).

[99] "Since the foregoing section has swollen out of all conscience, I shall do well to begin a new one." "The chapter just finished is also, for my taste, much too extended." "I will not look back, I will take care not to count the pages I have covered between the last Roman numeral and this one I have just written down" (Thomas Mann, *Doctor Faustus*, chaps. 4, 5, 9, trans. H. T. Lowe-Porter [New York: Knopf, 1948], pp. 21, 30, 70).

Tolstoy, Mann, Broch, Malraux were to transfer onto some of their characters the task of commentary and didactic discourse—going so far as to transform such scenes from *The Possessed, The Magic Mountain,* or *L'Espoir* [*Man's Hope*] into veritable colloquia of speculation. Nothing of the sort takes place in Proust, who, other than Marcel, has given himself no "spokesman." A Swann, a Saint-Loup, a Charlus, despite all their intelligence, are objects of observation, not organs of truth or even genuine interlocutors (we know, moreover, what Marcel thinks of the intellectual qualities of conversation and friendship): their errors, their absurdities, their failures and fallings-off are more instructive than their opinions. Even such figures of artistic creation as Bergotte, Vinteuil, or Elstir do not intervene, so to speak, as custodians of an authorized speculative discourse: Vinteuil is mute and Bergotte is reticent or trivial, and the meditation on their work reverts to Marcel;[100] Elstir begins, symbolically, with M. Biche's art-student antics, and the statements he makes at Balbec matter less than the silent teaching of his canvases. Intellectual conversation is a genre plainly contrary to Proustian taste. We know the disdain inspired in him by everything that "thinks"—like, according to him, the Hugo of the early poems, "instead of contenting himself, like Nature, with supplying food for thought."[101] All humanity, from Bergotte to Françoise and from Charlus to Mme. Sazerat, is before him like "Nature," entrusted with provoking thought, not expressing it. An extreme case of intellectual solipsism. Ultimately, and in his own way, Marcel is an autodidact.

The consequence is that no one—except the hero under certain conditions—is able or allowed to contest with the narrator his privilege of ideological commentary: whence the well-known proliferation of this "auctorial" discourse, to borrow from German critics a term which indicates both the presence of the author (actual or fictive) and the sovereign *authority* of that

---

[100] " 'Was this perhaps that happiness which the little phrase of the sonata promised to Swann and which he, because he was *unable* to find it in artistic creation, *mistakenly* assimilated to the pleasures of love . . . ' "(RH II, 1006/P III, 877).

[101] RH I, 1107/P II, 549.

presence in his work. The quantitative and qualitative importance of this psychological, historical, aesthetic, metaphysical
discourse is such, despite the denials,[102] that we can undoubtedly attribute to it the responsibility—and in one sense the
credit—for the strongest shock given in this work, and by this
work, to the traditional equilibrium of novelistic form. If the
Recherche du temps perdu is experienced by everyone as being
"not completely a novel any more" and as the work which, at its
level, concludes the history of the genre (of the genres) and,
along with some others, inaugurates the limitless and indefinite
space of modern *literature*, the cause is obviously—and this time
too despite the "author's intentions" and through the effect of a
movement all the more irresistible because involuntary—this in-
vasion of the story by the commentary, of the novel by the
essay, of the narrative by its own discourse.

The Narratee

Such speculative imperialism, such certainty of truth, could
lead one to think that the receiver's role here is purely passive,
that he is limited to receiving a message he must take or leave
and to "consuming" after the event a work that was completed
far from him and without him. Nothing would be more contrary
to Proust's convictions, to his own experience of reading, and to
the most powerful demands of his work.

Before considering this final dimension of the Proustian narrating instance we must say a more general word about this
personage that we have called the narratee, and whose function
in the narrative seems so variable. Like the narrator, the narratee
is one of the elements in the narrating situation, and he is necessarily located at the same diegetic level; that is, he does not
merge a priori with the reader (even an implied reader) any
more than the narrator necessarily merges with the author.

To an intradiegetic narrator corresponds an intradiegetic nar-

---

[102] "Hence the temptation for the writer to write intellectual works, which is,
however, a gross mistake. A work in which there are theories is like an object
which still has the ticket that shows its price" (RH II, 1009/P III, 882). Doesn't the
reader of the *Recherche* know what it costs?

ratee; and the narrative of Des Grieux or Bixiou is not addressed to the reader of *Manon Lescaut* or of *La Maison Nucingen*, but indeed only to M. de Renoncourt, only to Pinot, Couture, and Blondet; they alone are designated by the "second-person" marks present on occasion in the text, just as the "second-person" marks we find in an epistolary novel can designate only the epistolary correspondent. We, the readers, cannot identify ourselves with those fictive narratees anymore than those intradiegetic narrators can address themselves to us, or even assume our existence.[103] For we can neither interrupt Bixiou nor write to Mme. de Tourvel.

The extradiegetic narrator, on the other hand, can aim only at an extradiegetic narratee, who merges with the implied reader and with whom each real reader can identify. This implied reader is in principle undefined, although Balzac does turn particularly sometimes toward a reader from the provinces, sometimes toward a Parisian reader, and Sterne sometimes calls him Madam or Sir Critick. The extradiegetic narrator can also pretend, like Meursault, to address no one, but this posture— fairly widespread in the contemporary novel—obviously cannot change the fact that a narrative, like every discourse, is necessarily addressed to someone and always contains below the surface an appeal to the receiver. And if the existence of an intradiegetic narratee has the effect of keeping us at a distance, since he is always interposed between the narrator and us— as Finot, Couture, and Blondet are interposed between Bixiou and the nosy listener behind the partition, for whom that narrative was not intended (but, Bixiou says, "there is always someone off to the side")—it is also true that the more transparent the receiving instance and the more silent its evocation in the narrative, so undoubtedly the easier, or rather the more irresistible, each real reader's identification with or substitution for that implied instance will be.

It is indeed this relationship—despite some rare and fully

---

[103] A special case is the metadiegetic literary work, of the *Curious Impertinent* or *Jean Santeuil* kind, which can possibly aim at a reader, but a reader who in principle is himself fictive.

needless challenges we have already called attention to—that the *Recherche* maintains with its readers. Every one of them knows himself to be the implied—and anxiously awaited— narratee of this swirling narrative that, in order to exist in its own truth, undoubtedly needs, more than any other narrative does, to escape the closure of "final message" and narrative completion, to resume endlessly the circular movement from the work to the vocation it "tells" and from the vocation back to the work it gives rise to, and so on unceasingly.

As the very terms of the famous letter to Rivière make clear,[104] the "dogmatism" and "structure" of the Proustian work do not dispense with a continual resort to the reader, who is entrusted not only with "guessing" them before they are expressed, but also, once they have been revealed, with interpreting them and placing them back into the movement which both generates them and carries them off. Proust could not exempt himself from the rule he enunciates in the *Temps retrouvé*, a rule granting the reader the right to translate the universe of the work into his own terms in order then to "give to what he is reading its full general import": whatever apparent infidelity they commit, "in order to read with understanding many readers require to read in their own particular fashion, and the author must not be indignant at this; on the contrary, he must leave the reader all possible liberty," because the work is ultimately, according to Proust himself, only an optical instrument the author offers the reader to help him read within himself. "For it is only out of habit, a habit contracted from the insincere language of prefaces and dedications, that the writer speaks of 'my reader.' In reality every reader is, while he is reading, the reader of his own self."[105]

Such is the vertiginous status of the Proustian narratee: invited not, like Nathanaël, to "throw this book away,"[106] but to rewrite it, being totally unfaithful and wonderfully exact, like

---

[104] "At last I find a reader who *guesses* that my book is a dogmatic work and a structure!" (*Choix de lettres*, p. 197).

[105] RH II, 1031–1032/P III, 910–911.

[106] [Translator's note.] Nathanaël is the character addressed by the "first-person" narrator of Gide's *Les Nourritures terrestres* (*The Fruits of the Earth*).

Pierre Menard inventing *Quixote* word for word.[107] Everyone understands what is expressed by that fable, circulated from Proust to Borges and from Borges to Proust, and illustrated perfectly in the small adjoining drawing rooms of *La Maison Nucingen:* the real author of the narrative is not only he who tells it, but also, and at times even more, he who hears it. And who is not necessarily the one it is addressed to: there are always people *off to the side.*

[107] [Translator's note.] In Borges's story "Pierre Menard, Author of *Don Quixote.*"

Afterword

To conclude without useless recapitulations, here are some words of self-criticism, or, if one likes, of excuse. The categories and procedures put forward here are certainly not faultless in my eyes: it has been a question, as it often is, of choosing between drawbacks. In an area we regularly grant to intuition and empiricism, the proliferation of concepts and terms will doubtless have annoyed more than one reader, and I do not expect "posterity" to retain too large a part of these propositions. This arsenal, like any other, will inevitably be out of date before many years have passed, and all the more quickly the more seriously it is taken, that is, debated, tested, and revised with time. One of the characteristics of what we can call *scientific effort* is that it knows itself to be essentially decaying and doomed to die out: a wholly negative trait, certainly, and one rather melancholy to reflect on for the "literary" mind, always inclined to count on some posthumous glory; but if the critic can dream of an achievement in the second degree, the poetician for his part knows that he labors in—let us say rather *at*—the ephemeral, a worker aware of becoming un-worked.

Therefore I think, and hope, that all this technology—prolepses, analepses, the iterative, focalizations, paralipses, the metadiegetic, etc.—surely barbaric to the lovers of belles lettres, tomorrow will seem positively rustic, and will go to join other packaging, the detritus of Poetics; let us only hope that it will not be abandoned without having had some transitory usefulness. Occam, already uneasy about the progress of intellectual pollution, forbade us ever needlessly to invent creatures of reason—today we would say theoretical objects. I would be annoyed with myself if I fell short of this rule, but it seems to me that at least some of the literary forms designated and defined here call for further investigations, which for obvious reasons were not more than touched on in this work. So I hope to have furnished the theory of literature and the history of literature with some objects of study that are no doubt minor, but a little trimmer than the traditional entities, such as "the novel" or "poetry."

The specific application of these categories and procedures to the *Recherche du temps perdu* was perhaps even more offensive, and I cannot deny that the purpose of my work is defined almost exactly by the opposite view to what is expressed in the preliminary statement of a recent, excellent study on the art of the novel in Proust, a statement which no doubt meets immediately with the unanimous acceptance of well-thinking people:

> We did not want to impose on Proust's work categories external to it, or a general idea of the novel or of the way in which one should study a novel; we did not want a treatise on the novel, with illustrations taken from the *Recherche*, but concepts arising from the work, and allowing us to read Proust as he read Balzac and Flaubert. The only theory of literature is in criticism of the particular.[1]

We can certainly not maintain that here we are using concepts exclusively "arising from the work," and the description here of Proustian narrative can hardly be considered to conform to Proust's own idea of it. Such a gap between *indigenous theory* and critical method might seem inappropriate, like all anachronisms. It seems to me, however, that one should not rely blindly on the explicit aesthetics of a writer, even if he is a critic as inspired as the author of the *Contre Sainte-Beuve*. The aesthetic consciousness of an artist, when he is major, is so to speak never at the level of his practice, and this is only one manifestation of what

[1] Tadié, *Proust et le roman*, p. 14.

Hegel symbolized by the late flight of Minerva's owl. We do not have at our disposal one hundredth of Proust's genius, but we do have the advantage over him (which is a little like the live donkey's advantage over the dead lion) of reading him precisely from the vantage point of what he contributed to fathering (fathering that modern literature which owes him so much) and thus the advantage of perceiving clearly in his work what was there only in its nascent state—all the more nascent because with him the transgression of norms, the aesthetic invention, are most often, as we have seen, involuntary and sometimes unconscious. His goal was otherwise, and this scorner of the avant-garde is almost always a revolutionary despite himself (I would certainly say that that is the best way to be one if I didn't have the faint suspicion that it is the only way). To repeat it once more and following so many others, we read the past by the light of the present, and is not that how Proust himself read Balzac and Flaubert, and does one really believe that his were critical concepts "arising from" the *Comédie humaine* or the *Education sentimentale?*

In the same way, perhaps, the sort of *scanning* "imposed" here on the *Recherche* has allowed us, I hope, to reveal in that novel, under this new lighting, some aspects that Proust himself, and until now Proustian criticism, often overlooked (the importance of iterative narrative, for example, or of the pseudo-diegetic), or has allowed us to characterize more precisely features already spotted, such as anachronies or multiple focalizations. The "grid" which is so disparaged is not an instrument of incarceration, of bringing to heel, or of pruning that in fact castrates: it is a procedure of discovery, and a way of describing.

That does not mean—as readers may already have noticed that its user forbids himself all preference and all aesthetic evaluation, or even all bias. It has no doubt become evident, in this comparison of Proustian narrative with the general system of *narrative possibilities*, that the analyst's curiosity and predilection went regularly to the most *deviant* aspects of Proustian narrative, the specific transgressions or beginnings of a future development. This systematic valuing of originality and innovation is perhaps somewhat unsophisticated and altogether romantic as well, but today no one can entirely escape it. Roland Barthes in *S/Z* gives a highly convincing justification of it: "Why is the writerly [what can be written today] our value? Because the goal of literary work (of literature as work) is to make the reader no longer a consumer, but a producer of the text."[2] The preference for what, in Proust's text, is not only "readerly" (classical) but "writerly" (let us roughly interpret: *modern*) perhaps expresses the critic's desire, or even the poetician's, when in contact with the aesthetically "subversive" points of the text, to play a role vaguely more active than simply that of observer and analyst. The reader, here, believes he is participating in and to a minute extent (minute, but decisive) *contributing* to creation; and perhaps, by recognition alone—or rather by bringing to light features which the work invented, often without its author's knowledge—in reality he is. This contribution, or even this intervention, was, again let us remember, a little more than legitimate in Proust's eyes. The poetician for his part is also the "reader of his own self," and to discover is always (as modern science *also* tells us) somewhat to invent.

Another choice made, in this case a choice refused, will perhaps explain why this "conclusion" is not one—I mean: why readers will not find here a final "synthesis" in which all the characteristic features of Proustian narrative noted in the course of this study will meet and justify themselves to each other. When such convergences or correlations appear unchallengeable (for example, between the disappearance of summary and the emergence of the iterative, or between polymodality and the elimination of the metadiegetic), we have not failed to acknowledge them and to elucidate them. But it would be unfortunate, it seems to me, to seek "unity" at any price, and in that way to *force* the work's coherence—which is, of course, one of criticism's strongest temptations, one of its most ordinary (not to say most common) ones, and also one most easy to satisfy, since all it requires is a little interpretative rhetoric.

Now, if we cannot deny in Proust the will for coherence and the striving for design, just as undeniable in his work is the

2 Barthes, *S/Z*, p. 4.

resistance of its matter and the part played by what is uncontrolled—perhaps uncontrollable. We have already noted the *retroactive* nature (here as in Balzac or Wagner) of a unity belatedly won over material that was heterogeneous and not originally in harmony. Just as obvious is the part played by the incompletion due to the somewhat supplementary labor which the accidental stay of 1914 brought to the work. The *Recherche du temps perdu* was, without doubt, at least in Proust's mind, a "finished" work: that was in 1913, and the perfect ternary composition of that period (*Côté de chez Swann, Côté de Guermantes, Temps retrouvé*) bears witness to it in its own way. But we know what happened to it, and no one can claim that the present structure of the *Recherche* is the result of anything other than circumstances: one active cause, the war, and one negative cause, death. Nothing, certainly, is easier than to justify the action of chance and "demonstrate" that the *Recherche* finally, on November 18, 1922, found the perfect balance and the exact proportion which had been missing until then, but it is just this easy way out that we are rejecting here. If the *Recherche* was complete once, it is not so anymore, and the way in which it admitted the extraordinary later expansion perhaps proves that that temporary completion was, like all completion, only a retrospective illusion. We must restore this work to its sense of unfulfillment, to the shiver of the indefinite, to the breath of the *imperfect*. The *Recherche* is not a closed object: it is not an object.

Here again, no doubt Proust's (involuntary) practice goes beyond his theory and his plan—let us say at least that it corresponds better to our desire. The harmonious triptych of 1913 has doubled its area, but on one side only, the first panel necessarily remaining consistent with the original blueprint. This imbalance, or decentering, pleases us as it is and in its *unpremeditatedness*; and we will be very careful not to motivate it by "explaining" a nonexistent closure and an illusory design, and not to reduce improperly what Proust, apropos of something else, called the "contingency of the narrative."[3] Laws of Proustian narrative are, like that narrative itself, partial, defective, perhaps

---

[3] *Jean Santeuil*, Pléiade, p. 314. [Translator's note: my translation; the Hopkins translation, which is very free, is on p. 115.]

foolhardy: quite empirical and common laws which we should not hypostatize into a Canon. Here the code, like the message, has its gaps and its surprises.

But undoubtedly this rejection of motivation is in its own way a motivation. We do not escape the pressure of the signified: the semiotic universe abhors a vacuum, and to *name* contingency is already to assign it a function, to give it a meaning. Even—or especially?—when he is silent, the critic says too much. Perhaps the best thing would be, as with Proustian narrative itself, never to "finish," which is, in one sense, never to start.

Bibliography

Works by Proust

A la recherche du temps perdu. Ed. Pierre Clarac and André Ferré. 3 vols. Paris: La Pléiade, Gallimard, 1954. (Tr. *Remembrance of Things Past.* Trans. C. K. Scott Moncrieff and Andreas Mayor. 2 vols. New York: Random House, 1934, 1970.)

Jean Santeuil, preceded by *Les Plaisirs et les jours.* Ed. Pierre Clarac and Yves Sandre. Paris: La Pléiade, Gallimard, 1971. (Tr. *Jean Santeuil.* Trans. Gerard Hopkins. New York: Simon & Schuster, 1956. Tr. *Pleasures and Regrets.* Trans. Louise Varèse. New York: Crown, 1948.)

Contre Sainte-Beuve, preceded by *Pastiches et mélanges* and followed by *Essais et articles.* Ed. Pierre Clarac and Yves Sandre. Paris: La Pléiade, Gallimard, 1971. (Tr. [*Contre Sainte-Beuve*] *Marcel Proust on Art and Literature, 1896–1919.* Trans. Sylvia Townsend Warner. New York: Meridian, 1958. Tr. [selections from *Pastiches* and *Essais*] *Marcel Proust: A Selection from His Miscellaneous Writings.* Trans. Gerard Hopkins. London: Allan Wingate, 1948.)

Correspondance générale. Paris: Plon, 1930–1936.

Choix de lettres. Ed. Philip Kolb. Paris: Plon, 1965.

For various rough drafts or variants of the *Recherche,* see the following:

Du côté de chez Swann. Paris: Grasset, 1913.

Chroniques. Paris: Gallimard, 1927.

Contre Sainte-Beuve, followed by *Nouveaux Mélanges.* Ed. Bernard de Fallois. Paris: Gallimard, 1954.

Textes retrouvés. Ed. Philip Kolb and L. B. Price. Urbana: University of Illinois Press, 1968. And *Cahiers Marcel Proust.* Paris: Gallimard, 1971.

André Maurois. *A la recherche de Marcel Proust.* Paris: Hachette, 1949. (Tr. *Proust: Portrait of a Genius.* Trans. Gerard Hopkins. New York: Harper, 1950.)

Maurice Bardèche. *Marcel Proust romancier.* Vol. I. Paris: Les Sept Couleurs, 1971.

Critical and Theoretical Studies

Aristotle. *Poetics.*

Auerbach, Erich. *Mimesis: The Representation of Reality in Western Literature.* Trans. Willard Trask. 1953; rpt. Garden City, N.Y.: Anchor-Doubleday, 1957.

Balzac, Honoré de. *Etudes sur M. Beyle.* 1840; rpt. Geneva: Skira, 1943.

Bardèche, Maurice. *Marcel Proust romancier.* Vol. I. Paris: Les Sept Couleurs, 1971.

 Barthes, Roland. "Introduction à l'analyse structurale des récits." *Communications,* 8. (Tr. "An Introduction to the Structural Analysis of Narrative." *NLH,* 6 [Winter 1975], 237–272.)

———. "Le Discours de l'histoire." *Information sur les sciences sociales,* August 1967.

———. "L'Effet de réel." *Communications,* 11 (1968).

———. *S/Z.* Paris: Seuil, 1970. (Tr. *S/Z.* Trans. Richard Miller. New York: Hill and Wang, 1974.)

Bentley, Phyllis. "Use of Summary." In *Some Observations on the Art of Narrative.* 1947. Rpt. in *The Theory of the Novel.* Ed. Philip Stevick. New York: Free Press, 1967, pp. 47–52.

Benveniste, Emile. *Problèmes de linguistique générale.* Paris: Gallimard, 1966. (Tr. *Problems in General Linguistics.* Trans. Mary Elizabeth Meek. Coral Gables, Fla.: University of Miami Press, 1971.)

Blin, Georges. *Stendhal et les problèmes du roman.* Paris: Corti, 1954.

Booth, Wayne. "Distance and Point of View." *Essays in Criticism,* 11 (1961), 60–79. (Tr. "Distance et point de vue." *Poétique,* 4 [1970].)

———. *The Rhetoric of Fiction.* Chicago: University of Chicago Press, 1961.

Borges, Jorge Luis. *Discussions.* Paris: Gallimard, 1966.

———. *Other Inquisitions, 1937–1952.* Trans. Ruth L. C. Simms. Austin: University of Texas Press, 1964.

Bowling, Lawrence E. "What Is the Stream of Consciousness Technique?" *PMLA,* 65 (1950), 333–345.

Brée, Germaine. *Du temps perdu au temps retrouvé.* 1950; rpt. Les Belles Lettres, 1969. (Tr. *Marcel Proust and Deliverance from Time.* Trans. C. J. Richards and A. D. Truitt. 2d ed. New Brunswick, N.J.: Rutgers University Press, 1969.)

Brooks, Cleanth, and Robert Penn Warren. *Understanding Fiction*. New York: Crofts, 1943.

Daniel, Georges. *Temps et mystification dans A.L.R.T.P.* Paris: Nizet, 1963.

Debray-Genette, Raymonde. "Les Figures du récit dans *Un coeur simple*." *Poétique*, 3 (1970).

——. "Du mode narratif dans les *Trois Contes*." *Littérature*, 2 (May 1971).

Dujardin, Edouard. *Le Monologue intérieur*. Paris: Messein, 1931.

Feuillerat, Albert. *Comment Proust a composé son roman*. New Haven: Yale University Press, 1934.

Fitch, Brian T. *Narrateur et narration dans "l'Etranger" d'Albert Camus*. Paris: Archives des Lettres modernes, No. 34, 1961. 2d rev. ed., 1968.

Forster, E. M. *Aspects of the Novel*. London: Edward Arnold, 1927.

Friedman, Melvin. *Stream of Consciousness: A Study in Literary Method*. New Haven: Yale University Press, 1955.

Friedman, Norman. "Point of View in Fiction." *PMLA*, 70 (1955). Rpt. in *The Theory of the Novel*. Ed. Philip Stevick. New York: Free Press, 1967, pp. 108–137.

Genette, Gérard. *Figures*. Paris: Seuil, 1966.

——. *Figures II*. Paris: Seuil, 1969.

Greimas, A. J. *Sémantique structurale*. Paris: Larousse, 1966.

Guiraud, Pierre. *Essais de stylistique*. Paris: Klincksieck, 1971.

Hachez, Willy. "La Chronologie et l'âge des personnages de *A.L.R.T.P.*" Bulletin de la Société des amis de Marcel Proust, 6 (1956).

——. "Retouches à une chronologie." *BSAMP*, 11 (1961).

——. "Fiches biographiques de personnages de Proust." *BSAMP*, 15 (1965).

Hamburger, Käte. *Die Logik der Dichtung*. Stuttgart: Ernst Klett Verlag, 1957. (Tr. *The Logic of Literature*. Trans. Marilynn J. Rose. 2d. rev ed. Bloomington: Indiana University Press, 1973.)

Houston, J. P. "Temporal Patterns in *A.L.R.T.P.*" *French Studies*, 16 (January 1962), 33–44.

Huet, J. B. *Traité de l'origine des romans*. 1670.

Humphrey, Robert. *Stream of Consciousness in the Modern Novel*. Berkeley: University of California Press, 1954.

Jakobson, Roman. "Quest for the Essence of Language." *Diogenes*, 51 (Fall 1965), 21–37.

Jauss, H. R. *Zeit und Erinnerung in Marcel Prousts A.L.R.T.P.* 1965; rpt. Heidelberg: Carl Winter, 1970.

Lämmert, Eberhart. *Bauformen des Erzählens*. Stuttgart: J. B. Metzlersche Verlag, 1955.

Lefebve, Maurice-Jean. *Structure du discours de la poésie et du récit*. Neuchâtel: La Baconnière, 1971.

Lips, Marguerite. *Le Style indirect libre*. Paris: Payot, 1926.

Lubbock, Percy. *The Craft of Fiction*. London, 1921; rpt. New York: Viking, 1957.

Martin-Chauffier, Louis. "Proust et le double 'Je' de quatre personnes." In *Problèmes du roman (Confluences)*. 1943. Partially rpt. in *Les Critiques de notre temps et Proust*. Ed. Jacques Bersani. Paris: Garnier, 1971, pp. 54–66. (Tr. "Proust and the Double I." *Partisan Review*, 16 [October 1949], 1011–1026.)

Maurois, André. *A la recherche de Marcel Proust*. Paris: Hachette, 1949. (Tr. *Proust: Portrait of a Genius*. Trans. Gerard Hopkins. New York: Harper, 1950.)

Mendilow, A. A. *Time and the Novel*. New York: Humanities Press, 1952.

Metz, Christian. *Essais sur la signification au cinéma*. Vol. I. Paris: Klincksieck, 1968. (Tr. *Film Language: A Semiotics of the Cinema*. Trans. Michael Taylor. New York: Oxford University Press, 1974.)

Müller, Gunther. "Erzählzeit und erzählte Zeit." In *Festschrift für P. Kluckhohn und Hermann Schneider*. 1948. Rpt. in *Morphologische Poetik*. Tübingen, 1968.

Muller, Marcel. *Les Voix narratives dans A.L.R.T.P.* Geneva: Droz, 1965.

Painter, George D. *Proust: The Early Years* and *Proust: The Later Years*. New York: Atlantic–Little, Brown, 1959 and 1965. (Tr. Paris: Mercure, 1966.)

Picon, Gaëtan. *Malraux par lui-même*. Paris: Seuil, 1953.

Plato. *Republic*.

Pouillon, Jean. *Temps et roman*. Paris: Gallimard, 1946.

Raible, Wolfgang. "Linguistik und Literaturkritik." *Linguistik und Didaktik*, 8 (1971).

Raimond, Michel. *La Crise du roman, des lendemains du naturalisme aux années 20*. Paris: Corti, 1966.

Ricardou, Jean. *Problèmes du nouveau roman*. Paris: Seuil, 1967.

Richard, Jean-Pierre. "Proust et l'objet herméneutique." *Poétique*, 13 (1973).

Rogers, Brian G. *Proust's Narrative Techniques*. Geneva: Droz, 1965.

Romberg, Bertil. *Studies in the Narrative Technique of the First-Person Novel*. Trans. Michael Taylor and Harold H. Borland. Stockholm: Almqvist and Wiksell, 1962.

Rossum-Guyon, Françoise van. "Point de vue ou perspective narrative." *Poétique*, 4 (1970).

———. *Critique du roman*. Paris: Gallimard, 1970.

Rousset, Jean. *Forme et signification*. Paris: Corti, 1962.

Sartre, Jean-Paul. "M. François Mauriac et la liberté." 1939. In *Situations I*. Paris: Gallimard, 1947. (Tr. "François Mauriac and Freedom." In *Literary and Philosophical Essays*. Trans. Annette Michelson. New York: Criterion Books, 1955, pp. 7–23.)

———. *L'Idiot de la famille*. Paris: Gallimard, 1971.

Spitzer, Leo. "Zum Stil Marcel Prousts." In *Stilstudien*. Munich: Hueber, 1928. (Tr. "Le Style de Marcel Proust." In *Etudes de style*. Paris: Gallimard, 1970.)

Stang, Richard. *The Theory of the Novel in England, 1850-1870*. New York: Columbia University Press, 1959.

Stanzel, F. K. *Die typischen Erzählsituationen in Roman*. Vienna: Wilhelm Braumüller, 1955. (Tr. *Narrative Situations in the Novel: Tom Jones, Moby-Dick, The Ambassadors, Ulysses*. Trans. James P. Pusack. Bloomington: Indiana University Press, 1971.)

Tadié, Jean-Yves. *Proust et le roman*. Paris: Gallimard, 1971.

Todorov, Tzvetan. "Les Catégories du récit littéraire." *Communications*, 8 (1966).

———. *Littérature et signification*. Paris: Larousse, 1967.

———. "Poétique." In *Qu'est ce que le structuralisme?* Paris: Seuil, 1968.

———. *Grammaire du Décaméron*. The Hague: Mouton, 1969.

———. *Poétique de la prose*. Paris: Seuil, 1971. (Tr. *The Poetics of Prose*. Trans. Richard Howard. Ithaca, N.Y.: Cornell University Press; London: Blackwell, 1977.)

———. "La Poétique en U.R.S.S." *Poétique* 9 (1972).

Uspenski, Boris. *Poetika Kompozicii*. Moscow, 1970. (Tr. *A Poetics of Composition: The Structure of the Artistic Text and Typology of a Compositional Form*. Trans. Valentina Zavarin and Susan Wittig. Berkeley: University of California Press, 1973.) See also "Poétique de la composition." *Poétique*, 9 (1972).

Vigneron, Robert. "Genèse de *Swann*." *Revue d'histoire de la philosophie*, January 1937, pp. 67–115.

———. "Structure de *Swann*: Balzac, Wagner et Proust." *French Review*, 19 (May 1946), 370–384.

———. "Structure de *Swann*: prélentions et defaillances." *MP*, 44 (November 1946), 102–128.

———. "Structure de *Swann*: Combray ou le cercle parfait." *MP*, 45 (February 1948), 185–207.

Waters, Harold. "The Narrator, Not Marcel." *French Review*, 33 (February 1960), 389–392.

Wellek, René, and Austin Warren. *Theory of Literature*. New York: Harcourt Brace, 1949. (Tr. *La Théorie littéraire*. Paris: Seuil, 1971.)

Zeraffa, Michel. *Personne et personnage, le romanesque des années 1920 aux années 1950*. Paris: Klincksieck, 1969.

Index

Voice: narrative level (*cont.*)
diegetic—236-237, in Proust, 237-243, and metalepsis, 236-237, defined, 237, 240, and analepsis, 240-241, and person, 237, 247-248; metalepsis, 101n, 234-237; and immediate speech, 230; and analepsis, 231n; and status of narrator, 248; and narratee, 259-260
—person, 238, 243-247, in Proust, 247-254; defined, 215; and narrative level, 237, 247-248; shifts in, 246; narrator—and duration, 157, and mood, 211, and author, 212-213, 259, first-person, and final convergence, 221, not equivalent to hero, 223, homodiegetic, 245, heterodiegetic, 245, autodiegetic, 245, status defined and discussed, 248, and focalization, 251-252, functions of, 255-259; narratee—215n, 259-262, and repeating anachronies, 73. *See also* Reader; Receiver
—time of the narrating, 157, 215-223, in Proust, 223-227; and focalization,

199n; interpolated narrating, 216n, 217-218, 223; prior narrating (predictive narrative), 216, 217, 219-220; simultaneous narrating, 156n, 215n, 216, 217, 218-219, 223; subsequent narrating, 217, 220-223
Voyage narratives, 85n
Le Voyeur (Robbe-Grillet), 219n

Wagner, Richard, 149n, 154, 159n; *Parsifal*, 199, 253; *The Ring of the Nibelung*, 148-149
Warren, Robert Penn, 186, 189
Waters, Harold, 249n
Watson. *See* Doyle
Wells, H. G., 219
Woolf, Virginia: *To the Lighthouse*, 187
Words, narrative of. *See* Mood, distance
Writing, the: distinct from the narrating, 213, 214, 219-220, 229
Written narrative: and temporal duality, 34

Zola, Emile: *Germinal*, 191n

BEWARE OF THE TEMPTATION TO CONFIRM
FAIX NARRATIVE BY HIS (LITTLE AS IT IS) BIOGRAPHY
OR CONTEXT p 28

FAIx = narrator ⟹ HISTORY

FAIx ≠ narrator ⟹ FICTION p 213

+ importance of recipient / reader
↳ different modes of
interpretation

FAIx not as author but Translator p 230